Wings over Sakishima

Published by:
Fredio R. Samples
Snohomish, WA 98296-5435

Copyright © 2010 by Fredio Ray Samples. All rights reserved.
No part of this publication may be reproduced, transmitted, in any form or utilized in any form or by any means, electronic, mechanical, photocopying, recording, or by information storage and retrieval systems, without written prior permission of the author.

Best Wishes Always !
Fredio Samples

D1615908

Printed in the USA
ISBN 978-0-615-39668-2

Contents

Acknowledgments

For those of you listed here. It was with your encouragement and willingness to give me information that helped me write this story. I'm forever grateful to each of you.

Don Schroeder	John Miller
Sal Garcia	Margaret Johnson
Franklin E. Fairhurst	Quentin Schenk
Robert Allison	Stewart Wasoba
Forrest Glasglow	George Liebich
Tadashi Sonoda	Lloyd Wallen
George Hanover	George W. Artz
Ralph F. Watkins	William Lowenthal
Dick Knoth	Gene Fithian
Joe Nasello	Ben Heffer
Frank Murphy	Val Heffer
Adam Lewis	Marvin W. Rachal
Lyman W. Jeffreys	Larry Keyes
Ivor Jefferys	Jeff Davis
Robert Cloud	Gerald T. Fisher
Spencer F. Hatch	Robert S. Scott
Joe Stravers	Charlie Casello
Virgil Gooley	William Riggs
Bill Reddell	George Press Adams
Alvin B. Kernam	Harry Florence
Kyoko Takaesu	Trudy Florence
Walter Shackelford	Clark Nelson
Ralph E. Magerkurth	Doug Misamore
Bill Bever	Edward Anderson
Cactus Walters	Bill Denman
Terry Ann Walters	Heidi Denman Hogan

I'm forever indebted to my wife, Brenda Helen, for her patience and encouragement and for her time spent proof reading each chapter and correcting my many mistakes.

WINGS OVER SAKISHIMA
The Author

Fredio, at the age of 4 is shown here in this 1942 portrait. He often entertained the local neighbors by singing the popular WW-II song: "COMING IN ON A WING AND A PRAYER"

Fredio Samples was born in Corbin Kentucky on June 4, 1938. He enlisted in the U.S. Air Force in 1961 and served 4 years. After returning to civilian life he worked for thirty years for two U.S. Defense Contractors. He and his wife Brenda now live in Snohomish, Washington near Seattle.

WINGS OVER SAKISHIMA
INTRODUCTION
By Fredio Samples

Inspired long ago by a mysterious horrifying dream, driven by determination, reading old WWII declassified incomplete military records, conversing with aging airplane pilots, their crew members, navy ship crew members of the second world war, my experience of once living and working on the remote island of Miyako Jima located southwest of Okinawa at Sakishima Gunto after WWII, and the two journeys I made back to this region, motivated me to write this book.

What I have written and compiled here is the story of my experience and my undertaking to find the truth of the events that happen during WWII in the Japanese held islands of Sakishima Gunto. Sadly, in wars, all things will never be known. I hope that the information I have written in this book will instill in others to continue to search and eventually publish more of what happened during late 1944 and 1945 in these far away islands.

We must not forget those who flew the airplanes, the air crewmembers, the sailors and marines who sailed on the warships, and those who died during this war.
Their story should not be left untold. They should be given equal credit for their bravery and their part in bringing the war to a close in 1945 in the Pacific.

I will never forget the kindness and the friendship shown by the people of the beautiful Miyako Island to the American radar people who came, lived and worked there after the war. May the "Ghost of Nobaru" rest in peace.

DISCLAIMER

Writing this book has been a most challenging and a toiling experience. I'm not a professional military historian, although many of the daily military engagements described in this book were recorded from declassified military records. This book is not intended to replace any printed professional American military history of WWII. Due to limited resources for my research of the materials that was available to me while writing this story, I feel that I have done the best I could do. Therefore I shall not be held accountable or responsible for any inaccuracies, such as omissions of people, times, dates, places, events, military units, military hardware, ships or airplanes.

Glossary

Bogey	Unidentified Aircraft.
Bow	Fwd part of a water vessel.
Bridge	That part of a ship that is above the top deck. (The observation and Steering tower).
Caliber	The diameter of a bullet or inside diameter of a gun barrel.
Dumbo	A sea rescue plane- PBY Catalina, Martin PBM flying boat.
Ensign	Navy Officer Grade O-1, Same as: (2nd Lieutenant).
General Quarters	Ship Alert, orders given to man all stations.
Harbor lighter	A vessel that operates in the shallow waters of a harbor.
Heckler	A plane sent to fly near the enemy for the purpose of irritating them.
Judy	Fighter pilot has come into contact with the bogey.
Kamikaze	Means "Divine Wind". A name given to Japanese Special Forces Groups who trained their pilots to crash their planes into allied ships. A Divine Wind (thought to be a typhoon) had once destroyed a Mongol invasion fleet.
Lighter	Same as Harbor lighter.
Lugger	Small sailing vessel having two or more mast.
Port	Left side.
Revetment	A wall made of earth, sand bags, concrete, etc. To protect against enemy bombs, rockets and machine gun strafing.
Splash	Enemy plane shot down.
Starboard	Right side.
Stern	Rear section of a water vessel.
Sugar Dog	Small commercial ship having one mast.

Abbreviations

AA	(1) Anti-Aircraft (2) Air Artillery
AG	Air Group
AMMO	Ammunition
ASP	Anti-Submarine Patrol
BN	Bureau number
BuAer	Bureau of Aeronautics
CAP	Combat Air Patrol
CAL	Caliber
CDR	Commander
CIC	(1) Combat Information Center (2) Control Identification Center
CO	Commanding Officer
COMCAR	Commander Carrier
CV	Large Aircraft Carrier
CVE	Escort Carrier
CVEG	Escort Carrier Air Group
DD	Destroyer
DE	Destroyer Escort
GP	General Purpose
GQ	General Quarters
H	Hour of the day
HE	High explosive
HP	Horsepower
HVAR	High Velocity Air Rocket
IFF	Identification Friendly or Foe, sent from Airplane's transponder
(jg)	Junior Grade
LASP	Local Anti-Submarine Patrol
LCAP	Local Combat Air Patrol
LCI	Landing Craft Infantry
LST	Landing Ship Tank
Lieut.	Lieutenant
Lt.	Lieutenant
MCVG	Marine Carrier Air Group
MG	Machine gun
TCAP	(1) Tactical Combat Air Patrol (2) Target Combat Air Patrol
TBM	Torpedo Bomber (Letter "M" is manufactures code for General Motors)
TF	Task Force
TG	Task Group
TU	Task Unit
VC	Air Composite (used mostly, proceeding squadron numbers)
VF	Air Fighter " "
VT	Air Torpedo " "

Chapter 1
WINGS OVER SAKISHIMA

I enlisted in the US Air Force in January of 1961.There was the Military draft then and my number had came up to report for the US Armed Forces physical exam. I had loved airplanes ever since I was four years old and knew that the US Air Force was the place where I wanted to serve out my military obligation. My mind was made up as early as 1943. As a small kid I loved to lay in our front yard looking up into the sky, hoping to see the military airplanes fly over on their way from the factories to the war bases. When I would see them I would wave to them thinking they could see me and I was darn sure they were waving back. Just the sight of these airplanes thrilled me. My Mother bought me a child's military uniform and on the weekends she would dress me in my uniform, pin on my shinny wings and take me to the local park, where I would stand on top of a picnic table and sing the WW-II song, "COMING IN ON A WING AND A PRAYER."

After finishing my basic training in San Antonio Texas, I was sent to Keesler Air Force Base at Biloxi Mississippi for training in Airplane and missile radar detection and tracking. A few of us including myself was trained in a new program called "SAGE" (Semi-Automatic Ground Environment) of what was considered an advanced automatic system of radar and computer detection and tracking of aircraft and missiles that the US Air Force was going to operate and eventually replace their existing system of what they referred to as Manual radar operations. This SAGE system would require the use of a large computer that would compile information and flight data. The use of the SAGE program was a joint program between Canada and the U.S. and was tailored for the use in the far Northern regions for the early detection of any Soviet air penetration into North America. The SAGE system was also being implemented in Greenland and parts of North Dakota. Information from these radars and their computers was fed into "NORAD" (North American Air Defense Command) located at Colorado Springs Colorado.

Upon my completion of SAGE radar training at Keesler Air Force Base, I thought it was strange to received permanent duty orders assigning me to Tyndall Air Force base located in Panama City Florida. I didn't complain, for all of the other guys from my training class had received orders to report to bases in North Dakota. I felt fortunate to have received orders to a place having a warm climate. I was never fond of cold weather, so I didn't question my orders nor did I tell any of my friends where I had been assigned. When I arrived at the base in Florida, I discovered that they didn't have the new "SAGE" radar system in place and then it was clear to me that there must have been an error in my assignment orders. Faced with this problem, I now had to find a way to get my orders changed. For me to stay at this base and work here it would require that I be allowed to cross train into the manual radar operations that was the current operations at this radar site. I made myself useful by volunteering for every dirty hard job around the base squadron. This paid off shortly for afterwards I was offered the cross training.

The Manual Radar operations concept was patterned after a British WWII Radar network that was successfully used against the German Luftwaffe during the Bombing of Britain with some exceptions.

Manual Radar operations required search radar that would scan 360 degrees for a given range and detect a flying or floating object in the sky and in return display these objects on a radar scope. For the sake of measuring the altitude of these presented objects there was another type of radar called a height finder and it too fed its information into the radar room. The radar room was a dim lighted room inside a building having a large clear well lighted Plexiglas plotting board arranged in a vertical position and having the area of the radar station's responsibility transposed onto this board. All air traffic within this area of responsibility would be monitored by the Manual radar operators who were seated in front of this board. The radar operators would communicate with other airmen working behind the Plexiglas board. These airmen behind the board were called plotters. Whenever an aircraft or airborne object was seen by the radar operator on the radar scope, it would be referred to from that point on, as the "Target". The radar operator would relay the position of the target to the plotter. Using different colored grease pencils the plotter would enter the relative position of the target and the time the target was detected onto the backside of the Plexiglas board. Each color of the pencil used on the board meant a different level of urgency. Because the plotter was behind the board, this required that the plotter know how to print letters and numbers backwards so that it would be readable while viewing from the front side of the board. Now printing letters and numbers backwards was taught in military training school for manual radar operators who at times would be assigned to the plotter position behind the Plexiglas board. It became a standing joke among Manual radar operators. Uncle Sam had taught them a trade that they could use after their military service. Now that they knew how to write backwards, this qualified them for the job of advertising "Specials" on the glass windows of Super Markets.

It was now December 1963. I had been in Florida for 2 ½ years. The Cuban Missile crisis was now over and the US Air Force didn't need me watching off the coast of Florida for enemy airplanes or missiles flying north from Cuba on my radar. I had received orders to report to Travis Air Force base near Oakland California for deployment to Okinawa Japan. I had 12 months remaining on my 4 year enlistment and they planned to get that last year out of me on this overseas assignment. The Air Force had granted me a 15 day furlough in route to spend Christmas with my parents before reporting to my west coast departure base.

My plans after spending Christmas holidays in Kentucky were to catch a Greyhound Bus and travel North to Cincinnati Ohio, where I had planned to stop over for a short visit with my older brother and his wife, then continue on west to California. It was cold the last week in December in those Kentucky hills and a light snow lay on the ground. The day before I was to leave it began to snow again. I called the bus company to find out their bus schedule to Cincinnati Ohio and I was informed that their would be a delay of 24 hours due to a heavy snow fall on the highway leading to Cincinnati. They recommended catching a train. So I called the L&N railroad station and reserved two tickets on the first train leaving north the next day. My younger brother who was also home from college for the holidays decided that he would accompany me back to Covington Kentucky, a city just across the Ohio River from Cincinnati. I had never seen the Western part of the US or the west coast. So I was eager to get on my way. The rest of my trip across the western states was relaxing and interesting.

After arriving on the West coast, I spent a couple of days taking in the sights of San Francisco and Oakland California and then I reported to Travis Air Force Base and was given a seat on an airplane headed for Okinawa, a place I had heard of but knew very little about. I knew that there was a large battle fought there just before the dropping of the Atomic bomb on Japan in 1945. I also knew that Okinawa was a long ways from the United States and that the people there spoke Japanese. In a small instructions package that I was given just before boarding the airplane there was a small book titled "Basic Japanese Conversation Dictionary" I read this book from cover to cover during the long flight over the Pacific Ocean, thinking that I could learn a few important words like, "Where is the toilet?", "I need a taxi." I didn't know that I would find that the Okinawa people spoke Japanese with a different dialect. I heard that we would land at Kadena Air Force Base and I assumed there would be some instructions there as where I should go and whom I should contact when we arrived. I got out my orders and read them word by word. I was assigned to the 623rd AC&W squadron, Detachment # 1. I was to report to the 623rd AC&W Headquarters at Naha Air Force Base for transportation to Det. #1.When we arrived at Kadena Air Force Base I was informed that I would need to board a bus that would take me south to Naha Air Force Base and there I should report to the Squadron Headquarters shown on my orders.

After Japan surrendered in 1945 and was occupied by the US, Japan became the responsibility of the U.S. Military to protect it from any hostile aggression from other countries. A network of "Early Warning Radar" stations were constructed by the United States military that would monitor all air space off the coast of Japan, its home islands and territories. All airplanes or airborne objects detected on radars at these Early Warning remote stations would be reported back to a central located station called the "ADCC" (Air Defense Control Centers). In case of an unidentified airplane approaching the Japan coast. This airplane would be labeled unknown and the ADCC with its Commanders in charge would notify the nearest Interceptor squadron (see note) and they would deploy Fighter Interceptor airplanes to the general area where the unknown was spotted. The military term is called "SCRAMBLING". Once the interceptors arrive in the area of the target, a Radar Flight Controller at the nearest Radar station to the target would make contact with the Interceptors and assist the pilots in the intercept of the unknown target by giving the Interceptor pilots information such as the unknown's altitude, speed, direction and by giving the pilots vectors in compass heading needed to intercept the target.

Note: The Military word "Interceptor" is applied to a very fast armed military airplane that is sent to intercept and if necessary engage an enemy airplane before the enemy airplane can reach its target.

It became necessary to place some of these Early Warning radar stations on remote islands so that the radar coverage would overlap each station that was in the line up of stations that were up an down the coast of Japan including Okinawa and as far southwest as Taiwan. The Early Warning station would be first to detect enemy movement and first to report it. They were the Security guards of the sky working around the clock. The men at these stations were to detect and report all unknown aircraft and they also controlled all friendly aircraft in the skies in their airspace of responsibility much like the FAA does in their control centers for civilian passenger planes in the United States. Radar operators at Aircraft Control and Warning stations are trained to control aircraft, assist pilots with updated weather reports and airport conditions, and help keep airplanes on the correct headings.

Detachment #1 was a (EW) Early Warning Radar station located on Miyako Jima, an island 165 miles southwest of Okinawa. For transportation to Miyako from Okinawa the Air Force flew a C-47 there once a week and a well used left over WWII LSM-335 ship traveled between Okinawa and Miyako Jima carrying fuel and heavy supplies to the radar station when needed. If you were lucky while traveling between Okinawa and Miyako you got to ride on the C-47 going there and back. I wasn't that lucky the day I first traveled to Detachment #1. They said the day I traveled that I was needed to accompany much needed supplies that was loaded on the LSM. Under normal circumstances this ship would have stayed tied to the dock at Okinawa the day I left for Miyako. But for two weeks the weather had not been favorable for sailing and supplies were now running low at the radar station. We left at dusk and rode the high seas through the night in this flat bottom ship. During the trip our ship took on sea water over the ship's bow that flooded the "Well-hold" where supplies, mail and my luggage was stored. Seeing land the next morning was welcome site. We docked at Hirara Port on the northwest coast of Miyako Jima. There to meet the ship at the end of the dock was two American men sitting rather nonchalant in a military jeep. I was not sure what they represented for neither one of them was wearing a recognizable uniform. They were wearing Kaki shorts, White T-shirts and sandals on their feet. The way they were dressed was not what I was a custom to seeing military people wearing when on duty. It was their military rank pinned to their caps that I finally recognized.

Miyako Jima is a sub- tropical island that is located in the Sakishima Gunto Island group at the southwestern end of the Ryukyu Islands. In Japanese, Sakashima means: far away island. Miyako is closer to Taiwan than to Kyushu Japan. Miyako Jima is located at 24.45N latitude and 125.20E longitude. The island originated from coral, rising from the sea. Therefore the island is flat with the exception of one ridge near the center of the island. At the highest level of this ridge was the U.S. Air Force Station, 623rd squadron, Detachment-1. Previously it had been the 624th squadron when first built. Miyako Island is the largest of the eight islands that make up the Miyako Jima group. It is approximately 12 miles in length and 7 miles wide. The other seven smaller islands nearby are Irabu, Shimoji, Ikema, Ogami, Kurima,Tarama and Minna. Miyako Jima produces commercial brown sugar from its sugar mills and 85% of the island is made up of sugar cane fields therefore most of the natives are farmers. There are some fishermen who keep the island supplied in fresh fish and the natives grow their own vegetables near their homes. This region of Asia is prone to fierce Typhoons. The natives of this island consider themselves as being Okinawan. However, because of the 150 mile separation from the Island of Okinawa, the Miyako natives have developed their own unique dialect. Because of the distance from any other population, the island is considered isolated and the culture here remains much the same as it was long before the Japanese took control of the island. The habits and culture here resembles that of China, which is closer to Miyako than the main land of Japan.

The Ryukyu Islands in the older days were called the Lewchew Islands, a name that was believed to have derived from the Chinese language. The Kingdom of Lewchew was ruled by a King who lived in a Castle on top of a hill in the town of Shuri. Shuri is located just east of Naha in the southern half of the island of Okinawa. All of the ancient archives of the Lewchew islands that were kept at Shuri Castle were destroyed by fire during the siege of the castle by the American military in 1945. The Imperial Japanese Army had made their headquarters inside this castle during the battle for Okinawa.

In much earlier times, the Lewchew Islands were visited by trading ships in route between Southeast Asia, Philippines, Japan, Korea and China. These islands were an important link for trading between countries. Here trading ships from various countries could rest their crews while replenishing their food, water supply and make repairs to their ships if necessary.

The Lewchew people were peaceful and they had never seen the reason to have an army to protect their Kingdom. Japan was well aware of this and they begin to worry after noticing a great amount of European ships sailing through the islands. They became afraid that the Europeans would one day take over the islands by force and block Japan from their southern trading routes. Japan decided to protect their interest in the islands by doing the very thing that they thought that others might do and that was to invade the Ryukyu Islands and take control of the trade. So in 1609 the Japanese invaded the islands and took control of the trade, imposing heavy taxes on traded goods passing through the Islands. In 1853 Admiral Perry from the US sailed into Okinawa and went to visit the King, and while there, he promised the King that the Americans would defend Okinawa by building an American Army post there. But he was speaking only for himself for after he returned to America he couldn't find anyone who would agree that building a military base at Okinawa was a good idea. When Japan learned of the interest in Okinawa that the western world was having, this became too much for them. They sent an Army to be stationed at Naha Okinawa. This move on Japan's part didn't sit well with the Okinawan people and they begin to protest this move. Then, in a few years Japan made another move against the people of Okinawa. Under Emperor Mutsuhito Japan ordered King Sho Tai the King of Okinawa to report to Japan and then the Government of the Lew Chew-Okinawan Kingdom was terminated and the Japanese took over control of Okinawa and the Ryukyu islands in 1879. The Chinese now became very irritated with Japan over their take over of the Lew Chew-Okinawa islands and it was feared that a war might break out over this matter. China felt close to the islands and the island people and the Chinese liked trading with the Okinawans and using the islands to replenish their ships. The Okinawans were even sending their students to China for higher education and not to

Japan. Okinawa favored China as a big brother rather than Japan. General Grant from the U.S. who was in China on business was asked by the Chinese if he would try and defuse this matter between China and Japan by pressuring the Japanese into backing down on their control of the Islands. General Grant talked with the leaders of Japan and a deal was made. It was agreed to that the Ryukyu Islands be split up between the two powers. Written in the agreement in Japan was that the Island of Okinawa would remain independent on its own with a King in charge. Miyako, Ishigaki and close by Yaeyama would be given to China and the islands north of Okinawa would be given to Japan. After hearing of this agreement and of the offer by Japan to split up the islands between powers, there were some high ranking Chinese who let it be known that they didn't feel that Japan should have any of the islands that lay north of Okinawa and because of this the negotiations broke down and stalled. The two sides never came together again and nothing ever came of this agreement.

Back on Miyako Island, the Captain and the Sergeant give me a ride to the Radar station from the ship dock, but not before they introduced me to Hirara City by giving me a tour of the surroundings and this included a stop in one of their favorite clubs in Hirara City for a couple beers, make that three. Most of the section of Hirara City we drove through, I noticed that the buildings was low to the ground and made of wood. These structures were unpainted and the roofs were made of red tile. Small narrow unpaved alleys ran between and in front the buildings. Old men and women lined the alleys selling fish and vegetables. Small horses pulling two wheeled carts loaded with sacks of all types of materials blocked most of the alleyways. After leaving the city and on our way to the radar station the narrow road crossed over the single runway of Hirara Airfield. The road continued through a maze of tall sugar cane and then a couple miles south of the airfield we came upon the village of Nobaru. From here I could see the Nobaru ridge and the two familiar large white radar domes. One of these domes housed the 360 degrees search radar and the other one was used for measuring the height of aircraft for altitude readings.

After settling into my new quarters, the regular daily routine of working at the radar station and living the life of a GI was no different than what I had been doing before in the states for the last three years. The first couple months after arriving was spent getting adjusted to the food, the surroundings, new living quarters and learning a new language. My living quarters were in a two story barracks on the top floor where I shared the room with two other Airmen that worked on a different crew and shift than I did. The men stationed here at Miyako were warned that the Port City "Hirara" was not a safe place to be after dark. The reason for this warning was that many fishing boats and ships using the harbor were not checked closely for the nationalities of those who were coming onto the island. The main land of Communist China was close by. Chinese fishermen visiting the Miyako using the Hirara Port would leave their boats and come into the city at night and pay their respects to the many bars along the water front alleys. Here they would drink until they were drunken fools and then walk the alleys in numbers looking for trouble. We were also aware that the Communist knew we were there and the reason we were there. We had .30 caliber M1 and M2 Carbines to protect the Radar station but in case of an all out military assault on the island, we would not have been able to have held our ground or defend ourselves against machine guns. I thought this as being a problem worthwhile to inquire about, so I asked our station Commander if there was a defensive plan or escape plan in place incase we were ever attacked. His answer was: *"No, all of us here are considered expendable."* His answer shocked me and as far as I was concerned, it was unacceptable. If the U.S. Military was not going to have a plan to defend the station or give us a plan for an escape route, then I was going to plan my own escape route. During the next weeks I studied the native language and spent my free time near the fishing docks. I learned that the fishermen were eking out a living making two dollars a day. When the fishing boats were ashore, I had noticed that the fisherman slept on the boats or close by. I planned that one of these boats would become my transportation in case I needed to escape. I had put aside $100. With this money, I felt that I would be able to bribe a fisherman into delivering me to safety at Okinawa. I now felt at ease knowing that I had in my mind a plan of escape.

The nearby village of Nobaru was small and mostly inhabited by sugar cane farmers. There was no lighting in the village and this made it difficult to walk through after dark. A few times I would return from the Port City of Hirara by taxi after dark and the taxi driver would let me off in the village. This meant I had to walk through the village to the Radar station. One particular very dark, rainy, windy, night, I was making my way along the narrow road through the village when I begin to smell a familiar odor and not the odor that I would have welcomed. It was the sweet sour odor of what I had remembered years before of decaying human flesh while playing with my friend near holding vaults for the dead. These holding vaults were temporary vaults located in the City cemetery where bodies of the dead were kept until other arrangements were made for their final burial. That night and two more nights in session, I had troubling dreams. My world would be changed because of these dreams. What happened in these dreams inspired me to find the truth about this place and that I have done. I have asked myself many times if the dreams I had were caused by my imagination, or was it the Ghost of Nobaru who picked me to find the truth and tell their story?

Chapter 2
HORRIFYING DREAMS

I heard Japanese voices in the distance and I couldn't understand what was being said. I awoke and sat up in my bed and listened, but I heard nothing. Puzzled, I lay back down and went back to sleep. The next day I give this some thought but considered that I had had a dream. That night while sleeping the same dream repeated itself and I again heard the voices and they seemed to be closer and then I heard shouting and loud bursting sounds "rat-tat-tat, rat-tat-tat." I woke and was shaken by what I thought were the sounds of a machine gun. I got out of bed and went to the window and looked out into the black of the night. Everything was deadly quiet. It took me a long while to get back to sleep. I was now wondering what these dreams were about and why was I having them. Two dreams in a row and the second one was an extension of the first one. This disturbed me throughout the following day as I wondered what it might mean. That night while sleeping, just like the two previous nights, the dream repeated and continued on. Once again there were voices, the shouting, the sounds of the machine gun firing then the shouting stopped and I could here other people's voices. The voices seemed to be coming from the lower floor of the barracks. I dressed into my fatigue pants and shirt and went to my door and slightly opened it and peered out into the hallway. Peering down the hallway from the second floor level at the head of the stairs, I could see a dim light waving from below, casting shadows onto the second floor ceiling. The shadows resembled that of men struggling with something heavy as they made their way up the stairs. As they approached the top of the stairs I watched as they came in view. Three Japanese soldiers dressed in full WWII battle uniforms were carrying what appeared to be a machine gun, were now standing at the head of the stairs on the second floor of our barracks. Two men were carrying the machine gun by its tripod stand and a third soldier was hanging onto the handle of the gun. Right behind these soldiers was a Japanese officer. The officer had a flashlight in one hand and a sword in the other. The soldiers were busy with their load and had turned their backs to me at the head of the stairs and this give me a chance to duck back into my room. I closed and locked my door, then pushed my wall locker against the door, put on my shoes and strapped on my 45 automatic, pulled the gun from the holster, slid in a loaded clip in to the gun's handle, chambered a round into the barrel and put the safe on. I heard the Japanese officer shout. Then the firing of the machine gun started in the hallway of the second floor. Men begin to scream as the soldiers fired through the doors into their rooms as they lay in their bunks. I was alone in my room at the time. I quickly opened my window, kicked out the screen, climbed out and dropped to the ground below. As I looked to my right toward the south end of the barracks, I saw three Japanese soldiers. I pulled my 45 Automatic from its holster, pulled the hammer back, released the safety and drew a bead on the nearest soldier. I knew that I had to hold this gun steady and move the gun fast after the first shot to kill all three. The 1911 Army 45 Government issue automatic is a powerful gun. Each time it fires you will have to realign your eyes and the gun sights to the target. One of the three soldiers moved behind the barracks and out of my sight. This now could mean if I fire my gun, I possibly could only hit two of the soldiers and I surely would be giving away my position to the third soldier who would in return no doubt be reinforced by others. The three soldiers had not seen me, so I let the hammer down and put the 45 back in its holster and moved in the opposite direction away from the barracks and into the dense foliage of the ridge. I knew that I had to escape. That meant that I had to make my way north, and then off the ridge and through 4 ½ miles of sugar cane fields to the shoreline fishing camps. Narrow roads had been cut through these fields by farmers and my plan was to follow along side these roads, staying a few yards in the cane where I wouldn't be seen by passing traffic. Several Japanese army trucks passed during my journey. Each time I would lie down flat to the ground as they passed on by. When I arrived at the shoreline, I stopped a distance from the fishing boats tied up there and examined them and the surroundings. There were several docked close together and one boat was docked some distance from the others. I checked my holster making sure that my gun was still with me and ready if needed and I walked to the single boat that was a far distance from the others. The operator of the boat that I assumed to be a fisherman and the Captain was rolled in a blanket sleeping near the bow of his boat. I shook him awake. Very excitingly he responded in fairly good English by saying, "I thought all Americans on this island were dead and don't you know that you are the enemy?" I explained to him that I was not the enemy and I only wanted to escape from the island and that I would pay him 100 dollars to help me, by taking me in his boat to Okinawa and some extra money would be given to him upon our arrival. I knew that was more money than he would make fishing in three months. He said if I were to start my engine and leave now that it would look very suspicious for the fishing boats here normally leave around 0400. So he said that I should go to the back of the boat and lay down and he would cover me with a tarp and fishing gear. I boarded the boat and made my way to the stern where I laid down, curled up and waited for the fisherman to cover me. I must have laid there under the tarp and fishing gear for an hour or so before hearing an engine start from another boat. Then more boats started their engines. About this time my boat Captain raised the tarp just far enough to say in a very low voice that I should remain under the tarp until we were underway and far enough out that we could no longer see the land. He then started the boat engine and I could feel us moving away from the shore slowly out toward the breakwater. Once we were clear of the breakwater he sped up the boat and I could hear the pounding of the waves against the sides. The pounding of the waves and the high pitch of the engine noise is the last thing I remember before I awoke from my sleep and raised up in my bunk and looked around. My locker was not against the door as I had last seen it in my dream. One of my room mates was asleep in his bunk. I realized that I had had a horrifying dream and in the dream I had managed to escape while others didn't. The dreams that I had three days in succession seemed so realistic to me, so I asked myself, what was their meaning? Was it my imagination that brought on these dreams or was it the whispering "Spirits of Nobaru" asking for my help? I was compelled to start searching for the answer.

Chapter 3
REMINDERS OF WAR

I was shaken by this horrible dream, but I never told others about my dreams. I knew that no one would understand, for I didn't even understand them. I was walking one day in the port city of Hirara, when overhead I heard the droning of airplane engines. An older man and lady and two young children was walking ahead of me. As the airplane came closer the engines became louder the man suddenly stopped and looked up into the sky. He then grabbed the kids and motioned to the lady and they ducked behind a building. I looked around and saw other people moving off the street and in between buildings. I looked up and saw an Air Force four engine cargo plane fly over. The strange actions of these people when an airplane passed over made me wonder if these people were tourist from Tokyo or Hiroshima or maybe Nagasaki where they had witnessed aerial bombings during WWII. I was convinced that they were taking precautions by seeking shelter when they heard the airplane engines. One day, I decided to take a walk north of our radar station where there were lots of ground cover and heavy vegetation growing. In a clearing near the brush I noticed a round depression in the ground. At first I thought nothing of it but then I noticed it was very unique. The depression was a perfect circle and deeper into the ground at its center. About 15 or so feet from this depression was another depression with the same shape as the first one. I thought that these depressions could have been bomb craters. When I was in Okinawa prior to coming to Miyako Jima there were "Warning signs" posted about. You didn't dare walk anywhere unless it was posted: "Safe to walk". During WWII, I had heard that Japanese munitions such as live ammo, mortars, grenades and other explosives were buried by US army bulldozers as they made new roads and sealed off the entrances to caves. There were no warning signs here on Miyako Jima. As far as I knew, no American troops or their allies had come ashore at Miyako Jima during WWII and I knew nothing about the role this island might have played during WWII. I asked some of the local natives who lived nearby about the two depressions and they offered no clues for what might have made these. A month or so later on a Sunday, I had a day off from work and I planned to take a bicycle ride down to the southern coastline and see if I could find a beach to hang out for a while. I filled my canteen with water and was pumping up the tires when off in the distance I saw what looked like a cloud of smoke coming from the village of Nobaru. The cloud of smoke was moving in the same direction as the road that connected the village with the radar station. I caught a glimpse of a horse in front of the smoke and realized that what I had first thought was smoke was dust that was being kicked into the air by whatever this horse was pulling along behind it. I watched and as it got closer. I could see a man walking beside the horse leading it, and a young boy tagging along behind. The road from the village to the radar station had a horseshoe shaped curve in it just before it ran up in front of the squadron's orderly room. The island natives never came onto the station grounds unless they were escorted or they had been cleared to perform some type of work at the station. The man stopped his horse near the curve in the road and the young boy ran up to where I was standing. "Dozo- Dozo" (please- please) the boy said, while pointing toward the man and his horse. I was curious to why I was needed so I walked toward the man and his horse and as I got closer I suddenly stopped for I could see what the horse was dragging. My God it was a bomb! The horse had been dragging it by a rope. I just froze in place. The boy noticing that I had stopped ran up to me again. He picked up a stick and in the dirt he drew the letters USN. Then again he said, "Dozo- Dozo" and pointed to the bomb. I was frightened that I was standing so close, but I quickly thought it over. This bomb was lying still at this point. My thoughts were: if it was going to explode it had its chance to do so. I moved in closer and the old man bowed to me and the boy beaming with a smile pointed to the letters, USN stamped on the bomb. The bomb's size appeared to me to be a 100 pound bomb. What was it doing here on the island? I took the boy by the hand and walked back to our orderly room where I found the "OD" (officer of the day) and reported to him what we had there in the road. I will never forget the look on his face. The radar station's Air Force policeman was found and guards were posted along the road to warn any traffic that might come by. A call was made to Okinawa and an army ordinance team was flown out to the island to remove the bomb. Later that day I heard of how the bomb was treated. The bomb was loaded onto a barge and taken out a mile or so from shore and dropped into the ocean. 'Oh well," I thought, that bomb could have been dropped from a Navy carrier plane. The pilot may have known it was a dud or he may have dropped it for practice. After all, I was never told nor had I ever heard that there were ever any military actions on this island so what would have been on this island important enough to waste a good bomb? But I did think about the two depressions I had found that might have been bomb craters. One morning when our crew arrived for work we learned that the guard at the radar compound was sick and each of us would be taking turns throughout our shift, guarding the exterior of radar compound. When it became my turn to guard the compound, I discovered what appeared to be a base floor built of bricks formed side by side, end to end and sunken into the ground. The bricks covered the ground forming what appeared to be a floor, base or platform of some sort for a size of approximately 25 feet wide and 35 feet long. The bricks looked as if they had been laying there for a long while. My first thought was that this was the floor of a building that had been torn down and the floor made of bricks had been left there. At one end of these bricks I noticed two oval shaped pieces of concrete protruding upwards out of the ground about 4 inches. For several days I wondered about what this might have once been and I revisited the bricks and the oval shaped concrete pieces several times. I wondered if these bricks were formed to serve as a platform for a heavy gun. There would have been no better place on the island to have had an AA gun as a defense weapon as Nobarudake, for this was the highest point above sea level on Miyako Jima. I became more suspicious that war had come to this island in some form and I wanted to find out if this was true. I knew that in a few days I would be eligible for an R&R (what the military calls a rest and recuperation). I was planning to spend my 5 days of R&R at Naha Air Base on the island of Okinawa Shima and while I was there I planned to visit the base library and look up the Pacific war history for Sakishima Gunto. Unfortunately, I spent most of my R&R thumbing through books having no luck finding anything about the islands southwest of Okinawa. The battle of the big island of Okinawa Shima was well documented with war history. The invasion started on April 1, Easter Sunday, 1945. US Naval task forces made up of many battle ships, cruisers, aircraft carriers, destroyers, escort carriers, airplanes, fighters and bombers were all there while the Marines and Army ground forces went ashore. But there was no mentioning of Sakishima Gunto. So I returned to the island of Miyako Jima knowing no more about what I had seen or what I had dreamed. I served six more months at Miyako Jima and then my time was up and I was ready to return to the United States for discharge. After leaving the service, life moved on for me, but I never could forget what I had dreamed and what I had seen there on that island in 1964. It was in 1980 when I first met the late Edward Anderson, a retired United States Army Colonel who had been active in three wars. The US Air Force had hired him to be their local shipping representative at the Boeing Space Center in Kent Washington. When first meeting him, I learned that wood carving was his favorite hobby. One day I asked him if he would consider carving me a name plaque for my desk. He suggested that I should drop by his office and look at the one he had on his desk to see if it was what I had in mind. A day or so later I stopped in his office and while there he and I had a chat about our military experiences. Learning from Ed that he was on the Island of Okinawa during the mopping up of the last Japanese soldiers in 1945, I mentioned to him that I had been on the Island of Okinawa and that I had served at a radar detachment at Miyako Jima in 1964. I explained to him that due to some evidence I had seen on the island of Miyako Jima while I was there, I felt that some type of military action had taken place against the island. Although, I couldn't prove this for I couldn't find any written history to support my suspicions. Ed told me about a book written by the US Army's Historian Division, titled: "OKINAWA THE LAST BATTLE" and he offered to bring his copy of the book to his office where I could thumb through it. The next day I stopped by Ed's office and examined the book that he had brought. There were a lot of maps, pictures, charts and planning details in the book about the battle of Okinawa. There was the explanation of the planning for operations for the battle. The military operation was code named "ICEBERG." There were three phases of this operation shown. Phase III caught my attention right away for it was the planned invasion of the island of Miyako Jima. Selected and held aside for this invasion of Miyako Jima was the US Marine's V Amphibious Corps. According to the military planners, the reason Miyako Jima was of interest to the Americans was that it was suitable for the building of a long range airbase on its flat terrain and this would be a prime jumping off point for the later invasion of Japan. But Phase III of ICEBERG was cancelled after Japanese airbases on Okinawa were captured and found to be more suitable for bomber bases because Okinawa Shima was 150 miles closer to Japan's homeland. This was my first time to discover any mentioning of planned military action against Miyako Jima. My first real break came in 1997 when I became aware that there had indeed been US Military air action at the Sakishima Islands during the battle of Okinawa. I learned this after reading a book titled "Crossing the Line," written by Alvin Kernan. Alvin was a US Navy rear turret gunner who flew on a Grumman torpedo bomber in the Pacific. Alvin wrote in his book of bombing and strafing the Sakishima Gunto air strips and of the intense fire that he met from the Japanese AA guns that took the lives of his friends. I was now convinced that there was military action carried out on the Island of Miyako Jima and nearby islands during WWII. I could no longer doubt what I had seen on the island when I was there. I wondered about the awful dream that I had had for three days in succession back in 1964. Was there a meaning to the awful odor of death in the village of Nobaru the night I walked through the village? And what was the meaning in my dreams of the Japanese soldiers who entered our barracks and shot into the rooms, killing those who were asleep in their bunks? Were the Ghosts of Nobaru sending me a message in those dreams?

Japanese Army Bunker
at Nobarudake on Miyako Jima
Photo by Doc George

The top oval shape of this partly exposed concrete bunker entrance is what the Author of this book saw protruding above the ground only 4 inches when he was once guarding the U.S. Radar Station compound. This and other things later found is what convinced the Author that he should continue his search.

Chapter 4
THE WAR AND WHAT LAY AHEAD

Right after General MacArthur returned to the Philippines and secured that country, things begin to look very bleak for the Japanese. Most of their naval vessels were at the bottom of the sea and a large amount of their airplanes had been shot from the skies taking with them their best pilots. Japan was no longer on the offensive as that they had been the previous years starting with the bombing of Pearl Harbor on December 7, 1941. Now the only thing lying between the American advancing forces and Japan's home land was the sea and small Japanese controlled islands. On some of these islands the Japanese had stationed a few of what was left of their airplanes and a number of ground troops to protect their airfields. The Americans were advancing toward Japan at a rapid pace and this caused both sides to go into the emergency planning stages. The Americans were faced with the decision of where to attack next and build forward airfields and how to support the attack with men, ships, airplanes and supplies. The Japanese were trying to figure out where to deploy their remaining forces for a defensive blocking action. It became a cat and mouse game. In the Marianas, Saipan, Tinian and Guam had been captured. The Americans knew by early October 1944 that they would eventually have to deal with the Japanese in the Ryukyu Islands as they moved toward Japan's homeland. The island of Formosa that is now called Taiwan (not a part of the Ryukyu Islands), was under the control of the Japanese. Located in the East China Sea, southwest of Okinawa, the island was a jungle. The Japanese Army Air Force and land based navy had carved out airfields here, where they had stationed their bombers and fighters. Planes from these airfields had attacked the allied airbases in the Philippines only hours after they attacked Pearl Harbor in 1941, and again the Japanese sent their planes from these bases against General MacArthur's forces when they returned to retake the Philippines in 1944. The Americans made a plan to attack and take Formosa in 1945. The plan was code named "CAUSEWAY". Implementing this plan was favored by Admiral King and Admiral Chester W. Nimitz the Commander of the Pacific Fleet. To implement CAUSEWAY, it was going to require a combined military force consisting of all the flying forces of the Navy, Army and Marines along with a fleet of naval ships. On the ground it would require an undetermined amount the US Army and Marine ground troops. When the commanders of these forces were asked to give their opinion on CAUSEWAY, the Pacific Army commander, the Army Air commander and the commander of the 10th Army were not in favor of taking Formosa. After hearing the opinions of those for and those against "CAUSEWAY", Admiral King decided to delay the invasion of Formosa. On 3 October 1944 an order was given by the Joint Chiefs of Staff to attack the Ryukyu Islands located southwest of Japan.

On some maps, all of the Ryukyu Islands are shown as the Nansei Shoto- islands. On other maps they are listed in groups, such as Amami Shoto or Gunto which is a group very close to Japan's homeland. Next in line traveling southwest would be the Okinawa Shoto or Gunto and then last is the Sakishima Shoto or Gunto which is the greatest distance from Japan's home land and nearest to Taiwan. The Americans knew that

Okinawa Shima, the largest of the Ryukyu Islands, located at the threshold of Japan's southern tip was well fortified and the Japanese had airbases there with fighters and bombers that could attack the American fleet once they came into range. However, the taking of Okinawa whatever the cost would assure the Americans of a large anchorage and supply depot, airfields for bombers and deep seaports for ships that would be close to Japan's southern tip of Kyushu. Military planners put together a plan to invade Okinawa. The plan was named ICEBERG. It was scheduled to be implemented on 1- March 1945. However, due to delays in the Luzon operations, it was rescheduled for 1-April 1945.

KAMIKAZES

Earlier in the war, American fighter pilots were hearing that Japanese fighter pilots who expended all of their ammunition while dog fighting their opponent, sometimes elected to crash into his enemy's airplane rather than breaking off and heading for home. In almost every case, both airplanes would crash with almost certain death to both pilots. This act of suicide got a lot of attention from all American and British fighter pilots in the Pacific. It was in 1944 during the battle of Leyte Gulf when the act of suicide became a Japanese military operational tactic. On the island of Luzon in the Philippines, Japanese naval airplanes belonging to the 201 Air Group were fitted with 250 km bombs and sent to crash into the American ships in what was called "Crash diving." This tactic of crash diving was implemented by Admiral Takijiro Ohnishi, the Commander of the Japanese Navy's 1st air fleet in the Philippines and the planner of the Pearl Harbor attack. Pilots of air groups who performed this crash diving tactic later on in the war were called *Kamikazes,* meaning "Divine Wind." In early October 1944 the war was not looking favorable for the Japanese. They were running low on airplanes and ships and had no way to replenish them. It seemed to them at this time, that crashing what was left of their airplanes into the American aircraft carriers and other enemy ships was their only hope in slowing down or stalling the advancing American fleets. Young Japanese men were willing to give their lives for their country if asked to do so by their Emperor. Their willingness to take their own lives at Leyte was not left unnoticed by both sides. This was seen by the Japanese as a new worth-while tactic that was showing better results than attempting to bomb the American ships in the fleets from the air. Knocking out an aircraft carrier with a single plane crashing into it loaded with bombs was the same as destroying an airfield on land. Realizing this threat the Americans and British had to defend their ships by shielding them in some matter. Destroyers and Destroyer Escorts loaded with radar detection devices were positioned out a ways from the carriers. The destroyers formed a screen for the carrier's formations in places where they would be able to detect on their radar the enemy planes before they arrived over the carriers. American and British fighter airplanes were kept on constant Combat Air Patrol, ready to pounce onto any enemy or unknown airplanes if they were tipped off by the destroyer's radar men. Once alerted, the sailors and gunners aboard the carriers and other ships in the fleet would jump into action anytime enemy planes were spotted.

They would be searching the skies for any enemy planes that might have broken through their screen of airborne fighters. Stopping the Japanese *Kamikazes* by shooting them out of the air before they reached their target was the number one priority for the men on the ships. At first it was only the Japanese Navy air units who participated in crash diving. Later their Army Air Force units with their planes were trained to crash dive. Eventually, toward the end of the war they were using any type of plane that would fly and carry a bomb. The *Kamikaze* pilots were told to try and crash their planes into the elevator section of aircraft carriers. (*Crashing the elevator would cause the most damage to an aircraft carrier for the elevator is used to move the airplanes between the hangers and the deck.*) Loading airplanes with bombs and crashing them into ships was not the only suicide weapon that the Japanese had. They developed a special rocket propelled bomb that was flown by a suicide pilot. This controllable, piloted bomb having wings was designed to be carried into the air by a larger bomber type airplane and then detached from the bomber. A suicide pilot would then pilot the rocket to its final destination. This rocket bomb was called "Ohka" It was referred to in the western world as the "Baka" They also built small suicide boats powered by automobile engines that they hid near the shorelines. These were laden with explosions and could be piloted and rammed into ships at sea. The Baka flying bomb and the suicide boats later proved to be worthless. Another suicide weapon was a midget one man submarine, it was called the Kaiten. These were carried to their release point by a full sized submarine and then released. The nose of the Kaiten held a very high explosive that would detonate on impact. The Japanese claimed that they were used successively in sinking some American carriers and battleships. However, the US could never confirm these allegations. When the Japanese began to retreat from Manila in the Philippines, their Navy Air fleet moved their headquarters to Formosa. There they consolidated their Air Fleets and groups and re-assigned pilots and support personnel and formed special attack squadrons. A name used by these special attack forces to identify their group was *Shimpu*, meaning the same as *Kamikaze*. These Shimpu groups were formed into smaller squadrons and these were sent to airfields on the islands of Ishigaki and Miyako Jima, which are two of the larger islands belonging to Sakishima Gunto that are east of Formosa. From these two islands, the *Kamikazes* flew their airplanes and crashed them into the ships of the Americans and British during Operation Iceberg.

Author's Note

The forming of these special groups at Formosa may have not been known to the Americans at the time. The American planners may have thought that the retreating Japanese air fleet and groups moved what was left of their Philippine air resistance to their homeland. In the first days of April 1945 when the Americans began to send ground troops onto the island of Okinawa Shima and the Japanese began to crash dive into their naval fleet, reporters wrote that Kamikaze planes were coming from the home island of Kyushu. The Navy had stationed Radar picket ships between Okinawa and Kyushu for the purpose of alerting the fleet of enemy approaching planes and Combat Air Patrols were positioned over the area.

It was later discovered by the Americans that Kamikazes were not only originating from Japan's homeland bases, they were also flying from Formosa and airfields at Ishigaki and Miyako Jima. These airfields would have to be neutralized. This job was assigned to the British Pacific fleet who was Task Force 57 and to American CVE Escort Carrier's Task Units and their air squadrons and for them, it became a grinding daily task that lasted as long as the battle of Okinawa. The news results back home of these American and British Task Unit's daily operations were being over shadowed by the fierce battle at Okinawa Shima over 150 miles away. These Task groups of CVE's and their Air units never received the attention by the press or military history writers after the war that covered the history of operation "ICEBERG". It is my opinion that the story of Iceberg can't be complete without including the air battles at Sakashima Gunto. It might be that little was known at the time about the daily operation of these Task Units to anyone other than those men who were a part of the Task Unit. They were out to sea, many miles from the shores of Taiwan, Miyako Jima and Ishigaki Jima. No Allied ground troops were present on these islands to assess conditions. Only the pilots and their air crewmen who were sent to attack the islands could assess the damage after bombing and strafing either by seeing the conditions from the air or studying aerial pictures taken by cameras on photo- reconnaissance planes after the strikes. Ship and air records were classified and not made available to the press. In 1944, the average American had not heard of places called Saipan, Iwo Jima and Okinawa. They may have first heard these names from news reels and newspapers in 1945. War news released to the public about Operation Iceberg in 1945 was often misconceived by the general public. For an example, if a fighter pilot was shot down by AA fire at Miyako Jima or Ishigaki Shima, 165-200 miles from the island of Okinawa between 1-April 1945 and 24-June 1945, the pilot would be reported as missing in action during the battle at Okinawa. Why this would happen is because the pilot was shot down during Operation ICEBERG and Iceberg was about Okinawa.

Chapter 5
ULITHI ATOLL

The staging area for operation Iceberg was a large anchorage at Ulithi Atoll located in the Caroline Islands. The Americans had taken over Ulithi right after the Japanese evacuated the Atoll around September of 1944. Ulithi was about 1,150 miles south of Okinawa. The Navy Seabees built a sea supply base here where the allied fleet ships could rendezvous. At Ulithi, ships could be repaired, fueled, supplied with munitions and general supplies that would be needed for the invasion of Okinawa. Nearby in these Atolls was a place called Falalop, where there was a former Japanese airstrip that the Seabees improved. A recreation center was built nearby at a place called MogMog, where sailors and airmen would be allowed to have a few hours of R&R before having to head back to their duties. Ulithi could have been thought of as Commander Chester Nimitz's base camp of the Pacific.

STRATEGY

Admiral Nimitz believed that the air attacks against Japan from the heavy bombers in the Marianas and the navy's fleet carriers would force the Japanese to reinforce Kyushu Japan, the island of Formosa, the coast of China and the Ryukyu Islands. From these places it was thought that the Japanese would attack the allied ships with conventional and Kamikaze air attacks. Therefore, it was planned that ground forces once ashore would concentrate on capturing enemy airbases and facilities, early on in the islands. The capturing of airbases early on would enable land base aircraft to operate from these airfields against the enemy giving the United States the advantage of air superiority in the region. The Central Pacific Task Forces for the Ryukyu Island campaign was headed by Admiral R.A. Spruance who commanded Task Force-50. Task Force-58 with its fast carriers was a part of TF-50. Their job was to neutralize the Japanese airfields at Kyushu and Okinawa Shima. Task Force-57 also under TF-50 was the British Pacific Fleet. The British were charged with neutralizing five operational airfields on two islands southwest of Okinawa at Sakishima Gunto. *The American fleet would find later that they too would be needed at Sakishima Gunto and the British would be called on to strike Taiwan that was also called Formosa.*

SAKISHIMA GUNTO PREPARES FOR WAR

In the southwestern part of the Ryukyu Islands, the Japanese had not prepared the islands at Sakishima Gunto for war before 1944. Only a handful of soldiers were stationed there. As the Americans advanced toward the Japanese homeland, the Japanese military planners decided to start a military build up just in case the Americans were planning to island hop their way to the Japanese homeland. The Islands of Ishigaki and Miyako Jima would offer to the Americans, if taken, a base for long range bombers. The Japanese were correct in their thinking, for the Island of Miyako Jima was to be taken and used for a long range bomber base according to phase III of operation Iceberg. In 1944 there was one Japanese Navy Airfield on Miyako Jima. It was located near the harbor city of Hirara and went by the name of Hirara Airfield. Its runway was surfaced with crushed packed coral. In 1944, by using local labor including high school students, two more airfields were built. An Army airfield having two separate runways was built at Nobaru near Nobarudake. This airfield was mistakenly called Nobara by the Americans and the British. Another airfield having one runway was built on the Westside of the island near Yonaha. The Americans called this airfield Sukama. With no time to build quarters for the Japanese troops when they began to arrive, the local school buildings were taken over by the military and made into their headquarters. A Navy Garrison was positioned near Hirara and was to defend that Airfield with heavy AA guns and a special forces Navy team were to operate from the shore their hidden suicide boats incase the enemy tried to land near the harbor. At first an attempt was made to recruit and train troops for the buildup. But after a troop transport ship was torpedoed and sank while attempting to ship nearly 300 newly trained specialized troops to Miyako, it was decided to transfer experienced troops from other assignments. Soldiers from Japan's 28th Division stationed in Manchuria commanded by Lieutenant General Senichi Kushibushi were ordered to report to Miyako Jima. The 28th Division soldiers were trained to fight the Russian Army. They were a rugged bunch. They were older, experienced and considered the best. They were a Cavalry Regiment and a Mountain Artillery Regiment. Horses were not needed at Miyako jima, so the Cavalry left most of them behind and the men became infantry foot soldiers. In September the IJA 59th and 60th Brigades from Manchuria arrived at Miyako. Local men from Okinawa and the Sakishima islands were also recruited to complete the build up. With the troop strength now completed, General Kushibushi distributed his troops between Miyako and Ishigaki. At the peak of the build up, Miyako alone was defended with a force of 31,000 men. Sent to Miyako were cannons and howitzers ranging from 7cm to 20cm, medium sized tanks to protect the coastline and airfields. All heavy weapons were staged by a battle plan that was drawn up based on the knowledge learned from how the Americans had attacked other islands. General Kushibushi and his planners knew that once the battle began that he could not expect additional soldiers for there was no way to safely transport them. His army would meet the Americans at their landing site with full force and then hope for a protracting battle. What the IJA feared the most was the Americans would land on the southern coast where the land was level with the ocean and advance across the flat island with their tanks. If this happened the plan was to make a final stand at the highest point of land on the island near the newly built cave headquarters at Nobarudake. There were many diseases on the Sakishima Islands and no control to eliminate them. Malaria was a major problem caused by disease carrying mosquitoes. An attempt was made to fill in the swamps to rid the mosquitoes of their nesting places. The IJA medical staff didn't have the knowledge or training to treat the disease. Medical supplies were already in short supply and there was no plan in sight to receive more. Fresh clean drinking water was always in short supply. Early on planners had requested well digging machinery to be sent to the island, but none had reached the island. Thirty thousand plus soldiers and an undetermined amount of island civilians were going to need food and water daily. Everyday they were dying from Malaria, lack of sanitary conditions and malnutrition. Plans were made to catch rain water for drinking. Fishing parties were formed and sweet potatoes and soy beans were planted. Rice was not grown there. Rice was imported from

Taiwan before the US submarines arrived. The fishing parties had to brave enemy subs and airplanes while fishing for food and the fishing stopped after 1- April 1945.

EARLY AIR STRIKES

Air strikes against Kyushu Japan and Okinawa Shima were necessary before 1-April 1945, the planned assault date of Okinawa Shima. The U.S. high command felt that they didn't know enough about Okinawa to land ground forces there without first studying the island. This meant flying over these places and photographing the surroundings. It was decided that since Leyte was to be moved on by MacArthur's forces around the 20th of October 1944, that any planes they sent on reconnaissance missions would also bomb and strafe air installations and the ship harbors. It was thought that any of these installations that were damaged or put out of service could hinder the Japanese from supporting the oncoming battles in the Philippines. So, on the 10th of October 1944 planes were sent to Kyushu and Okinawa Shima. The weather was not always favorable this time of the year and it was difficult to get good aerial photos. Admiral Mitsher's Task Force-58 and his fast carriers attacked Formosa and surroundings on the 12th and 13th of October. *The first American bombs fell on Miyako Jima and Ishigaki Jima on the morning of 10 October 1944. One raid was in the morning and another in the afternoon. A ship was sunk in the harbor and some airplanes on the ground were destroyed at Hirara Airfield. The American planes came again on the 13th and one of the planes was shot down and the pilot was captured.* Bomber aircraft belonging to the Army Air Force stationed in China attacked Formosa and shipping on the sea nearby. Attacks again were made on the 2nd through the 4th of January 1945. Okinawa was attacked and a sweep was made down through the Ryukyu Islands as far as Formosa. The weather was not good and the bombing was performed through cloud cover. On the 9th of January Task Force-58 launched a strike at Formosa along with Army Air Force bombers from China, and after Formosa the fleet turned east and struck airfields and shipping at Miyako Jima. On 9-January the *USS ESSEX CV9*, with Task Group III, sent planes belonging to *Air group-83* to attack Miyako Jima. Formosa was again attacked on the 21st of January and afterwards the fleet turned toward Sakishima Gunto in the Ryukyu Islands to bomb and take aerial photos. On the 15th of February Lieutenant Cutaiar from the US Patrol Bomber Squadron VPB-111 flying his PB4Y-1 Liberator, bombed and strafed a radar station at Miyako Jima with 3-100# G.P. bombs and 200 rounds of .50 caliber ammunition. On the 23rd of February, Lieutenant (jg) Paris flying his PB4Y-1 Liberator from the US Patrol Bomber Squadron VPB-111 sighted two barges near the Miyako Jima coast, containing what was reported to be 300 Japanese soldiers. He executed a bombing and strafing attack against the two barges. The two barges were sunk and it was reported that 200 of the soldiers were killed. On 5 March Lieutenant J. W. Holt flying a Navy PB4Y-2 Privateer belonging to the US Patrol Bomber Squadron VPB-119, sighted 3 barges about 3 miles off shore at Miyako Jima's harbor and four Japanese Destroyer escorts and 7 merchant vessels anchored inside of the harbor. Approaching at a low altitude the gunners strafed and sank all three barges. The Japanese fired their AA at the bomber from the Destroyer escorts and shore batteries hitting the planes instrument panel and its hydraulic fluid lines were severed. This damage forced Lieut. Holt to return to his base. On the 6th of March Lieutenant (jg) A. L. Althans flying a PB4Y-2 Privateer from

Patrol Bomber squadron VPB-119 squadron attacked three small merchant ships near Ishigaki Jima. One ship was hit admidship with a single 100# bomb, sinking it and another ship was left with its deck burning and the third ship was reported to have had minor damage. On the 8th of March, Lieutenant Comdr. R.C. Bales flying his PB4Y-2 Privateer from the US Patrol Bomber Squadron made a direct hit with a 250# G. P. Bomb on a three hatch merchant ship near Ishigaki. At 0600H on the 23rd of March, 16 FG-1D Corsair fighter bomber planes from *Air Group-6* were launched from the *USS HANCOCK CV 19* for targets at Sakishima Gunto. Each plane was armed with 6 five inch High Velocity rockets. The weather over the targets was bad and the results of the raid couldn't be seen. It was thought that the runway at Sukama Airfield at Miyako Jima was damaged. The next day at 0559H *HANCOCK* launched 16 FG-1D Corsairs each armed with four five inch H.V. rockets; the target was Miyako Jima, 180 miles away. The fighters reported encountering enemy's 75mm, 20mm and machine gun fire while over the target. Destroyed were three out of four twin engine planes sitting on Hirara field. Two AA positions were rocketed with direct hits. Three ships were rocketed and left burning along with a spreading fire at the main jetty in Hirara port. All of the shipping around the harbor was attacked. All aircraft returned to their carrier. AT 0740H the following airplanes were launched from the *HANCOCK* to attack Miyako Jima. From Squadron *VB-6,* 9 SB2C Helldivers, each armed with 2-500# General Purpose bombs, Squadron *VT-6,* 13 TBM-3 Avengers, each armed with 4-500# G.P. bombs, Squadron *VBF-6,* 6 FG-1D Corsairs, each armed with four H.V. rockets and Squadron *VF-6,* 4 F6F-5 Hellcats, each armed with .50 caliber wing guns. All bombs and rockets hit targets on Sukama and Nobara Airfields at Miyako, leaving the runways cratered. All airplanes returned safely. (*Nobara and what is now called Nobaru are one of the same places.*) At 1124H *HANCOCK* launched 17 FG-1D Corsairs, each armed with four 5 inch rockets for a strike at Ishigaki Jima. Rockets were fired through overcast and the damage caused to the targets couldn't be determined because of the cloud coverage over the target. One of the planes was hit by flak and the pilot was forced to make a water landing. Other planes stayed in the area, circling the downed plane until they ran low on gas. One of these planes that had been circling ran out of gas and had to make a water landing and the pilot was picked up by a US Destroyer. The other pilot who was hit with flak was later rescued by a British ship. At 1350H the following airplanes were launched from the *USS HANCOCK*. From Squadron *VT-6,* 11 TBM-3 Avengers, each armed with 4-500# G.P. bombs, Squadron *VB-6,* 10 SB2C4 Helldivers, each armed with 2-500# bombs and Squadron *VBF-6,* 6 FG-1D Corsairs, each armed with four 5 inch rockets. All bombs were dropped and rockets were fired. The target was Hirara Airfield on Miyako Jima. The target was covered in a cloud layer and the bombing was made by radar, all airplanes safely returned to the carrier.

TENSE TIMES AT MIYAKO

Large enemy planes were seen flying very high over Miyako during January of 1945. These were thought to be planes that were doing reconnaissance work, so the people on the island became very nervous. Rumors ran high and everyone was tense. It now seemed probable that the island would be attacked from the sea, for the Japanese Army HQ moved from the schools in Hirara city out to Noharadake and established themselves in housing at the north end of Noharadake. Adjacent to their new quarters, a cave had been dug into the side of the dake to be used for the Army Headquarter's last stand against the enemy. Around the middle of February the people of Miyako learned that the Americans were attacking Iwo Jima. Word was spread through the island that everyone should expect a land war at Miyako and that everyone who was fit and able should prepare to fight the enemy when they landed. In March two supply ships were attacked by enemy bombers while their crews were unloading their cargo at Hirara port. A military ship laying mines around the island also came under attack and all three being hit with bombs slipped to the bottom of the ocean with the loss of 115 men. Now word reached the island that Iwo Jima was in American hands and the enemy was gathering at Ulithi in the Caroline Islands for their next plan of attack. The people were wondering if the next enemy attack was going to be Miyako or Okinawa or both. The answer was just a few days away. Bombs from enemy aircraft rained on Miyako Jima on the 30th of March as the people nervously looked out of their bomb shelters. So far, this was the most enemy airplanes that had come to attack the island. The Japanese had learned from previous assaults on their islands by the Americans that just before landing their troops from the sea they would heavily bomb and strafe. Miyako people were sure this meant their island was next. It was later learned that this attack against the airfields and the island's port was part of the Americans plan in disabling the airfields and aircraft at Sakishima Gunto while taking Kerama Retto near Okinawa.

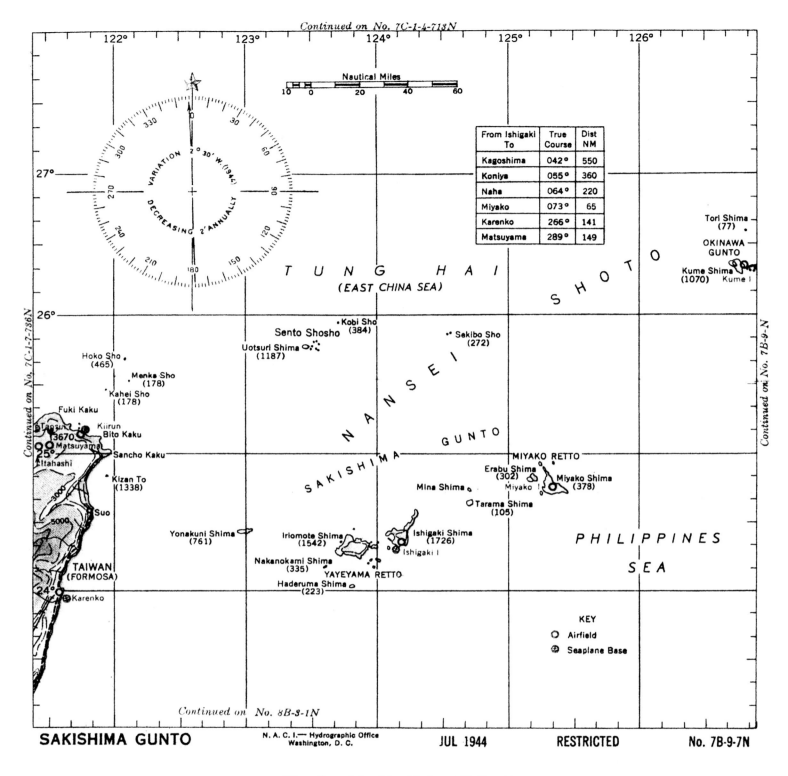

Continued on No. 7C-1-4-713N

From Ishigaki To	True Course	Dist NM
Kagoshima	042°	550
Koniya	055°	360
Naha	064°	220
Miyako	073°	65
Karenko	266°	141
Matsuyama	289°	149

KEY

⊘ Airfield

⊕ Seaplane Base

Continued on No. 8B-3-1N

SAKISHIMA GUNTO

N. A. C. I.— Hydrographic Office
Washington, D. C.

JUL 1944   RESTRICTED   No. 7B-9-7N

Map furnished by Robert S. Scott

Robert S. Scott was an aviation radio man and the tail gunner who participated in the bombing and strafing at Okinawa and Sakishima Gunto. His air squadron, VC91 was attached to the USS SAVO ISLAND CVE-78 and USS MAKIN ISLAND CVE-93. He flew aboard the TBM Avenger torpedo bombers that were escorted by FM-2 Wildcat fighters. The fighters strafed the Airfields at Sakishima Gunto and the TBM's followed, dropping their bombs. On their bombing runs Bob noticed that the antiaircraft fire was as heavy at Sakishima Gunto as any he had seen at Okinawa.

AIRFIELDS AT SAKISHIMA GUNTO
1945

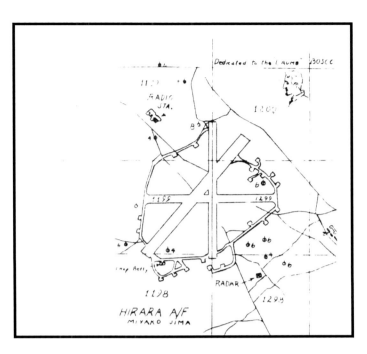

HIRARA MIYAKO JIMA Japanese Navy
Airfield 1945 Three runways
NE-SW 300 X 4800 ft.
E-W 320 X 5000 ft.
SE-NW unknown

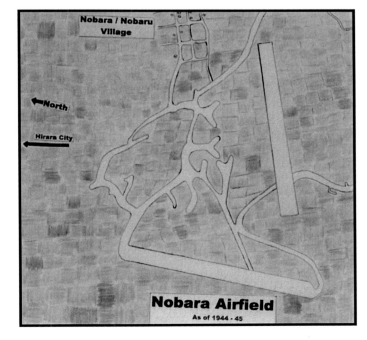

NOBARU/NOBARA MIYAKO JIMA
Japanese Army Airfield 1945
Two runways
NE-SW 175 X 4600 ft.
E-W unknown

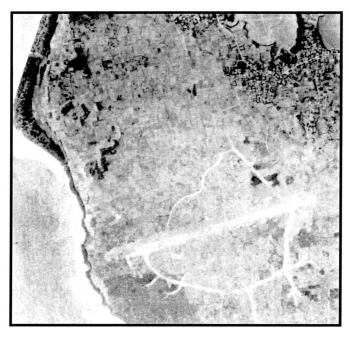 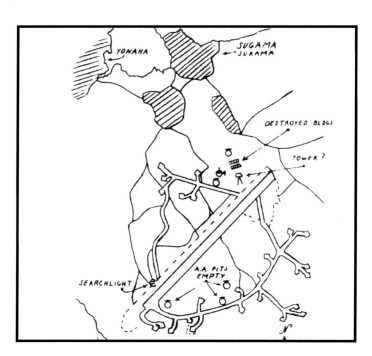

SUKAMA MIYAKO JIMA AIRFIELD 1945
One runway. Size unknown

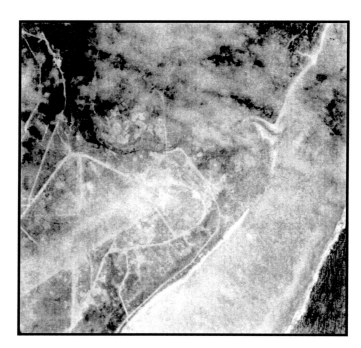 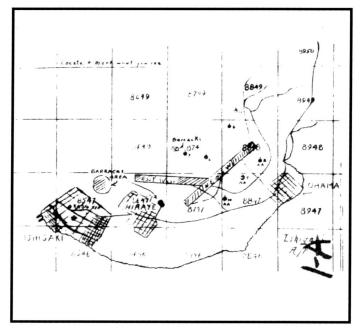

ISHIGAKI JIMA Japanese Airfield
Two runways
NE-SW 320 X 5000 ft.
E-W 490 X 4700 ft.

Note: Photo and Drawing of MIYARA AIRFIELD at ISHIGAKI are not available.
Airfield Photos are from The National Archives. Drawings from G.P. Adams.

A Japanese KAMIKAZE pilot salutes as he receives his sortie orders.
The two bars on his sleeve indicate that he is a Naval Lieutenant.
(Courtesy of the US Naval Institute)

A Comrade Tightens the "HACHIMAKT" for a Japanese KAMIKAZE Pilot
ready to sortie, 1944-45

The ancient Samurai, in preparing for battle, wound this folded white cloth about their heads to confine their long hair and to keep perspiration from their eyes. The Hachimaki thus came to symbolize mainly courage and pre-battle composure, and so was worn by all the Kamikaze pilots.

(Courtesy of the US Naval Institute)

Lieutenant General Toshiro Noumi
1894-1945

Japanese Army Commander at Miyako Jima
at Sakishima Gunto

Home residence: Omichi Kiatsu Ichihara at Hiroshima

Graduated from Military school and Army University

As a foot soldier he became a Lieutenant Colonel

In 1940 he became the Headquarters chief for the Military Police

As a Major General he was Commander of the Military Police at Formosa/Tiawan

Promoted to Lieutenant General he took over as 28th Army Division Commander at
Miyako Jima Sakishima Gunto on 12 January 1945

He ended his life with poison in 1945 after he learned that he was being linked to killings
in Shanghai China where he was a police commander in 1940

It was also alleged that he gave the order to kill an American pilot who was being held
captive at Miyako Jima in 1945 while he was the Army division commander there

Chapter 6
THE
BRITISH AND AMERICAN
DAILY OPERATIONS AT
SAKISHIMA GUNTO

The British Pacific Fleet "BPF" was formed on the 22nd of November 1944. The fleet was made up of ships, airplanes, sailors and pilots from BRITAIN, AUSTRALIA, NEW ZEALAND, and CANADA. The BPF fleet had successfully attacked oil refineries under Japanese control in SUMATRA in January 1945. The fleet sailed from SYDNEY, AUSTRALIA near the end of February 1945 to their forward base at MANUS ATOLL in the Admiralty Islands. When they were needed to support "OPERTION ICEBERG", *the Allied battle code name for the Okinawa Operation in the RYUKYU Islands*, the British left MANUS on 18 March 1945 and arrived at ULITHI ATOLL, the massive US supply and staging area in the CAROLINE Islands on the 20th of March. Three days later with Vice Admiral Sir Bernard Rawlings, their Commander at sea aboard *KING GEORGE V,* and Vice Admiral Sir Philip Vian in charge of the Air Operations, the fleet sailed from ULITHI and arrived at their assigned station near SAKISHIMA GUNTO. They were to be the British Pacific Fleet Task Force-57, a partner with the American Task Force 58 in Operation Iceberg. Their battle station was a position southwest of the larger American Task Force-58 who was assembling near OKINAWA SHIMA. BPF would be at the American's rear and left flanks and their job would be the neutralizing of the Japanese airfields on the islands at SAKASHIMA GUNTO and nearby FORMOSA now called TAIWAN. The Japanese "Special Strike Forces" in FORMOSA were going to be using these special airfields for staging and refueling of their Kamikaze airplanes that were on their way to dive into American and Allied ships near OKINAWA. Admiral Rawlings assembled on his battle station near SAKISHIMA GUNTO two battle ships, five cruisers, eleven destroyers and four Aircraft carriers. He also had brought a fleet train that was waiting off in the distance, ready to re-supply and refuel his warships. Admiral Rawlings would report to Admiral Spruance the US 5th fleet commander during the first part of Iceberg and Admiral Halsey the US 3rd fleet commander later when Halsey took over for Spruance. *It should be noted here that while BPF was under Admiral Spruance, the 5th fleet Commander, the British would be called Task Force-57, and when they were under Admiral Halsey, the 3rd fleet Commander, they would be called Task Force-37.* The four British carriers of Task Force-57 were commanded by Vice Admiral Sir Philip Vian. The Carriers were the *HMS INDOMITABLE, HMS ILLUSTRIOUS, HMS INDEFATIGABLE* and *HMS VICTORIOUS* and later *HMS FORMIDABLE,* that replaced *ILLUSTRIOUS.* These carriers had a variety of airplanes onboard. The bombers were the American built Grumman designed TBF Torpedo bombers. The fighters were American built modified F4U Corsairs. Other fighters were the American built F6 Grumman Hellcats, British built Seafires and Fireflys. Then there were two bi-winged, sea rescue and fleet spotter planes called the "Walrus". These were stationed on the aircraft carrier *HMS VICTORIOUS.* In the Pacific, the Avenger Torpedo bombers were loaded with General Purpose bombs and used extensively against the islands as a light bomber. The Seafire was the British navy's version of the land based Supermarine Spitfire. Because of its long nose it was not very popular as a carrier based plane. The wings on the Corsairs had to be modified by shortening the wing tips. This was done so the planes would fit under the deck on the British carriers. The Fairey Firefly was a two seat fighter and held it's own in combat. The Supermarine Walrus was an armed float sea rescue plane and a spotter. One disadvantage for the British Air-Arm was that they never developed their carrier based planes into "Night Fighters"

In the morning hours of the 26th of March the first British strike took place against the airfields at MIYAKO JIMA at SAKISHIMA GUNTO. Through out the day nearly 75-80 fighters and bombers took action against the three airfields at MIYAKO JIMA. One fighter and one bomber were reported lost during this raid. On the 27th there was a repeat of strikes against MIYAKO. Targeted on this raid were barracks, a radio station and airfields. There were no strikes called for on the 28th of March due to a typhoon warning. On the 29th and 30th the fleet pulled back from their station to refuel from their fleet train. On the 31st, fighters patrolled the islands seeing very little activity. After three days in a row of action, the ships on battle station would begin to run low on fuel and supplies and they would have to be replenished. When they pulled away from their battle station to be re-supplied by their fleet train, the plan was that carrier based planes from American aircraft carriers would take over the task of attacking the SAKISHIMA GUNTO airfields while the British were away.

On 1 April, word reached the Japanese military on MIYAKO JIMA that the American 10th Army had landed on the beaches at Okinawa. Special Forces planes (Kamikazes) from TAIWAN landed on the airfields at ISHIGAKI and MIYAKO. They were fueled and checked out while their pilots rested and received up to date information before leaving to find their enemy targets.

1 April 1945 *Easter Sunday* **(L-DAY)** While the US ground forces were going ashore at OKINAWA SHIMA, enemy planes were spotted heading for the British carriers. One strafed *INDOMITABLE* and the Battle ship *KING GEARGE V*. Four enemy planes were splashed. A few minutes later one broke through and a Kamikaze dived into the *INDEFATIGABLE'S* deck. The flight deck of the British carriers was made of steel and this crash only slightly damaged the carrier's deck. She was back operational in less than an hour. There were a few casualties reported. Another enemy plane dropped a bomb very close to the destroyer *ULSTER* causing her engine room to flood and she reported some casualties. She was later towed away by another destroyer. BPF launched a fighter sweep attacked against Japanese aircraft seen on the ground at ISHIGAKI and HIRARA airfields, later they reported 14 aircraft damaged in this raid. Back at the fleet another Kamikaze dove and clipped the edge of *VICTORIOUS'S* flight deck and crashed over the side. This caused no damage to the carrier.

The Americans took note of the 3 inch thick steel decks on the British carriers. The flight decks of the American carriers were made of wood. Airplanes crashing into the steel decks were like a fly hitting a window. After a kamikaze would hit the British carrier's deck, the ship crews would sweep the airplane crash remains over the side and they would be back in full operation in 30 minutes. Repair of the American wooden decks after being hit by a Kamikaze could cause a carrier to be taken out of service for several days and even weeks in some cases. However, there was a couple of down sides to the steel decks on the British carriers. The weight of these decks caused the British carriers to burn more fuel per mile and when these ships were operating in the tropical regions, the sailors complained about the hot steel on the bottoms of their feet. One lad told the story of how he and his shipmates would bind layers of card board to the bottom of their shoes in order to build up a space between the bottoms of their feet and the steel on the deck. Some would say at high noon the steel would get so hot that you could fry eggs on the decks.

2 April (L-plus-1) British fighters again swept the islands. In the afternoon the BPF pulled back from their combat station and went for re-fueling. Now, The American carrier planes were diverted to SAKISHIMA GUNTO to continue the attacks on the islands until the British returned.

3 April 1945 (L-plus-2) Twelve F6F Hellcats from *VF-30* squadron stationed on the American *USS BELLEAU WOOD CVL-24* were launched for strikes at MIYAKO JIMA. The 12 fighters were rigged with 6 rockets on each plane. The target was the SUKAMA airstrip on the west side of MIYAKO JIMA. Only one single engine plane was seen shielded in a revetment. The plane was strafed without seeing fire or an explosion raising the possibility that it was either a dummy or an inoperable plane. The plane was also hit with a rocket and now can be considered destroyed no matter what its prior status was. Barracks like structures adjacent to the airfield were strafed and rockets hits were also made on them causing fires. A lighthouse on the north tip end of MIYAKO got the attention of all striking groups who strafed it thoroughly and expended their remaining rockets at it. Some small boats were strafed in a northeastern cove of the island. All planes returned. All rockets and 15,500 rounds of .50 ammo was expended. No enemy damage was noted on the returning airplanes.

Note: Airplanes from three large American Aircraft carriers and Naval Patrol Bombers were often sharing the same air space over the islands at the same time.

Lieutenant (jg) F.D. Murphy from the US Patrol Bombing Squadron VPB-119 sighted two merchant ships at MIYAKO JIMA. On his first bombing run against the ships, he dropped a single 250# bomb that hit one of the ships and blew it to bits. He then strafed the second ship. As he passed over it at 300 feet the ship blew up, sending pieces of metal and debris up through the bottom of his Privateer bomber causing a considerable amount of damage to the plane.

At 0605H on 3 April, 15 F6F Hellcats from *VBF-17* were launched from the *USS Hornet* plus fighters from the other fast carriers in Task Group 58.1. The fighters strafed NOBARA airfields, installations and AA (anti-aircraft) positions with 11,000 rounds, damaging all targets. One enemy single engine airplane, thought to be a *"Zeke"* on the ground was destroyed and another damaged. Nine fighters attacked HIRARA Airfield and revetments, firing 3,200 rounds of ammo damaging one twin engine airplane on the ground. The fighters strafed the town of HIRARA, boats, docks and warehouses with 4,200 rounds starting numerous fires. All of the fighters returned to their carriers. One

Hellcat lost a belly fuel tank to AA fire. Twelve Hellcats from *VF-17* took off from the *Hornet* and joined other carrier fighter units at 0705H. Eleven Hellcats were fitted each with a 500 lb G.P Bomb. The target was ISHIGAKI JIMA. Seven bombs were dropped on the airfields and enemy AA targets. On the airfields two 'Betty" bombers were burned and 11 single engine airplanes and 3 twin engine airplanes were damaged. Four bombs were dropped on the town of ISHIGAKI damaging warehouses and docks. A radio station at HIRAKUBO SAKI was strafed at the north end of the island and two AA positions were knocked out. Moderate medium and some heavy AA were encountered over the airfield during the runs. One pilot took aerial pictures while over the airfield. All fighters returned to their carrier were it was discovered that one Hellcat had taken a 20mm hit in the Starboard wing. All bombs were dropped and 7,000 rounds of ammunition were expended.

At 0823H, the *USS BENNINGTON CV-20* launched 4 of her F6F-5 Hellcats from *VF-82*, 12 TBM Avengers from *VT-82, 12 SB2C-4E* Helldivers from *VB-82* and 6 F4U-1D Corsairs from their Marine squadron *VMF-123*. The four Hellcats accompanied the strike group to MIYAKO JIMA to obtain photographs. Because of 8/10 cloud cover at low altitude, photos of any value couldn't be taken. Planes attacked NOBARA Airfield in a strafing bombing and rocket run. Also some parked aircraft were strafed. Meager AA fire was encountered during this attack.

At 0827H, 12 F6F Hellcats from *VF-17*, 12 TBM-3 Avengers from *VT-17* and *12 SB2C* Helldivers from *VB-17* took to the air from the *USS HORNET CV-12*. Ten of the Hellcats were loaded with 500 lb G.P. bombs having 4-6 hour delayed fuses. Two Hellcats carried cameras. All of the Hellcats were each fully loaded with 2,400 rounds of ammo and each plane was carrying 400 gallons of fuel. Their target was HIRARA Airfield at MIYAKO JIMA. The 4-6 hour delay bombs were dropped on HIRARA Airfield by the first division. Bombed also were revetments along the NE-SE runway. Two twin engine planes were damaged on the runway. Strafing attacks were made at KURIMA, BORA towns and on the lighthouse at the north tip of MIYAKO JIMA. Fires were started in two towns resulting from the strafing. Four planes strafed small boats at OGAMI SHIMA, six luggers and a town on IKEMA SHIMA. Prior to the photo run, it was reported that a "Betty" bomber may have been damaged on HIRARA Airfield. The Photo team took photographs of the three airfields on MIYAKO JIMA and after finishing they strafed the town of HIRARA and a town on the south end of IKEMA SHIMA. Another division of Hellcats were directed to accompany a division of bombers and a division of torpedo bombers in an attack on some watercraft which were sighted in Junk Bay (*YONAHA BAY*) on the west side of MIYAKO. The fighters attacked ahead of the bombers. After this they all joined in on the bombing of HIRARA Airfield destroying two more twin engine planes. All airplanes on this raid returned to their carrier and none reported any damage to their planes. All bombs were dropped and 19,200 rounds of ammo were expended. The bomb tactics were: From 10,000 feet start a 40 degree glide and release the bombs at 1,200 ft. altitude.

Another strike launched at 0830H from the *HORNET* was 12 F6F Hellcats from *VF-17*, 10 TBM Avengers from *VT-17* and 10 SB2C Helldivers from *VB-17*. The target was

MIYAKO JIMA. On this raid 9-500# General Purpose bombs were dropped on shipping at IKEMA and at the north end of MIYAKO causing damage to shipping and to the nearby docks. Thirty four 500# bombs, 8 of these having 24 hour delay fuses were strewn along the SW-NE airstrip at HIRARA Airfield. A total of 2,500 rounds of .30 cal. and 3,900 rounds of .50 cal. ammunition were expended on the MIYAKO JIMA airfields and targets at IKEMA SHIMA. Some ground AA was observed and six dummy airplanes were seen at HIRARA Airfield.

Seven *VF-30* F6F Hellcats from the carrier *BELLEAU WOOD* took to the air at 0830H in route to MIYAKO JIMA. Each was carrying two 500# G.P. bombs. Their target was the airfield at SUKAMA. Because of low overcast the fighter planes were forced to spot the target through rifts in the clouds, position themselves for the run, and start down hoping to be on target when they broke through the overcast and with no opportunity to correct aim before release. The bombs fell along the north edge of the runway. Two bomb hits were seen on the runway, probably made by torpedo bombers. All planes dropped their bombs. 2,000 rounds of .50 ammunition were expended while strafing. Enemy AA was meager. All seven Hellcats returned and no damage to the planes was reported.

At 0837H another bombing strike was initiated. This time 12 SB2C Helldivers from *VB-17* left the *HORNET* in route to MIYAKO JIMA. Seven of the Helldivers were carrying two each 500# G.P. bombs and five had two each 250# G.P bombs. The weather was cloudy and there was 12 miles visibility. A stacks aft freighter was spotted off the NW coast of MIYAKO and the Helldivers initiated an attack from 10,000 feet. During the dive the pilots noticed that this ship was already gutted and aground. Some of the planes released their bombs and some didn't. After breaking off from the freighter attack the bomber group hunted for targets of opportunity such as small boats, airfields and other targets. Some meager heavy automatic AA fire was encountered. All planes returned to the carrier. No damage was reported. All bombs were dropped and a total of 900-20mm rounds of ammunition were fired.

At 1024H, Three F6F-5 Hellcats from *VF-82* and seven F4U-1D Corsairs from *VMF-123* left the *USS BENNINGTON CV-20*. Their mission was to strike the runway at ISHIKAKI JIMA with 500# bombs and rockets. This was accomplished by the three Hellcats. Two single engine airplanes parked near the runway were damaged. Action taken by the Corsairs is not known. One of the Hellcats was hit in the port wing by very accurate enemy AA that was believed to have been a 25mm shell. This airplane did return to base along with the others.

At 1035H 16 F6F Hellcats from *VF-17* from the *HORNET* were launched along with fighters from other carriers in Task Group 58.1. All of the planes were loaded with 1 each 500# G.P. bomb. Twelve of these bombs had a standard fuse attached while the other 4 planes, their bombs were fused for a twenty four hour delay. The target was IRIOMOTE JIMA, where an airfield that had previously been reported to have been under construction. The attack on this airfield was cancelled when it was noticed by the attacking division that all work on the field had been stopped. The fighters flew around the southern and western side of the island and spotted the minor naval base at

SHIRAHAMA near the inlet of FUNAUKE KO. Seen here were thirteen 60 foot landing boats on the ramp and in the water, boat building and maintenance facilities, Two "Sugar Dogs" (*Code name for small merchant ships with one mast*) anchored off shore, and a barracks area at the base. These became the target for the 16-500# G.P. bombs and 20,000 rounds of .50 cal .machine gun ammo that was delivered in 5 attacks. All of the landing boats were destroyed or rendered inoperative. Barracks and maintenance buildings were left burning and the two "Sugar Dogs" were damaged. A radar station at YAYEME and the town of AKASAKI were strafed. Time over the target was 1 hour 5 minutes. All planes returned. Minor damage was reported to the Port wing on one of the returning fighters.

Released from the *USS HORNET* at 1151H on 3 April 1945 were 14 F6F Hellcats of squadron *VBF-17* that were assigned a fighter sweep of IRIOMOTE JIMA in SAKISHIMA GUNTO. Each Hellcat was fitted with 1-500# G.P. bomb with a fuse setting of .025. One of these Hellcats would be the photographic plane. Each of the 14 planes carried 2,400 rounds of ammunition, and each was fueled with 400 gallons of aviation gasoline. The weather was hazy and the cloud ceiling was 1,500 feet. The fighter group searched for a reported airfield at HAEMI ZAKE but was only able to locate a construction site having 15-20 small buildings where the airfield was reported to be. A bombing attack was made on the buildings and bombs were dropped among the buildings causing slight damage. Following this bombing raid the fighters strafed a town at KURO SHIMA starting fires. Before returning to the carrier; the planes made strafing attacks on some small boats and a pier at a town on the west side of KOHAMA JIMA and they strafed a village on HATOMA JIMA. The photo plane was able to photograph the entire perimeter of IROMOTE Island. All planes returned to the carrier after being airborne for 4 hours and each plane having 100 gallons of fuel remaining in their tanks. There was no reported damage to their airplanes and no AA or enemy planes were seen.

At 1155H, eleven F6F Hellcats of squadron *VF-30* launched from *USS BELLEAU WOOD* CVL-24. Each plane was carrying two 500# G.P. bombs. The target was HIRARA Airfield on MIYAKO JIMA. Some parked planes that were observed on HIRARA, included one "*Helen*" that looked operational. This plane was bombed and the damage results were unknown. One "*Topsy*" in a revetment sustained a direct hit by a 500# bomb, two single engine fighters in a double revetment took a direct hit by a 500# bomb and approximately 12 single engine types, mostly "*Zekes*", dispersed around the field were thoroughly strafed and two rocketed. These planes were gray in color and bore no visible markings and may have been dummies. The runways on this field were cratered by seven hits by 500# bombs. One bomb was placed at the intersection of the runways. Two bombs were placed in the southwest end of the northeast-southwest runway. Another hit was at the east-west runway near its west end. Another hit was at the north end of the north-south runway. Very well camouflaged barracks and other buildings located east of the airfield were bombed, rocketed and strafed. No reported damage was reported to the eleven returning airplanes. Meager AA was reported while over the airfield.

At 1345H, 10 TBM Avengers of *squadron VT-17*, 12 F6F-5 Hellcats of *VF-17* and 10 SB2C Helldivers of *VB-17* left the *HORNET* for an attack on shipping an the runways at MIYAKO JIMA. No shipping was found, so the attacks were made on the airfield and its installations. Sixty percent of twenty eight 500 pound bombs dropped on the airfield struck the runways, principally the SW-NE runways. Two bombs of four directed at AA batteries east of the runways were reported hits. Likewise, half of a four-bomb load dropped on AA batteries north of the field found their mark. Four bombs were laid along the southern taxiway of the airfield where the pilots reported revetments. Eight of the bombs carried 24 hour long delay fuses. These were dropped on airstrip and taxiway. The 10 *VT-17* planes expended a total of 2,750 rounds of .50 cal ammo, 1,150 rounds of .30 cal on airfield targets and other targets of opportunity. Fires were started by strafing the town of IKEMAZOE on IRABU SHIMA. Heavy to meager AA was reported by the Avenger pilots. All planes returned to the carrier. Duration of the attack was 2.5 hours. No damage was reported to the returning planes.

At 1349H, 9 F6F-5 Hellcats of *VF-17*, 2 Hellcats of VB17, 10 TBM Avengers of *VT-17* and 10 SB2C Helldivers from *VB-17* from the *HORNET* were launched for the airfields at MIYAKO JIMA. The Hellcats dropped 7 of their 500# G.P. bombs onto HIRARA airfield revetments and runways reporting serious damage to both. Twelve single engine planes were reported hit with 5 of the 12 being destroyed. After the attack on the airfield the sweep strafed HIRARA harbor, a sea truck and 4 luggers (*Two mast sailing ships*) and then they set course for IRABU where the town of IKEMAZOE was strafed several times. Four fires were left burning there. This fighter division then returned to the carrier leaving one of their Hellcats to fly cover for the photographic team. This single Hellcat strafed SUKAMA Airfield and some barracks and concrete buildings on the northern peninsula of the island. Prior to the last photo run on the island during a pull out from a low level strafing a Hellcat was hit with several rounds of medium AA, blowing the port stabilizer and elevator off and making two large holes in the port wing. The pilot was able to climb back to 8,000 feet and join up with his division and fly back to the Task Force straight and level at 135 knots. He reported that he could not control his plane at speeds less than 115 knots, he couldn't bring his control stick back and that he couldn't extend his tail hook for landing. He was told to fly ahead of the others and bail out. He climbed to approximately 8,500 feet rolled over on his back and jumped. His chute opened and his division circled him in tight turns all the way down. A destroyer of the formation reached the pilot's parachute within one minute after it hit the water, but the pilot was missing. Although a thorough search of the area was conducted until darkness, the pilot was not found.

At 1354H, Eight F6F-5 Hellcats from *VF 30* aboard the carrier *USS BELLEAU WOOD* were launched. Their target was NOBARA Airfield on MIYAKO JIMA. These fighters were fitted with two 500# bombs on each plane. The East –West runway was attacked by one Hellcat, placing two 500# bombs just west of the middle of this runway. Other bombs were dropped just east of the middle and near the west end. Another Hellcat hit the east end with one bomb. A "*Zeke*" was strafed that was parked off the north edge of the west end of this runway which refused to burn. A bomb was placed in a clump of trees to the north from which heavy AA fire had been received on a morning strike. A

"*Topsy*" was strafed that was parked off the south edge of the west-end of this runway without damage results being known. Two planes attacked the North-South runway and scored a bomb hit near the south end of this runway and two bombs were placed near the middle. The second section of this division attacked the East –West runway, making a hit at the east end and a hit at the west end. The barracks and buildings located north of the east end of the East-West runway were strafed. All bombs were dropped and 1,850 rounds of .50 cal. ammunition were expended. All airplanes returned to the carrier. No damage was reported to the airplanes.

3 April at 1358H, 10 Helldivers of *VB-17* took to the air. The bombers were each carrying one 1000# G.P. bomb and 2 each, 250# G.P. bombs. HIRARA Airfield including AA positions, buildings, revetments and runways were strafed and bombed. All of the bombs hit their targets considering that the airfield was partially obscured by clouds. After the bombing runs, the pilots moved their Helldivers to the town of HIRARA on MIYAKO and the town of IKEMAZOE on IRABU and strafed both towns with their 20mm guns starting numerous fires before returning from the raid. Meager, accurate heavy AA automatic weapons fire was encountered over HIRARA Airfield during the bombing run. All bombers returned without encountering any damage during the strike.

At 1503H, six F6F-5 Hellcats from *VF-82* took off from the *USS BENNINGTON*. One airplane was fitted with one 500# bomb and others were fitted with 8 rockets. The Hellcats was to strike targets of opportunity on ISHIGAKI JIMA. The fighters located the HEGINA emergency airfield a short distance northwest of ISHIGAKI and they seriously damaged two hangers there. The field is small, about 1,600 square feet with an extension off on one side which gives a little longer runway. The surface was made of sod. No aircraft were sighted on the ground during the attack. Two medium sized hangers existed with good revetments. There were rifle pits noted to the east of the field. Attacked next was MIYARA Airfield with a strafing run. No lucrative targets were found on this airfield. IRIOMOTE Island to the west was looked over but no airfields were found. Six luggers were strafed that were seen in a cove on the western side of the island. The fighters then returned to base as scheduled. 3,000 rounds of ammunition were fired and all bombs and rockets were expended. There was no damage to the returning fighters.

At 1505H, eight F6F-5 fighter bombers of *VB-17* and *VF-17* got underway for a strike on ISHIGAKI JIMA Airfield. This time they were fitted with 1000# G.P. bombs. Five of these bombs had long delay fuse settings. The fighter bombers' guns were fully loaded. The fighters and fighter bombers arrived over their target at 1600H at an altitude of 8,500 feet and the fighter bombers started their bombing run with a 60 degree dive, releasing their bombs at 2,000 feet with a recovery at 1000 feet. Airplanes and buildings near the runway were seriously damaged. After the bombing run, three additional strafing runs were made on revetments and parked aircraft on the field. One division made an additional strafing attack on MIYARA Airfield. All airplanes returned to the carrier. One Hellcat suffered extensive damage to its rudder and starboard, inboard flap.

On the ground the people huddled in makeshift bomb shelters while the island was being attacked for the last three consecutive days. Noises made by the attacking enemy planes were the roar and the revving of their engines, the firing of their machine guns, the frightening sound of the rockets and bombs exploding all around. Then there were the sounds of the Island's Air Artillery in the highlands firing their large guns at the enemy. All of this together was absolutely deafening. This was far beyond anything the people of MIYAKO JIMA had ever been subjected to. Everything on the island had suffered some type of damage during these attacks. Many animals that were out in the open were killed. The enemy planes dropped some bombs that didn't explode when they first made contact with the ground. These were identified and watched very carefully for it was not known when they would explode. Everyone stayed far away and clear of these bombs.

4 APRIL 1945 *Haven't learned of any action taken this day at SAKISHIMA GUNTO.*
5 APRIL 1945 *USS OAKLAND (CL95) with TG 58.4, strikes SAKISHIMA GUNTO.*

6 April 1945 (L-plus-5) On *the 6th of April the Japanese implemented the first attack of their plan 10-GO, called Kikusui, meaning "floating chrysanthemums". This plan was to be 10 separate attacks on the American and British fleets, using all the airplanes available from their Army and Navy. They would be a mixed group. Some bombers, fighters and Kamikazes would make up the attacking raids. Each of the 10 attacks would last as long as the Commanders felt that the attack was effective. So that no leaks could be made to the Allies of when one of these 10 attacks would start, no pre-planned starting dates were established. The decision to implement an attack could be decided whenever the Japanese Commanders called for it.*

The British returned to their battle station at SAKISHIMA relieving the Americans. A Kamikaze attempted to crash into the *HMS ILLUSTRIOUS* and as it came near the ship its wing hit the ships island structure and this spun the plane into the sea. A bomb aboard the plane exploded causing some minor damage to the carrier's structure. Two enemy planes were reported shot down and one British plane was lost to friendly fire.

7 April (L-plus-6) The British Fleet was requested to concentrate on FORMOSA and had to pull back from SAKASHIMA GUNTO and prepare for this. The American Escort carriers and their Air Groups would now again be assigned the job of neutralizing the airfields at SAKASHIMA GUNTO. The US 7th Fleet planes attacked and damaged planes parked on MIYAKO'S NOBARA Airfield. Lieutenant J.W. Holt from US Patrol Bomber squadron VPB-119 spotted and attacked a Japanese merchant ship in a cove at MIYAKO JIMA. His Privateer bomber met intensive anti-aircraft fire from all sides. After he finished his run against the ship he withdrew over the MIYAKO JIMA Airfield. There he spotted five Japanese "Oscar" fighter airplanes on the field. He strafed the planes, destroying two of them and damaging the remaining three. Crewman Henry B. Babe was slightly wounded during the attack. The bomber took hits that severed the rudder control cables and one engine was knocked out along with a fuel cell being damaged. The crew was able to stabilize the rudder and the plane made it back to its base safely.

The job of neutralizing the airfields at MIYAKO *and* ISHIGAKI JIMA *would now be assigned to RearAdmiral Calvin T. Durgin and his Escort Carriers and their Air Groups while the British were concentrating on Formosa. Under Durgin's command, were Task Units made up of CVE Escort Carriers, DD Destroyers and DE Destroyer Escorts. The Air Groups aboard most of the Escort Carriers operated with the Grumman TBM Avengers and General Motors FM-2 Wildcats, Although, the Grumman F6 Hellcats and Goodyear FG1 Corsairs operated from some of the larger Escort carriers and those with improved catapults. Durgin's main combat Task Units on Combat station were: TU 52.1.1, commanded by R. Admiral C.A.F. Sprague and other Commanders during the period of Operation Iceberg. TU 52.1.2 was commanded by R. Admiral Felix B. Stump and TU 52.1.3 was commanded by R. Admiral William D. Sample. Durgin also had some Escort Carriers in reserve. These carried out such support duties as transporting new planes, pilots and air crewmen to other combat carriers and to land stations. Some of these would be brought up to relieve Escorts on Combat stations.*

The Escort Carrier was often called a Jeep Carrier and often referred to as the baby Carrier. It was smaller than the Navy's Fast Carriers. Therefore, it couldn't carry aboard as many airplanes as the large carriers. However, it was easier to maneuver in and out of combat zones and especially around the smaller Pacific islands. Escort carriers performed their first duty in the Atlantic Ocean while escorting ships that were carrying war materials to England. Some of its duties were to replenish the larger fast carriers with airplanes. Air groups from the Jeep carriers furnish CAP, Combat Air Patrol and ASP, Anti-Submarine Patrol for convoys crossing the ocean. They furnished Fighter and Torpedo/bomber type airplanes to support island landings and their planes performed air to ground bombings of enemy airfields, The planes from these baby carriers supported ground troops by bombing enemy positions and bombing enemy AA gun positions, enemy ships and the Escorts conducted training for Air Groups. Admiral Nimitz once said that the Escort carriers became a lot more than its name implied. All Escorts carriers were not the same in size. It was only late in the war that a standard size Escort carrier was designed and several of these were built in Washington State by Henry Kaiser.

Early in the war, some civilian oil company transports were converted into Escort carriers by adding a landing deck nearly 550 feet long and 115 feet wide to the top of their hull. The Escorts had a speed of 18-19 knots. Each carrier accommodated a ship crew, including their air crew of approximately 800. Up to 25 airplanes could be handled aboard each vessel during combat conditions. These large Escort Carriers could hold enough fuel to stay on battle station longer than other escorts. They could even fuel the Destroyers and Destroyer Escorts in their Task Unit. Four of these modified tankers were assigned to Admiral Durgin's task group and were under the Command of R. Admiral Sample of TU 52.1.3. They were: USS SANGAMON CVE 26, formerly Esso "Trenton", USS SANTEE CVE 29, formerly Esso "Seakay", USS SUWANNEE CVE 27, formerly civilian tanker "Markay" and USS CHENANGO, formerly civilian Esso tanker "New Orleans". It's fair to say that these civilian ships brought into the US Navy earlier, had served as fleet Tankers and Oilers before being converted to Escort Carriers in early 1942. They were seasoned veterans of the War by the time they reached SAKISHIMA

GUNTO. These four escort carriers had been in action in North Africa in operation Torch in 1942 and had seen plenty of action in the Pacific before becoming a part of operation Iceberg. They earned the name: "THE INDISPENSABLES".

What one Sailor who later became the USS SANGAMON'S historian wrote about the SAKISHIMA operation: "This group of islands including ISHIGAKI and MIYAKO, on which the enemy had airfields for launching attacks against shipping around OKINAWA. It became the task of the SANGAMON'S group to keep these fields inoperative. The islands became what our Air Group called our Baby. Since our carriers of the unit took over the routine patrols, every flight from the SANGAMON to SAKISHIMA was either a strike or Target Combat Air Patrol." Ref. Don Schroeder's history of the USS SANGAMON.

Rear/Admiral Sample, Commander of Task Unit 52.1.3 Carrier Division 22, took up his position 120 miles east of MIYAKO JIMA the morning of the 8th of April with his four modified tankers that had been made into Escort Carriers. There was the *USS SANGAMON CVE 26 with AIR GROUP 33, USS SUWANNEE CVE 27 with AIR GROUP 40, USS SANTEE CVE 29 with AIR GROUP 24* and *USS CHENANGO* with *AIR GROUP 25.* Because these four Escort Carriers were the larger of the bulk of Escort carriers in the American fleet. All four of these Escort carriers had Air Groups that flew the Grumman F6 Hellcats as fighters and their fighter bombers were TBM Avengers. Even though the Avengers were originally designed as a Torpedo plane, they were used very effectually in the latter part of the war as bombers.

As for the Air group designators, I have chosen to use the parent Air group (AG) number only when referring to the Air groups on the four larger CVE carriers. The US Navy Designation for the Air groups on these four Escort carriers is CVEG-#. For an example, The SUWANNEE had CVEG-40 at SAKISHIMA GUNTO, Meaning Escort Carrier Air group 40. Now, the Air groups were often broken down into Squadrons. The Avengers of Air group 40 might belong to VT-40, meaning Air Torpedo 40 Squadron. The Hellcats might belong to VF-40, meaning Air Fighter 40 Squadron. In some cases there were the letters VTB in front of an Air Squadron number, meaning Air Torpedo Bomber or VFB, meaning Air Fighter Bomber. Now to make this more confusing some of the later Air groups were replaced with what were called Composite squadrons. In that case they had the letters VC in front of the number, meaning Air Composite. For an example: VC-91.

8 April (L-plus-7) Launched from the *USS SUWANNEE* from *AG-40* were 4 Hellcats for Tactical Combat Air Patrol, 7 for Local Combat Air Patrol, 2 for Local Anti-Submarine Patrol and 2 Avengers were sent for Air Observers. An additional 24 Hellcats and 13 Avengers were launched to make strikes on the islands of MIYAKO and ISHIGAKI SHIMA. On MIYAKO JIMA the primary target was HIRARA Airfield where one plane on the ground was destroyed. Gun positions around the field were bombed, strafed and rocketed. Expended were 7-500# General Purpose bombs, 70-100# G.P. bombs and 134-5 inch High Explosive rockets. A small tramp steamer was set fire north of HIRARA by strafing. On the Bomber strip at ISHIGAKI JIMA, 4-500# G.P. bombs, 20-100# G.P. bombs and 58-5 inch H.E. rockets were expended on the runway, installations and gun positions. The *USS SANTEE'S AG-24 planes* were launched at 0549H and 1045H. Fifteen fighters and 8 TBM Avenger bombers were sent to attack HIRARA Airfield at MIYAKO where they cratered the runways and destroyed one "*Betty*" bomber and one "*Tony*" parked on the ground. In a later run on the airfield again the runways were bombed and an ammunition dump was destroyed. Expended on the two runs were 15-500# G.P. bombs, 80-100# G.P. bombs and 110 H.E. rockets. *USS SANGAMON'S AG-33* launched 5 Avengers and 9 Hellcats for MIYAKO JIMA and ISHIGAKI JIMA and 4 more Avengers later in the day were launched for ISHIGAKI JIMA. Eight Hellcats and 4 Avengers were launched to find targets of opportunity at SAKISHIMA GUNTO. Several Hellcats flew CAP and LCAP. One Hellcat returning crashed into the *SANGAMON'S* catwalk, causing no injuries. *AIR Group-25* from the *USS CHENANGO* launched 8 planes for CAP and ASP and 20 fighters and 8 Avenger bombers for a strike on the runways at ISHIGAKI JIMA. The runways were cratered; revetment areas and AA emplacements were damaged, and some houses were hit in targets 7660 and 7459 causing fires. (*7660 and 7459 are the grid zone numbers marked on the pilots attack map.*) On this strike *CHENANGO* planes dispensed 20-500# G.P. bombs, 80-100# G.P. bombs and 142-rockets. *CHENANGO'S AG-25* reported that their Air Skipper, Lieutenant Commander RICHARD W. ROBERTSON'S plane was hit over ISHIGAKI JIMA and he had to bail out a few miles offshore. Several hours later when he was picked up, it was determined that he had drowned while waiting to be rescued by the PBM (Dumbo).

9 April (L-plus-8) Twenty four Hellcats and 12 Avengers of *AG-40* were launched from the *USS SUWANNEE,* The target was MIYAKO and ISHIGAKI JIMA. One group hit MIYAKO airstrips, gun positions and installations in the town of NOBARA *The correct name of this town in "Romaji" is NOBARU. (See note and the end of this day.)* This group dropped 15-500# G.P. bombs, 79-100# G.P. bombs and 145-five inch High Explosive rockets. The second group hit ISHIGAKI'S bomber strip, damaging the airfield, gun positions and revetment areas. This group expending 40-100# G.P. bombs and 78-5 inch H.E. rockets. *USS SANTEE* made two launches of *AG-24* fighters and bombers for a strike on targets at MIYAKO JIMA. Bombs were dropped and rockets were fired at AA positions, buildings, warehouses and a radio station. Expended from 15 fighters and 8 bombers were 15-500# bombs, 80-100# bombs and 152 H.E. rockets. From *SANGAMON'S AG-33,* four night fighters were launched at 0336H to heckle and intrude over MIYAKO and ISHIGAKI JIMA and 4 Avengers were sent to bomb at ISHIGAKI. Also, several of *SANGAMON'S* Hellcats flew LCAP through out the day and 4 Avengers flew LASP. *CHENANGO* launched 12 Hellcats and 6 Avengers for a strike in the town of ISHIGAKI. Airfield runways were cratered and hits were made in dispersal areas. Expended were 8-500# G.P. bombs, 64-100# G.P. bombs and 80 rockets. An accident on the recovery of airplanes on the *CHENANGO* caused three deaths and 7 airplanes to be destroyed when a Hellcat landed and its tail hook broke after catching the arrester wire. The plane continued on forward floated over the barriers and crashed into other planes spotted on the deck. A large fire broke out aided by gasoline that flooded the deck, causing ammunition and rockets to cook off. Serious damage to the vessel was prevented by immediately changing course to the left to bring the wind across the starboard bow. The *CHENANGO* was out of operations for a short period to clean up and to bury their dead at sea. Some of their planes were sent temporarily to the *USS SANGAMON* until they completed their damage clean up. They continued scheduled operations the next day.

Note: More often in their reports the Americans and their Allies referred to one of the Airfields and its nearby village located on MIYAKO JIMA as "NOBARA." The true MIYAKO name is "NOBARU."

10 April (L-plus-9) *Air Group 33* from the SANGAMON started this day very early by sending 4 night fighting Hellcats to strike MIYAKO and ISHIGAKI. (*The USS SANGAMON was the only carrier of the four having night fighters*) Throughout the rest of the day they sent 10 Hellcats and 2 Avengers to strike MIYAKO JIMA. They sent 10 Hellcats and 10 Avengers to ISHIGAKI JIMA and launched 15 of their Hellcats for LCAP. *Local Combat Air Patrol.* Air Group-*40* Hellcats and Avengers from the *SUWANNEE* took to the air to find targets at MIYAKO and ISHIGAKI JIMA. Twelve F6F fighters and 10 TBM torpedo bombers hit the two islands for the third straight day. On MIYAKO JIMA, one "*Betty*" bomber was burned on the ground. One fuel storage tank was burned on a bridge east of NOBARA Airfield and the "RADAR" installation located on the hill east of NOBARA at NOBARU was hit with rockets. Airstrips were pocketed with bombs. On MIYAKO JIMA, 24-500# G.P. bombs, 32-100# G.P. bombs and 112-5 inch H.E. rockets were expended. Four Hellcats struck ISHIGAKI installations and airfields with 4-500# G.P. bombs and 24 five inch H.E. rockets. *USS SANTEE* in two launches sent 4 Avengers for Local Anti-Submarine patrol, 11 Hellcats and 8 Avengers for a strike at ISHIGAKI JIMA. Bombing strikes were made against ISHIGAKI Airfield and AA positions. Expended were 18-500# bombs, 32-100# bombs, 8-350 depth charges and 114 H.E. rockets. Their Commanding Air Officer of *AG-24*, Lieutenant Cdr. Rexford John Ostrum crashed into the sea after being hit with enemy AA while leading an attack on enemy installations at ISHIGAKI JIMA. He jumped from his airplane without his parachute opening and was not seen thereafter. R/Admiral W. D. Sample shifted his flag from the *USS SUWANNEE* to the *USS SANGAMON*. The transfer of Admiral Sample and his staff was completed by the *USS DREXLER DD 741*. The *USS SUWANNEE* left the battle station formation and sailed to KERAMA RETTO near OKINAWA to be re-supplied.
The American re-supply base for the four Escort carriers in this Task Unit at SAKISHIMA GUNTO was at KERAMA RETTO, off the southwest coast of OKINAWA. This Retto had been captured and made into an American supply center just a few days before the landing of troops on OKINAWA SHIMA.

11 April (L-plus-10) *SUWANNEE*, while headed to KERAMA RETTO launched 8 Hellcats to fly Local Combat Patrol (LCP). These Hellcats were instructed to land on the *CHENANGO* at SAKISHIMA when they return. The *SUWANNEE* was anchored at berth K-9 while being replenished and afterwards got underway to join the other three CVE carriers on station at SAKISHIMA GUNTO. Meanwhile, *SANGAMON* had launched 12 Hellcats for LCAP duty and 8 more to strike ISHIGAKI and MIYAKO while the USS *SANTEE* at 1300H launched 4 Hellcat fighters for a strike at ISHIGAKI JIMA, where they dropped 4-500# bombs and fired 24 rockets, resulting in burning a warehouse. Launched from the *SANTEE* for Local Anti-Submarine Patrol (LASP) were six *AG-40*

Avengers. The *CHENANGO* was on General Quarters most of the night. At 0900H and 1500H she launched a total of 8 fighters and 4 torpedo bombers for strikes on airfields at NOBARA Airfield at MIYAKO and ISHIGAKI Airfield. Airfields and runways were cratered at both airfields and hangers and other buildings were damaged at NOBARA. One enemy airplane, a "*Tony*" was destroyed on the runway at ISHIGAKI. Expended on targets were 20-500# bombs and 62 HVA rockets. The British Pacific fleet, TF-57 took up a Battle position 40 miles from the Island of FORMOSA and they sent out about 40 bombers and the same number of fighters. Their planes commenced attacking the airfields on the North end of the island. However, bad weather in the area hampered their operations considerably. They continue attacking Formosa the next day while the American Task unit 52.1.3, located 200 miles east of them, bombed and strafed the airfields at SAKISHIMA GUNTO.

12 April (L-plus-11) The *SANGAMON* launched from her deck at 0953H eight Hellcats for LCAP and four Avengers belonging to the *USS CHENANGO'S AG-25* for LASP duty. The *SUWANNEE* while heading to be refueled, sent 11 Hellcats out for LCAP and 4 Avengers were sent for LASP. At 0920H, fighters from her group reported that they shot down one Japanese "*Myrt II*". The Destroyer Escort *USS SEDERSTROM DE-31* recovered an empty Japanese parachute and a few minutes later Destroyer Escort *USS TISDALE DE-33* recovered the body of a Japanese pilot near the crash site. The *SANTEE* put up 14 planes as she prepared to head for KERAMA RETTO with the Destroyer Escort *USS EISELE DE-34*. The *CHENANGO* reported that their Skipper had downed one 'TONY' over MIYAKO JIMA.

April 13th. Word arrived that President Roosevelt had died in the afternoon of the 12th of April. His Son, LT. Commander Frank Roosevelt, Captain of the nearby Destroyer Escort, USS COUVERT M. MOORE was notified and was flown back to the US.

On the 13th of April near Formosa a Japanese plane was mistaken for a friendly plane and was not fired on as it came in low over the British Pacific fleet's carrier INDOMITABLE. The plane dropped a bomb that bounced off the deck without exploding. At the same time a British friendly fighter who was in pursuit of this Japanese plane was mistaken for an enemy plane and was shot down.

On the 13th of April there was a Task unit change made at SAKISHIMA GUNTO. Rear Admiral Felix B. Stump's Task Unit 52.1.2 (ComCarDiv24) was called upon to replace Rear Admiral Sample's very tired American Task unit 52.1.3. Sample would move his unit to the south east of Okinawa to the waters at 24.58 degrees north-129.03 degrees east. This change involved a different type of CVE Escort Carrier and a different fighter plane to attack SAKISHIMA GUNTO targets. The Escort Carriers in Task Unit 52.1.2 were the "Casablanca Class" Escort Carriers. These Escort carriers were often called "KAISERS", named after the ship's builder: Henry Kaiser. These were designed on the drawing board and built entirely new as Escort Carriers. They had two elevators and one catapult and their overall length was 512 feet, 3 inches x 65 feet 2 inches wide. Their speed was rated at 19 knots. These were built under a war time contract by Henry Kaiser between 1942 and 1944 in Vancouver, Washington. These carriers had Air Squadrons stationed aboard that the Navy called Composite Squadrons indicated by the letters VC in front of their squadron number. The airplanes were Grumman TBM Avenger torpedo bombers and FM-2 Grumman designed, General Motors built, Wildcats. The earlier Wildcats built by Grumman were know as F4's. When the Grumman Company became over extended with demands for later designed airplanes such as the F6 Hellcats, they had General Motors, Eastern Division, build the FM-2 Wildcats. The FM-2 Wildcat engine has more horsepower than the F4 Wildcat and the vertical stabilizer holding the rudder was taller than the F4 Grumman built Wildcats. Task Unit 52.1.2 with the newer Kaiser Escort Carriers had been near OKINAWA, supporting the landings of troops and protecting Task Force 58 from air attacks before being called upon to help neutralize the airfields at SAKISHIMA GUNTO. New names of Escort Carriers such as MARCUS ISLAND, SAGINAW BAY, SARGENT BAY, PETROF BAY, RUDYERD BAY, TULAGI and MAKASSAR STRAIT would now relieve the previous Escorts Carriers at SAKISHIMA GUNTO.

13 April (L-plus-12) Nine Avengers were launched at 1400H from the *USS SAGINAW BAY* and 12 FM-2 Wildcats were launched from the *USS TULAGI'S VC-92 Air group* and 4 Wildcats were launched from the *USS MAKASSAR STRAIT*. These planes were to strike HIRARA, SUKAMA and NOBARA airfields at MIYAKO JIMA. The nine Avengers were split into three groups and each group was to attack one of the three airfields. Prior to each attack the Wildcats were to attack the runways, strafing and rocketing and the Avengers would follow, unloading their bombs and rockets. HIRARA Airfield was hit first by the first group of Avengers as they followed the Wildcats of *VC-97*. The field appeared to be operational but cratered. Eight-500# bombs were dropped and landed on the runways and taxiways. Ten rockets were fired into the revetments along the runway. One Avenger dropped a bomb that landed close to a single engine bomber causing some damage to the plane. Light moderate AA fire was encountered during the attack coming from a direction northeast of the field. A large fire was noted by the attacker upon leaving the area. SUKAMA Airfield was the next group's target, so they started their attack from the west flying eastward following the *VC-92* Wildcats. This field seemed to be operational and it was noted that 6 planes on the ground appeared operational. Seven 500# bombs and 12 rockets struck the runway, taxiways and revetments. The planes on the ground were hit, but the damage was undetermined. No AA fire was seen near the field, but upon retiring, some light AA fire on the northeast coast knocked out the Plexiglas on the port side of the second cockpit of one Avenger. NOBARA Airfield was the last of the three attacks. The Avengers were preceded by 4 Wildcats from *VC-92*. The fields didn't appear to be operational. However, 5 planes on the ground did look operational. Seven 500# bombs and 10 rockets were released on to the runways and buildings nearby. Some light meager and medium intensified AA come from east of the field. All 3 of the airfield attacks took a total of 25 minutes. The bombing runs begin at 9,000 feet in a 30 degree glide while releasing the bombs at 3,500 feet. The weather was extremely suitable for these attacks. Following the attacks, the groups rendezvoused 10 miles northeast of the island at 5,000 feet and then they returned to base. One fatality occurred when Lieutenant (jg) N. "Jack" Link's Wildcat from the *USS TULAGI'S VC-92* Air group exploded and crashed east of HIRARA Field at MIYAKO JIMA. Another incident was that an AA shell exploded near the cockpit of one of the

Wildcats belonging to *VC-97*. Flying shrapnel caused injury to the fighter pilot. However the pilot managed to land safely on the *USS MAKASSAR STRAIT*.

Note: The number of rockets shown to have been launched on these three strikes is from the Avengers. Information on the number of rockets fired by the Wildcats that preceded the Avengers on each bombing strike is N/A. Lieutenant Jack Link the FM-2 Wildcat pilot that crashed east of HIRARA Field at MIYAKO JIMA is mentioned in the narration written by Lt.(jg) Spencer Hatch of Air Group VC-92 shown elsewhere in this book.

The *USS PETROF BAY'S VC-93* planes attacked ISHIGAKI JIMA and reported that two of their fighters were shot down and the pilots were rescued. One TBM Avenger that returned had suffered a hole in the right wing. The wing was replaced and the airplane was ready to fly the next day. *MARCUS ISLAND CVE-77* launched 12 of their Wildcats as part of a strike group against aircraft and facilities at SAKISHIMA GUNTO. In addition they launched 8 planes for direct support, 8 planes flew Tactical Combat Air Patrol, 2 planes were assigned as spotters and 2 flew Local Anti-Submarine Patrol for a total daily count of 32 Sorties. They reported that they had destroyed six Japanese planes on the ground at ISHIGAKI JIMA. *RUDYERD BAY CVE-81* launched her planes today for strikes on MIYARA Airfield at ISHIGAKI.

Note: The planes from USS PETROF BAY, VC-93 AIR SQUADRON that were in the air on the 13th and reported that they had seen dummy planes on SAKISHIMA runways. The Japanese had built these from cane and straw. This type of decoy would often fool fighter and bomber pilots. The Japanese hoped to draw their enemy closer to the ground where they would waste bombs and rockets firing at these dummies and the Japanese gunners could then take advantage of these low flying airplanes with their AA fire. This trick fooled some of the less experienced pilots.

14 April (L-plus-13) *RUDYERD BAY* planes were launched for Combat Air Patrol and Target ASP and others were assigned strike aircraft for targets at HIRARA Airfield and SUKAMA Airfield and installations on MIYAKO JIMA and ISHIGAKI JIMA. On this raid there were a total of 86-100# G.P. bombs, 68-5 inch rockets and 5,100 rounds of .50cal.ammo expended. One TBM Avenger failed to return to base after the strike. *MAKASSAR STRAIT*, together with the other carriers in the unit, maintained a continuous two planes for LASP and 8 planes for LCAP from dawn until sunset. Task unit 52.1.2 planes continued strikes against ISHIGAKI and MIYAKO JIMA. Nine Avengers and 4 Wildcats struck ISHIGAKI Airfield in the early morning, hitting AA positions, airplanes inside revetments, runways and buildings on and near the field. Eight Wildcats hit a new airfield near HEGINA on ISHIGAKI JIMA, strafing revetments, AA emplacements, and planes near the runway. A "*Tony*" was fired on in the air and damaged but managed to get away. The plane was not pursued because the fighters were low on fuel. Eleven planes were destroyed on the ground and 16 were reported damaged. In addition, buildings near the fields were hit and left burning, AA positions hit, revetments damaged and runways cratered. One Wildcat, side number 13, Bureau No. 74085 was shot down by enemy AA fire over ISHIGAKI JIMA. At 1700H, the Pilot was reported being in his raft 6 miles and bearing 210 degrees true from ISHIGAKI Airfield. Two planes from the strike group from this ship orbited his position until relieved on station by other planes from Task Unit 52.1.2. Rescue operations were not completed before darkness, with the result that the covering airplanes were forced to return to base and rescue attempts were deferred until the following morning. In addition to this plane loss, other planes that were damaged were: Avenger side number 32, having Number 11 and 13 engine cylinders riddled, the propeller pitted, and the engine cowling torn. Avenger side number 25, the stabilizer was shot off, the elevator hinge fitting was broken and the fabric was torn, also the left wing was punctured. Avenger side number 23, 2 ½ square feet of the left wing area was demolished, including the ribs, stringers, skin and the longerons. A wing change was necessary for this plane. *USS TULAGI* had her *VC-92* planes attacking ISHIGAKI JIMA on this day and one of their TBM Avengers lost a wing on its second run over the airfield. The pilot bailed out but the two crewmen, Harold A. Morrissey and Darrell L. Booth went in with the plane. *MARCUS ISLAND* and her Air Group sent 14 planes against facilities on MIYAKO JIMA. Eight of her planes flew Target Combat Air Patrol, 12 flew Local Combat Air Patrol, 2 planes flew Anti-Submarine Patrol and 4 were assigned the duty of flying cover for the Dumbo rescue plane and performing a night intruder strike on the ISHIGAKI Airfield. Air group *VOC-1* from *MARCUS ISLAND* reported that they had destroyed 4 enemy planes on the ground this day at MIYAKO JIMA.

15 April (L-plus-14) At 0730H, *USS SAGINAW BAY* launched four Wildcats from *VC-88* Composite Squadron. Each was fitted with 6 High Explosive Rockets. The target was ISHIGAKI JIMA. The four Wildcats of *VC-88* were assigned Target Combat Air Patrol over ISHIGAKI JIMA. They were to be used to cover a strike group who would be arriving at a latter date. However, the strike group composed of Avengers and Wildcats from *VC-93* didn't communicate with the leader of *VC-88* when they arrived. The *VC-93* Avengers and Wildcats started to dive on the island, so the CAP leader led his division in a strafing and rocket attack on the two airfields, picking out gun emplacements. One Wildcat fired rockets into a "T" shaped building and others struck the airfields. No AA fire was encountered. One TBM belonging to *VC-97* stationed on the *MAKASSAR STRAIT*, engaged in another strike and crashed south of ISHIGAKI Airfield about 100 yards inland from the southern coast. The 4 Wildcats of *VC-88* resumed CAP over the target. On another strike this day, 9 Avengers and 4 Wildcats from *SAGINAW BAY'S VC-88* attacked HIRARA Airfield at MIYAKO JIMA. The Avengers were divided into three sections of four planes per section. Each section had a specific runway for its target. The first division leader led his section from the west, hitting the East-West runway. The next section hit the North-South runway, and the last section hit the Northeast-Southwest runway, attacking from the Northeast. (*See note marked * at the end of this day.*) All three attacks were coordinated so that only a slight amount of time existed between attacks of each section. FM-2 Wildcats preceded the Avengers, strafing the runways. All bombs were dropped on these first runs. After the bombing runs, all planes rendezvoused to the east of the island and begun a section run. Four planes per section abreast of each other came in strafing and rocketing. The fighters preceded the bombers in this strafing attack. These bombing runs begin at 10,000 feet altitude at a 40 degree glide, and the bombs were released at 3,500 feet. The rocket run begin at 8,000 feet, pulling out at 2,500 feet. The damage done was considerable. A total of 25-500# G.P. bombs hit the runways, leaving them well cratered. Three planes on the ground were hit. One heavy AA position located west of the northern tip of the North-South runway that was spotted and hit on the 14th of April was again hit on this run with 3 bombs and 3 rockets. A medium AA gun position was rocketed and several revetments were bombed and rocketed. A great amount of AA fire was encountered on the previous strikes. The heavy caliber fire was meager and inaccurate. The medium fire was intense and fairly accurate. The light fire was intense and inaccurate. All the planes returned to base. Twelve Avengers and 7 Wildcats belonging to *VC-93* from the *PETROF BAY* took to the air to attack airfields at ISHIGAKI JIMA. One of the Wildcats was hit and had to ditch in the water. Its pilot was later rescued. Another Wildcat that was launched later from the carrier was shot down near MIYAKO and its pilot, a Flight Commander was rescued from the sea. The *SAGINAW BAY* launched twelve Avengers and 4 Wildcats. They teamed up with 6 Avengers and 6 Wildcats from the *MARCUS ISLAND* for MIYAKO JIMA. Each of these 18 Avengers was loaded with 3-500# G.P. bombs and 4 H.E. rockets. The 12 Wildcats were carrying 6 High Explosive rockets per plane. The Wildcats took off before the Avengers and they flew Target Combat Air Patrol until the Avengers arrived. At 1500H Wildcats loaded with 6 H.E. rockets were launched from the *SAGINAW BAY.* This was to be a fighter sweep of MIYAKO JIMA Airfields. Aircraft in revetments were the principal targets. On this sweep, seven aircraft found at HIRARA Airfield was damaged. Also a medium AA gun position was struck with a direct hit with rockets and strafing. Another medium AA gun position was damaged with one rocket and strafing at NOBARA Airfield. *RUDYERD BAY* sent her *VC-96* airplanes to participate in striking the airfields and installations at MIYAKO and ISHIGAKI JIMA. These planes expended 15-500# bombs, 70-5 inch H.E. rockets and 18,500 rounds of .50 cal. *MARCUS ISLAND'S VOC-1* flew 43 sorties today. Thirty three of the planes flew strikes and sweeps against ISHIGAKI airfields. Eight of their planes were assigned to Combat Air Patrol duty and 2 were assigned to ASP duty. Three enemy aircraft were reported destroyed on ISHIGAKI Airfield. *MARCUS ISLAND* reported that one of her fighters was shot down by AA and it crashed at sea and there was no report on the fate of the pilot. *USS MAKASSAR STRAIT* received word that their Wildcat pilot was rescued from the sea after being shot down on the 14th near ISHIGAKI. *MAKASSAR STRAIT* launched 32 sorties. Eight of which were Local Combat Air Patrol, Two were Local Anti Submarine Patrol and 10 were on a strike mission. The strike mission was made up of 6 Avengers and 4 Wildcats, which struck ISHIGAKI airfields and vicinity in the morning hours, expending 49-100# G.P. bombs, 4 Napalms and 36-5 inch H.E. rockets on the targets. No air opposition was encountered. Two enemy planes were destroyed, 7 probably destroyed and 19 damaged on the ground. Revetments and AA positions were struck by bombs and rockets. The Napalms were effective. Several buildings were fired, including a building believed to house Japanese planes. Intense AA fire was noted. Avenger side number 31, Bureau No. 68767, was reported to have been shot down over ISHIGAKI Airfield. The plane flamed on landing. One parachute was observed, opening, but no personnel were seen after the plane struck. Pilot, Lieutenant V.L.Tebo and his air crewmen: W.H.Loyd and R. Tuggle Jr. were aboard this Avenger. (See note marked ** at the end of this day.) Planes that flew over the scene later in the day were not able to add any information. In addition to this downed plane another Avenger was hit by AA severely damaging the left wing and a Wildcat was hit, damaging its left wing and flap. In the afternoon, 8 Wildcats made up a 4 plane

Target CAP over ISHIGAKI and a 4 plane TCAP over MIYAKO JIMA airfields. SUKAMA and HIRARA airfields on MIYAKO JIMA were strafed. A *"Betty"* Bomber seen on HIRARA Airfield was damaged. Buildings around SUKAMA Airfield were left burning. Near ISHIGAKI Airfield, AA positions and trucks moving along the roadway were strafed, with undetermined results. Later 4 fighters, making up the second TCAP over ISHIGAKI Airfield during the afternoon, fired 24 rockets into a radio station between ISHIGAKI Airfield. and the town of SHIRA. No definite results were observed. No air opposition was encountered and AA was light, meager and inaccurate. At the conclusion of the day's missions, ISHIGAKI Airfield was reported cratered and non-operational. HIRARA and SUKAMA airfields were non-operational, and NOBARA Airfield seemed operational for fighters. At 2205H, *USS MAKASSAR STRAIT* in company with the Destroyer Escort *USS DENNIS,* left for KERAMA RETTO to rearm.

Note* The Northeast-Southwest runway, once a part of HIRARA Airfield at MIYAKO JIMA during the war is now the active runway today. It is the only remaining runway left from WWII on the Island. It has been lengthened for jet service and is now the active single runway at the "MIYAKO JIMA AIRPORT".

Note** There will be more intriguing information later in this book about the fate of the pilot and crewmen from the MAKASSAR STRAIT and VC-97 Squadron who were shot down on 15 April 1945 at ISHIGAKI JIMA. (See note 4 page 149)

It was on this day that Marine Air Squadron VMF (N)-542 from YONTAN Airfield OKINAWA started their night missions against the RYUKYU chain of islands including strikes against MIYAKO JIMA. They would later earn the "Presidential Unit Citation" for their action.

16-17 April (L-plus-15-16) The BRITISH PACIFIC FLEET, Task Force 57 was back on station at SAKISHIMA GUNTO relieving the American Escort Carriers and again striking the island's airfields. The British had replaced her carrier, *HMS ILLUSTRIOUS* with *HMS FORMIDABLE.(Action by the British for these two days is not available.)*

18 April (L-plus-17) Admiral Sample moved his American Task Unit 52.1.3 into the SAKISHIMA GUNTO battle station while the British were fueling their carriers. (*The USS SANGAMON with Air group 40 aboard would start flying dust to dawn missions. This tactic would keep the Japanese from repairing their runways at night after they had been cratered by bombs throughout the day.*) So the *SANGAMON* turned into the wind and launched 4 Hellcats at 0200H for ISHIGAKI and MIYAKO JIMA. At 0406H they launched 4 more Wildcats and 4 Avengers for the two islands. Admiral Sample shifted his flag and administration from the *SUWANNEE* and came aboard the *SANGAMON*. At 1645H, 8 Hellcats were sent out for CAP duty and later two more Hellcats were launched for TCAP for MIYAKO and ISHIGAKI JIMA. At 1935H while recovering airplanes it was reported that a Hellcat, number 13, Bureau number 71372, piloted by Lieutenant (jg) J.H. Bateman was reported missing near ISHIGAKI JIMA. By 2230H, *SANGAMON* had launched 4 more Hellcats for CAP over the two islands. The USS *SUWANNEE'S* planes got into the action by flying 48 sorties including 18 Hellcats and Avengers for TCAP, LCAP and LASP. Sixteen of their Hellcats and 17 Avengers struck ISHIGAKI JIMA, expending 50-500# G.P. bombs, 65-100# G.P. bombs and 249-5 inch H.E. rockets, hitting runways and installations. Three Hellcats teamed up with other groups and struck HIRARA Airfield on MIYAKO JIMA. Here they expended 3-500# G.P. bombs and 22-5 inch High Explosive rockets, hitting the airstrip and ammo dump nearby. The *SANTEE*, who lost all of her ship's electrical power in the early morning, repaired the problem and launched a total of 41 planes. Fifteen of her fighters and bombers were assigned strike duty over the two islands and she had 18 planes assigned to LCAP and LASP and 8 more for TCAP. *CHENANGO* had her planes over MIYAKO supporting strikes by other Air groups. In two strikes on runways at NOBARA and HIRARA airfields, the runways were bombed and cratered, revetments and emplacements were damaged and a radio station near HIRARA was hit. Expended were 22-500# bombs, 40-100# bombs and 119 rockets. Thirty two planes were launched for CAP and ASP. The *USS SANTEE* launched her first strike with 4 fighters at 0930H for a strike on ISHIGAKI Airfield. The runway was cratered with 4-500# bombs and 24 H.E. rockets. Eighteen planes from this carrier were assigned to fly LCAP and LASP. One Avenger was sent as a photo plane. Planes launching again at 1200H and 1400H from the *SANTEE* struck NOBARA Airfield at MIYAKO. Twelve fighters and 8 torpedo bombers cratered the runways with 6-500# bombs, 32-100# bombs and 112 H.E. rockets

Today it was reported that ERNIE PYLE, a beloved writer of war correspondence who was covering the action on Okinawa was killed on the island of IE SHIMA near Okinawa.

19 April 1945 (L-plus-18) USS *SANGAMON* launched two *AG-33* Hellcat night fighters at 0033H for Combat Air Patrol over ISHIGAKI and replaced them with two Wildcats at 0227H. At 0445H, 8 Hellcats and 4 Avengers were airborne for CAP duty at MIYAKO JIMA. An Avenger was sent to MIYAKO AND ISHIGAKI for a message drop and one Avenger and four Hellcats were sent on a photographic mission. *Air Group-40* from the *USS SUWANNE* flew 54 sorties today. Eighteen Hellcats flew Target Combat Patrol (TCAP), Local Combat Air Patrol (LCAP) and 2 Avengers were on Local Anti-Submarine Patrol (LASP). One Hellcat was launched to take photos. Twenty Wildcats and 16 Avengers from *SUWANNEE* flew strike missions against MIYAKO and ISHIGAKI JIMA. NOBARA Airfield at MIYAKO JIMA was hit with 4-500# General Purpose bombs. Parking areas and installations on ISHIGAKI JIMA was hit with 48-500# G.P. bombs, 36-100# G.P. bombs and 65-5 inch High Explosive rockets. The *CHENANGO* sent *AG-25* Hellcat fighters and Avenger bombers to MIYAKO to strike runways at SUKAMA, NOBARA and HIRARA airfields. The runways were cratered and fires were started in storage buildings and barracks. One enemy plane, a *"Frances"* was caught on the ground and destroyed. Expended were 27-500# G.P. bombs, 38-100# bombs and 107 air rockets. Thirty two planes were assigned CAP and ASP. The *USS SANTEE* made three strike launches consisting of a total of 24 planes. Strikes were made at ISHIGAKI JIMA, where warehouses were set fire, At MIYAKO, the NOBARA Airfield runways were bombed through the overcast leaving them cratered. Expended were 32-500# bombs, 32-100# bombs and 147 H.E. rockets. Eighteen planes belonging to *AG-24* flew LCAP and LASP.

20 April (L-plus-19) The British Pacific Fleet returned to attack SAKISHIMA GUNTO for one day. Her planes attacked the islands dropping 75 tons of bombs on airfields at MIYAKO and ISHIGAKI JIMA. Several ships, barracks and a radar station were hit with rockets. One Avenger, ditched a few miles off the coast of ISHIGAKI. Later this day the British Pacific Fleet set sail for LEYTE and San Pedro Bay in the Philippines for replenishing and major repairs.

In absence of Task Force 57 on the 21st of April, American escort carriers and their planes took over. The British were not to return until the 4th of May.

21 April (L-plus-20) Admiral Sample with TU 52.1.3 and his "INDISPENSABLES" was back on battle station on the 21st of April and the *USS SANGAMON* at 0415H started launching her planes. Through out this day they launched 21 Hellcats and 9 Avengers to strike ISHIGAKI and MIYAKO JIMA. Twenty two Hellcats were launched for Local Combat Air Patrol. The *SUWANNEE* placed 10 Avengers on Local Anti-Submarine Patrol, 3 Hellcats for Target Combat Air Patrol and 2 Hellcats were to fly photograph duty. Seven Hellcats and 5 Avengers hit MIYARA Airfield on ISHIGAKI JIMA dropping 25-500# G.P. bombs and 20-100# G.P. bombs. *SUWANNEE* then set sail with a couple of destroyers for escorts for KERAMA RETTO for ammunition and supplies. Planes from the *SANTEE* joined in by furnishing 12 fighters and 8 torpedo bombers, striking runways, gun positions and buildings at MIYARA Airfield on ISHIGAKI JIMA with 28-500# bombs, 32-100# bombs and 136 H.E. rockets. Eighteen planes from the *SANTEE* flew TCAP, LCAP and LASP. *USS CHENANGO* reported encountering heavy AA while her planes made 3 strikes on HIRARA, NOBARA and SUKAMA airfields and one strike on ISHIGAKI and HEGINA airfields. Expended were 38-500# G.P. bombs, 48-100# G.P. bombs and 221 rockets. *AG-25* destroyed two enemy "*Tojo*" airplanes on the ground at MIYAKO. One of *CHENANGO'S* F6F-5 fighters was hit by AA over ISHIGAKI and the pilot had to make a water landing. He was rescued the next morning after spending the night in his life raft.

Today, an American ship reported rescuing the crew from the British Avenger that ditched near ISHIGAKI on the 20th of April.

22 April (L-plus-21) The *USS SANGAMON* started this day off by launching strike aircraft at 0230H for ISHIGAKI JIMA and MIYAKO JIMA. Through out the day they launched 32 Hellcats and 8 Avengers for strikes at airfields and 2 Hellcats for CAP and one Avenger for message dropping. During *SANGAMON'S* dusk strike over MIYAKO JIMA 25-30 Japanese planes warming up on the NOBARA runways were spotted. About this time 7 Japanese "*Oscars*" appeared and tried to attack the American planes in the air. The torpedo bombers pressed on their bomb and rocket strike against the planes on the ground, causing extensive damage and setting the planes on fire. Then they returned to their carrier base while the Hellcats engaged the 7 Japanese "*Oscars*" in the air, downing 5 of them. Then 4 more "*Oscars*" joined in the fight. Hellcat night fighter airplanes from the *SANGAMON* joined in and shot two more "*Oscars*" down. It was reported that one Hellcat was shot down over ISHIGAKI and the pilot was Lieutenant (jg) R.F. Eckstein, although this was not confirmed. *CHENANGO* and her plane carried out strikes against ISHIGAKI, MIYARA and HEGINA airfields. Runways were cratered and dispersal areas were damaged. A bridge was damaged near HEGINA. Fifty five-500# G.P. bombs, 61-100# G.P. bombs and 255 rockets were expended on targets. Thirty planes flew CAP and ASP. *USS SANTEE* launched planes for three strikes at MIYAKO JIMA. Twelve fighters and 8 torpedo bombers hit the runways, dispersals and barracks at NOBARA, HIRARA and SUKAMA airfields. Expended on the targets were 28-500#

bombs, 32-100# bombs and 120 H.E. rockets. Thirty planes from the *SANTEE* flew LCAP and LASP.

23 April (L-plus-22) The *USS SANGAMON* launched 27 Hellcats and 11 Avengers, 20 of these planes were to strike MIYAKO and ISHIGAKI JIMA, the other 7 were to fly Combat Air Patrol at both islands. One Hellcat was reported down at sea, east of ISHIGAKI and its pilot Lieutenant C.M. Reynolds was reported to have been seen holding onto a life raft that was dropped to him. The *USS SUWANNEE* returned from being replenished with supplies at KERAMA RETTO. Her Air Group flew 40 sorties including 12 Hellcats on LCAP, 8 Hellcats for TCAP at SAKISHIMA and 4 Avengers flew Local Anti-Submarine Patrol. Eight Hellcats and 8 Avengers hit ISHIGAKI AND MIYAKO airfields and installations. Twenty 500# G.P. bombs, 30-100# G.P. bombs and 20-5 inch H.E. rockets were expended. One "lugger" was strafed, fired and left sinking. Planes from the *USS SANTEE* in three launches sent 36 fighters and bombers for strikes on NOBARA Airfield at MIYAKO resulting in damaging the two runways and dispersals nearby. One TBM-3 Avenger torpedo bomber from *AG-24* off the *SANTEE* was hit by AA while on an east to west run over NOBARA Field. TBM-3 Avenger B/N 68688 crashed in flames and exploded upon ground impact east of NOBARA Airfield at MIYAKO. One parachute was seen landing between the two runways. Aboard the plane was Pilot Ensign Joseph. F. Florence, crewmen R.J. Murphy and C.E. Boley. The three men were listed as missing in action. **(See note at the end of this day's action)** On the 3 strikes, planes from the *SANTEE* expended 52-500# bombs, 64-100# bombs and 170 H.E. rockets. 10 planes from *SANTEE* flew LCAP and LASP. The *CHENANGO* launched planes to attack ISHIGAKI and MIYAKO. At ISHIGAKI the ISHIGAKI Airfield was bombed and the runway cratered and there were possible damage to an AA position. NOBARA Airfield at MIYAKO was bombed and fires were started in some storage buildings. One single engine plane was destroyed on the ground at NOBARA. Sixteen 500# G.P. bombs, 24-100# G.P. bombs and 99 rockets were expended on targets. At 2025H the *CHENANGO* left for KERAMA RETTO.
NOTE: It was later learned after the war that the one parachute seen at the crash site was that of Pilot Ensign Joseph Florence. He was the only survivor from the crash of his TBM Avenger after the bombing attack on NOBARA Airfield at MIYAKO JIMA. More is written elsewhere in this book about his captivity and demise.

24 April (L-plus-23) *SANGAMON*, with a speed of 18 knots and a heading of 190 degrees into the wind, she commenced launching 10 Hellcats and 4 Avengers at 0517H to strike ISHIGAKI and MIYAKO JIMA. Word was received that Lieut. C.M. Reynolds who crashed into the sea on 23 April was rescued by a "Dumbo" (*Navy slang for the PBY Catalina and the Martin PBM flying boats*) and taken to KERAMA RETTO near Okinawa where he would be returned to this carrier. Admiral Sample, Commander of Division 22 and his flag was transferred with his staff from the *USS SANGAMON* to the *USS SUWANNEE*. At 1919H the *SANGAMON* left formation and headed for KERAMA RETTO to receive ammunition and pick up their pilot who had been rescued. *USS SANTEE* made launches at 0600H and 0830H sending a total of 16 planes for attacks at MIYAKO JIMA where they hit barracks and left them burning. Expended on targets were 12-500# bombs, 16-100 bombs and 40 H.E. rockets. Twenty two airplanes were launched for LCAP and LASP. *USS SUWANNEE* Hellcats and Avengers from *Air group 40* struck HIRARA Airfield at MIYAKO JIMA, hitting runways and installations with 46-500# General Purpose bombs and 63-100# G.P. bombs. One hundred fifteen High Explosive 5 inch rockets were expended against AA positions and revetments.

25 April (L-plus-24) Fourteen Hellcats and 12 Avengers from the *USS SUWANNEE* struck HIRARA and NOBARA airstrips and AA positions on MIYAKO JIMA. 38-500# G.P. bombs, 44-100# G.P. bombs and 92-5 inch H.E. rockets were expended on this sweep. One of the Avengers from *AG-40* was shot down by Japanese AA and no survivors were seen. The three men aboard the crippled TBM Avenger were pilot Lieutenant F. Collura, and crewmen C.H. Powell and C.A. Steward. The *CHENANGO* re-joined the group after returning from KERAMA RETTO and sent her planes against ISHIGAKI, MIYARA and HIRARA airfields. At ISHIGAKI and MIYARA, runways were cratered; fires were left burning in buildings and camouflaged disposal areas. Two enemy planes were set fire on the ground. At HIRARA Airfield at MIYAKO, buildings and a radio station was damaged. Fifteen fighters and 14 bombers dropped 31-500# G.P. bombs, 56-100# bombs and fired 185 rockets. Eighteen planes were assigned CAP. The *SANTEE* launched 22 Hellcats and 8 Avengers for strikes against MIYAKO and ISHIGAKI Airfield runways. On both islands, runways were cratered from bomb hits and dispersals and barracks were damaged. A *"Tojo"* and a *"Betty Bomber"* were destroyed on the ground. Expended were 16-500# bombs, 32-100# bombs, 22-350# depth charges and 174 H.E. rockets. Twelve airplanes were launched from the *SANTEE* for LCAP and LASP. At 1125H it was reported that Hellcat F6F-5 B/N# 77942 belonging to *AG-24* from the *SANTEE* piloted by Lieutenant (jg) G.W. Freeman was seen to have crashed into the sea near ISHIGAKI after failing to pull out of a dive on MIYARA Airfield. At 1940H the *USS SANTEE* departed from Task Unit 52.1.3 in company with *USS BUTLER DE339* and *USS FULLAM DD474* in route to KERAMA RETTO for replenishing of ammunition and supplies.

26 April (L-plus-25) The *SANGAMON* returned from KERAMA RETTO and joined the *SUWANNEE* and *CHENANGO* on their battle station at SAKISHIMA GUNTO and she started her early morning launching of airplanes at 0349H. Four Hellcats and 4 Avengers took to the skies on a heckler mission at ISHIGAKI and MIYAKO JIMA and again at 0532H, *CHENANGO* launched 8 Hellcats for a strike on the two islands and at 1606H, 8 more Hellcats were sent for a strike on the islands. Meanwhile R/Admiral Sample, his flag and his staff who was commanding from the *SUWANNEE* while the *SANGAMON* was at KERAMA RETTO, returned to his ComCar 22 Commanding position on the *SANGAMON*. The *SUWANNEE* had 3 of her Hellcats and 7 Avengers striking HIRARA Airfield and AA positions at MIYAKO JIMA. These planes dropped a total of 22-500# G.P. bombs, 28-100# G.P. bombs and 8-5 inch H.E. rockets. Planes from the *CHENANGO* struck ISHIGAKI and MIYAKO JIMA. A radio station at ISHIGAKI was rocketed at the north tip of the island and numerous fires were set in the town area, also the ISHIGAKI and MIYARA Airfield runways were bombed and cratered and targets in the dispersal areas were hit. Over on MIYAKO JIMA, HIRARA Airfield runways were cratered and targets in the dispersal were hit. *CHENANGO* also furnished 30 Airplanes for Combat Air Patrol and Anti-Submarine Patrol. Bombs and rockets expended on these strikes by *AG-25* planes were 24-500# G.P. bombs, 68-100# General Purpose bombs and 202 rockets were fired.

One of CHENANGO'S air crewmen on an Avenger explained to others after returning from a strike, "you couldn't tell if the Japanese were shooting at our plane, for there were no tracers like you would normally see from AA fire. I figured that the Japanese AA gunners were using non-tracer heavy caliber impact-fuse AA."

27 April (L-plus-26) SANGAMON'S early launches consisted of 12 Hellcats and 4 Avengers. One of the Hellcats would fly a message drop to Task Unit 32.1.1 near OKINAWA and the other planes would strike ISHIGAKI and MIYAKO JIMA. The *SANGAMON* also launched 12 Hellcats in the afternoon and evening for targets at MIYAKO JIMA. Four of these Hellcats launched in the evening would stay around and heckle the island after dark. *SANTEE* planes struck both ISHIGAKI and MIYAKO airfields at SAKISHIMA GUNTO. Airfield runways were cratered and dispersals were hit by bombs and rockets from 15 fighters and 8 torpedo bombers, expending 38-500# bombs, 60-100# bombs and 114 H.E. rockets. Ten planes flew LCAP and LASP. One Hellcat was sent on a special mission to cover a PBM Dumbo to a point 40 miles north of FORMOSA in an unsuccessful effort to locate and rescue a member of the crew of a US submarine. *CHENANGO* launched her planes to strike ISHIGAKI and MIYARA runways, leaving them cratered and damaging dispersal areas. Also a strike was made on NOBARA Airfield, dispersals and fuel areas. One of the Avengers from *CHENANGO* that was on Anti-Submarine patrol was given an incorrect bearing by the controlling base and the pilot became lost but was later located by IFF (*airplane transponder code*). He then ran out of fuel about 20 miles short of the formation and had to ditch. All members of the plane were rescued by a PBM (Martin Mariner). Bombs and rockets dispersed were 12-500# bombs, 40-100# bombs and 96 High Velocity rockets. *SUWANNEE* launched 15 Hellcats and 11 Avengers. They struck the island of ISHIGAKI, MIYARA Airfield and nearby barracks. Expended from the *SUWANNEE'S* planes were 27-500# G.P. bombs and 40-100# G.P. bombs. A fighter sweep dropped 8-500# G.P. bombs on HIRARA Airfield and strafed luggers at the dock at IKEMA JIMA. One Avenger crashed on ISHIGAKI. No survivors were seen near the crash site. The Pilot and crew members of this Avenger were: Lieutenant C. R. Campbell, J.R. Loughridge and E.A. Zahn of *Air Group 40.*

28 April (L-plus-27) While the four larger CVE's of Admiral Sample's TU 32.1.3 were fueling southeast of OKINAWA, Escort carriers from Task Unit 32.1.1 were sent to SAKISHIMA GUNTO from OKINAWA to take over air operations against ISHIGAKI and MIYAKO JIMA. The *USS SHAMROCK BAY CVE 84* launched 4 of *VC-94's* Avengers to strike MIYAKO JIMA. They were to meet up with other planes launched from three other Escort carriers for a strike against the NOBARU Airfield. They all reached the island and preformed a coordinated attack against a revetment area to the east of NOBARU Field. Cloud conditions were ideal for this attack. There was a cloud layer over the island with a 3,000 foot ceiling except for the area right over the field. This made it possible for the planes to make most of their runs from the north over the cloud layer, break out in the clear over the target and escape to the clouds to the south. The original plan of attack called for one division of Wildcat fighters to precede the Avengers and one to follow. Just before the first run there became some confusion to which planes would lead the run, so *VC-94* Avengers went first and the others followed. The bombs were released at 4,000 feet, all planes releasing simultaneously. All bombs of *VC-94's* Avengers, which were 4-500# G.P. and 6-100# G.P. bombs being armed for .025 sec. delay, appeared to land in the target area, but actual damage could not be determined. *VC-94* planes were followed by the other Wildcats and Avengers in the other groups. A similar attack was made on three earth covered revetments near the center of the same airfield, in which planes could be seen through the mouths of the revetments. Planes from the *SHAMROCK BAY* dropped 3-500# G.P. bombs and 6-100# G.P. bombs on this target, again with unobserved results. The bomb fuses were armed for .025 second delay. After this attack and the planes were rendezvousing to the north of HIRARA Airfield, they were rocked by explosives from 8-10 burst of heavy and medium AA apparently coming from the vicinity of the airfield. No damage was done to the planes. For the remainder of the period over the island, planes were divided into two units, each consisting of Wildcats and Avengers. One unit was directed to attack targets of opportunity in the southern part of the island and the other unit which included *VC-94's* Avengers went to the northern part of the island. Three structures on the northern peninsula, two of which appeared to be barracks, were attacked with .50 caliber ammo and rockets. One of the structures was camouflaged as a hay stack. One of the barracks disintegrated when struck by two rockets. The hay stack was hit by two rockets and burst into flame with black smoke rising to 4,000 feet, indicating an oil stores. The unit next attacked two groups of small boats on the northwest side of the island. Of the six in the first group of boats, three 10-12 footers were damaged by strafing with 500 rounds of .50 caliber ammo. The second group also consisted of six boats. One 500# G.P. bomb and two 100# G.P. bombs were dropped in the midst of these. Three 20-30 foot boats are believed to have been sunk as a result of this bombing attack. *USS SAVO ISLAND CVE 78* sent airplanes from her *VC-91* squadron to strike ISHIGAKI airfields. A total of 12 Avengers and 16 Wildcats struck airfields and installations in a morning and afternoon strike. Expended were 22-500# G.P. bombs, 53-100# G.P. bombs, 132-5 inch rockets and 13,900 .50 caliber ammo. Four AA placements were destroyed; revetments at the edge of the northeast-southeast runway were hit. It was noted that airplanes seen on the ground appeared to have been damaged by earlier strikes. These were fired on to assure complete damage. *USS FANSHAW BAY CVE 70* launched 16 Wildcats for sweeps of ISHIGAKI and MIYAKO JIMA, 16 Wildcats and 4 Avengers for support missions and 4 Wildcats for scramble missions. They destroyed one single engine aircraft on the ground, made a probable hit on a *"Val"* and one *"Tony"*, damaged 5 single engine aircraft, and damaged two AA guns and one barge. They expended 8-500# G.P. bombs, ten 100# G.P. bombs and 216-5 inch H.E. rockets. The enemy AA fire was intense and accurate. Wildcat, B/N 74401 piloted by Lieutenant W.L. McNett was shot down in flames and he was not recovered. The pilot was listed as missing in action. Ten planes sustained damage. Four had major and 6 had minor damage. All 10 of these made it back and landed aboard the carrier. Enemy aircraft was reported in the vicinity and the carrier went to General Quarters. Four Wildcats were scrambled but they didn't make contact with the enemy planes, although, it was reported later that 3 *"Zekes"* were splashed by planes from another carrier in this formation. After bogeys were reported in the general area and being called to General Quarters three times, *USS STEAMER BAY CVE 87* launched a division of Wildcats for Local Combat

Patrol. The division was vectored in the direction of two bogies closing from the northwest. The interception succeeded and one *"Zeke"* was splashed. Two other enemy planes were chased for 25 miles. In the encounter one of the Wildcats was riddled when a *"Zeke"* got on his tail. The pilot was uninjured and was able to splash the *"Zeke"*. The Air division leader destroyed the second *"Zeke"* making the total, 3 *"Zekes"* splashed for *VF-90*. *USS MAKIN ISLAND* made three strikes on MIYAKO JIMA. They put 19 Wildcats and 12 Avengers over MIYAKO. The Avengers were split with two bomb load types. Six having 2 each 500# G.P. bombs and the remaining 6 having 10 each 100# G.P. bombs. The Wildcats were fitted with 6 each high explosive rockets. Having clear skies and visibility of 25 miles they made 2 strikes at NOBARA Airfield and one strike at HIRARA Airfield. The Avengers released their bombs at 2,500 feet, pulling out at 1,500 feet and the strafing was performed from 100 feet above the ground. The first strike was on the southwest end of NOBARA Airfield, hitting warehouses and then hitting revetments on the east side of the field. On the second strike on the NOBARA Airfield, the southwest end of field was again targeted. Also struck were barracks located on the northeastern coast of MIYAKO JIMA, south of SHIMAJIRI. On the third strike, HIRARA Airfield was targeted. A shop at the west side of the field and revetments were struck and a large fire was started in a fuel dump. On one of the strikes at NOBARA, one of the Avengers was seen to peel off to the left in a run from 7,000 feet at 70 degrees then snap to the right lessening the angle to 60 degrees. Four rockets appeared to be fired hastily and then the starboard wing came off. As it fell the wing's ailerons were observed to be shredded. (*ailerons are small flaps on each wing that controls the airplane's right-left roll.*) The plane rolled over on its back, gas coming from the right tank and crashed. It had already made a bombing run, releasing 10-100# bombs and was then carrying 8 H.E. rockets. There was no AA observed around the stricken plane. Killed was the pilot: Lieutenant (jg) D.E. Glasgow, crewmen, G.F. Cota, G. Douvos and photographer H.M. Hansen. These men were from Air Composite squadron *VC-84* stationed on the Escort Carrier *USS MAKIN ISLAND.*

29 April (L-plus-28) The four "INDISPENSABLES" with R/Admiral Sample commanding were back again on the SAKISHIMA GUNTO battle station. USS *SANGAMON* commenced launching 4 Hellcats and 4 Avengers at 0331H to strike ISHIGAKI and MIYAKO JIMA. A second group of 8 Hellcats were launched between 0528H and 0533H for the same two targets. In the afternoon, 9 Hellcats and 5 Avengers, one of these to be on a photo plane were launched to strike ISHIGAKI. Upon returning one of the Avengers crashed at sea. The pilot and one of the crewmen were rescued. The second crewman, E.A. Desjarlais was reported missing. *SUWANNEE* planes, 15 Hellcats and 8 Avengers hit ISHIGAKI Airfield, MIYARA Airfield and dispersal areas on ISHIGAKI. They dropped 45-500# G.P. bombs and 32-100# G.P. bombs. Twenty four Hellcats flew LCAP and 8 Avengers flew LASP. At 1940H *SUWANNEE* left the formation with *DD GUEST and DE EDMONDS* for KERAMA RETTO for replenishment of supplies. *SANTEE* planes from *AG-24* got in on the action with 13 Hellcats and 16 Avengers by hitting the HIRARA runways and dispersals with 44-500# bombs, 64-100# bombs and 114 H.E. rockets. One *"Tony"* and two *"Oscars"* were destroyed on the ground. Fourteen of *SANTEE'S* planes flew LCAP and LSAP. *CHENANGO* making up the 4th CVE in formation launched her 8 Hellcats early, for a sweep of ISHIGAKI, MIYAKO and IRIOMOTE islands. Fourteen 100# G.P. bombs were dropped on the ISHIGAKI dispersal areas. Another strike of 8 Hellcats and 8 Avenger torpedo bombers struck the runways at ISHIGAKI and MIYARA airfields, expending 30-500# G.P. bombs and 32-100# G.P. bombs. Eight fighters and 6 bombers were launched at 1300H for ISHIGAKI. There the runways were cratered and dispersal areas were damaged with 10-500# bombs and 60-100# bombs. 4 Hellcats flying TCAP struck an ammunition dump at NOBARA at MIYAKO JIMA with 8-500# bombs exploding it, causing fires in a nearby dispersal area.

Task unit 52.1.2 merges with Task unit 52.11.

30 April (L-plus-29) *USS SANGAMON* launched 22 Hellcats and 7 Avengers to strike ISHIGAKI and MIYAKO JIMA. Seven additional Hellcats were launched for Local Combat Air Patrol and 6 Hellcats were launched for hecklers. The pilot and his radio man from one of the striking Avengers suffered shrapnel wounds from anti-aircraft fire during the bombing strike. The wounds were not serious and the men were treated and later returned to duty. One Hellcat was shot down and its pilot, Lt. (jg) Walter Baskett was last seen on a reef one mile off ISHIGAKI JIMA. An Avenger was sent, having instructions to drop a life raft to the downed pilot near the reef off the coast of ISHIGAKI. *USS SANTEE* launched a total of 33 planes from her deck for today's strikes planned for ISHIGAKI and MIYAKO JIMA. At MIYAKO, a radio station was burned, HIRARA Airfield runways were bombed and cratered and dispersals rocketed. At ISHIGAKI JIMA, two "*Tonys*" and 3 single engine planes were destroyed on the ground. Runways were cratered and dispersals were rocketed. Expended were 15-500# bombs, 64-100# bombs and 202 H.E. rockets. *CHENANGO* planes launched an early strike on ISHIGAKI and HEGINA airfields causing damage to runways and designated targets in the dispersal areas and setting fires to some barracks. Seven enemy airplanes caught on the ground at ISHIGAKI were destroyed. These were two "*Vals*", one "*Betty*", and 4 single engine planes. Planes launched from *CHENANGO* to strike NOBARA Airfield cratered the runways and targets were hit in the dispersal areas and a radio station was attacked and set fire on IRABU SHIMA. Expended in this attack were 24-500# bombs, 68-100# bombs and 202 rockets. One of *AG-25's* airplanes from *CHENANGO* was hit by AA over ISHIGAKI Airfield but the pilot managed to get it back to the carrier. One Avenger was hit in the wing over MIYARA Airfield by AA. The hydraulic system and flaps were damaged and a wing was set on fire. The pilot made a landing in the water 12 miles south of MIYAKO JIMA and the pilot and crew was rescued by a life guard submarine.

1 May 1945 (L-plus-30) *USS SANGAMON* started this day by launching 2 Hellcats to fly heckler sorties over MIYAKO and ISHIGAKI JIMA. (*Heckling the Japanese through the late evening and early darkness periods was found to slow down their process of repairing the runways that had been cratered by bombing attacks through out the day.*) At daylight, 8 Hellcats and 5 Avengers were sent to strike ISHIGAKI JIMA. Also a Hellcat was dispatched with a message to Task Unit 52.1.1. Six Hellcats left on a search mission around noon. Commencing at 1531 hours, *SANGAMON* launched 8 Hellcats and 5 Avengers for strikes on ISHIGAKI and MIYAKO JIMA. Four Hecklers were sent to

ISHIGAKI and MIYAKO at 1756 hours. Two more Hellcats were launched at 2115 hours for a sweep of SAKISHIMA GUNTO. *SUWANNEE'S* planes struck ISHIGAKI JIMA, hitting airfields, barracks and revetments. Due to a heavy cloud layer over the target, damage was undetermined. The division expended 18-500# G.P. bombs, 20-100# G.P. bombs and 62-5 inch H.E. rockets. Four Hellcats and 6 Avengers hit NOBARA Airfield and revetment areas on MIYAKO JIMA with 16-500# G.P. bombs, 24-100# G.P. bombs and 51-5 inch H.E. rockets. Fighters also strafed six luggers near IKEMA Island. *USS SANTEE* at 1300H and 1500H launched 31 planes for a strike on MIYAKO JIMA. Runways at the airfields were cratered, dispersals were rocketed, and a radio station, barracks and several boats were damaged on their first run. On the second run, runways were again cratered, dispersals hit and an AA position was rocketed. Ten flights were furnished for the purpose of Local Combat Air Patrol and Anti-Submarine Patrols and one Hellcat was flown as a photo plane. Bombs dropped on the two missions were 47-500#, 64-100# and a total of 192 rockets were fired. USS *CHENANGO* launched planes to support strikes through out the day at NOBARA, ISHIGAKI and MIYARA. Targeted were runways and dispersal areas. Expended on these targets were 194-100# G.P. bombs. Eighteen planes were launched for CAP and ASP. Later *CHENANGO* proceeded to KERAMA REETO with *USS DREXLER* and *USS MASSEY*. (*KERAMA RETTO was located approximately 110 miles NE of the Task Unit's assigned combat position.*)

2 MAY (L-plus-31) USS *SANGAMON* launched 6 hecklers for ISHIGAKI JIMA and MIYAKO JIMA between 0030H and 0410H. At dawn 12 Hellcats were sent on a sweep of ISHIGAKI and MIYAKO. Four of these 12 were assigned LCAP duty. *SUWANNEE* sent 8 of her Avengers for a sweep of MIYAKO JIMA. The Avengers expended 16-500# G.P. bombs, 32-100# G.P. bombs and 48-5 inch H.E. rockets. 20 Hellcats were launched for LCAP and TCAP and 3 Avengers were assigned LASP. Hellcat #15 ditched 11 miles from the formation and the pilot was rescued with no injuries by the Destroyer, *USS FULLAM DD-474*. *USS SANTEE* launched 4 Hellcats at 1500H armed with a total of four 500# bombs and 16 H.E. rockets for a strike on ISHIGAKI Airfield. Twenty eight planes were launched for LCAP and LASP and one plane for a photo plane. Dispersals were bombed and rocketed and one single engine plane on the ground was destroyed.

On this day a rumor was circulating around that Adolf Hitler was dead.

3 May (L-plus-32) At 0230H the *USS CHENANGO*, *USS MUSTIN* and *USS STACK* returned from KERAMA RETTO and joined the SAKISHIMA GUNTO formation and took up the stations they were assigned. *SANGAMON* launched 8 Hellcats and 6 Avengers for their early morning strikes at ISHIGAKI and MIYAKO JIMA. One Hellcat was also sent at this time for a message drop. It was reported that the radioman of one of the Avengers was hit in the shoulder by a piece of enemy anti-aircraft fire during an attack on MIYAKO JIMA and his wounds were later treated aboard the ship and he was released back to duty. Later in the day the *USS FULLAM* came along side the *SANGAMAN* to transfer Admiral Sample and his staff to the nearby *SUWANNEE*. In the afternoon four Hellcats were sent out for CAP duty at ISHIGAKI and MIYAKO JIMA. At 1919H the *SANGAMON, DENNIS DE405* and *FULLAM DD474* left the carrier formation and proceeded to KERMA RETTO to rearm. Today planes from the *SUWANNEE* flew 52 sorties at SAKISHIMA. Sixteen of her planes struck ISHIGAKI boat yards and airfields, damaging 3 luggers and 4 small boats. Sixteen planes hit targets of opportunity on MIYAKO JIMA. Twenty planes were sent out for LCAP and LASP duty. Twenty four 500# G.P. bombs, 32-100# G.P. bombs and 24-5 inch High Explosive rockets were expended from *SUWANNEE'S* planes. The *CHENANGO* planes reported a low cloud ceiling over SAKISHIMA GUNTO targets which hindered their strikes. Planes from this carrier assigned Tactical Combat Air Patrol struck barracks near ISHIGAKI Airfield with 8-100# bombs and 24 rockets. A second strike by TCAP planes two hours later cratered the ISHIGAKI runway and damaged dispersal areas. Expended on this strike were 7-100# G.P. bombs and 24 rockets. *SANTEE* launched 24 flights off her deck. Four Hellcats were placed on Tactical Combat Air Patrol and 20 flights were assigned Local Combat Air Patrol and Local Anti-Submarine Patrol.

With SANGAMON already in route to KERAMA RETTO. Admiral Sample and his three remaining "INDISPENSABLES", SUWANNEE, CHENANGO, and SANTEE and their Destroyers and Destroyer Escorts moved out of SAKISHIMA GUNTO, making way for the return of the British Fleet.

4 May (L-plus-33) The *USS SANGAMON* and her escorts *USS DENNIS* and *USS FULLAM* reached KERAMA RETTO near Okinawa at 0700H and the *SANGAMON* anchored at Berth K-99 for replenishment. A smoke screen was laid in the harbor during this time. Through out the day enemy aircraft had been active and several times the carrier was on General Quarters. *SANGAMON* and her two escorts left KERAMA RETTO at 1830H. She had been replenished with ammunition, bombs, aircraft spares and fresh provisions. Barely underway at 1850H, a group, possibly 9-12 unidentified planes were detected at a distance of 29 miles, bearing 200 degrees. *SANGAMON* and her escorts went to General Quarters. Land based Corsair fighters providing Combat Air Patrol for the vicinity and they were vectored out 20 miles to intercept the approaching unidentified aircraft and they claimed to have found and destroyed 9 Japanese planes, although some enemy planes got away. After the three ships went to General Quarters, the destroyer *FULLAM* and the destroyer escort *DENNIS* formed an AA defense screen with the *DENNIS* 1,000 yards ahead of the *SANGAMON* and the *FULLAM* 1000 yards astern of the carrier on a course of 190 degrees- True and a speed of 18 knots. At 1902H a *"Tony"* was sighted bearing 160 degrees- True, distance 3-4 miles, position angle 15 degrees. The *"Tony"* flew down the port beam at about 2 miles until it reached the port quarter. Here the plane was taken under fire by all ships plus the *USS SPEARS* who was on patrol in the vicinity. As the carrier swung left the *"Tony"* went into a dive for the ship and narrowly missed, carrying away the starboard radio antenna and crashing about 25 feet off the starboard beam. Three sailors went overboard. The *SANGAMON* continued to turn into the wind and two F6F night fighters were launched. These planes later landed at YONTAN Airfield, OKINAWA. The ship turned out of the wind and continued south. At this time there were still unidentified aircraft reported to the southwest and also indications that window was being used. (*WINDOW- is a form of radar jamming.*) At 1930, night fighters were sent out to investigate and just after they disappeared into the low hanging clouds a twin engine Japanese *"Nick"* was sighted on the starboard quarter at

290 degrees-True distance 3 miles, position angle 15 degrees. This plane was taken under fire, but it continued on a northerly course, and disappeared into the clouds. Shortly it reappeared directly astern as it dove from the base of the clouds for the ship. It was burning from engine to engine as it crashed into the flight deck amid ship at 1933H. A terrific explosion occurred and heavy fires immediately broke out on the flight and hangar decks. At 1940H the bridge was cleared of all personnel by order of the Captain. The Captain, Navigator, Captain's Orderly, and Helmsman remained. Numerous personnel were reported as having either been blown over the side or to have jumped. Various ships in the area closed to pick up personnel and to render assistance. The ship swung to the left to bring the wind on the starboard beam to facilitate fighting the fire. By 1955H all communications from the bridge and control were lost. After steering control was lost an attempt was made to steer by varying speed of the engines. The ship was swinging slowly starboard with heavy fires burning in most of the hangar and also on the fuel deck as gasoline and oil flowed down from the hanger deck. Large fires were burning in the parked planes on the flight deck admidship enveloping the port and starboard catwalks between frames 53 and 79. Large quantities of .50 caliber, 20mm and 40mm ammunition exploded on the hangar deck, flight deck, in clipping rooms and on the catwalks at the guns. The planes parked aft of the after elevator were all jettisoned both port and starboard with help of destroyers who came long side, passed up lines attached to planes, then backed away hauling the planes over the sides. Sixteen planes were jettisoned in this manner. By 2005H steering control was established at Battle II and at 2015H control of the ship was assumed at Battle II. Steering by magnetic compass and at 10 knots speed. At 2020H the *USS HUDSON* who had been assisting in the plane jettisoning came along side to the starboard to help fight the fires aft of the island. The *HUDSON* very skillfully and courageously came very close aboard in the face of the fire and the exploding ammunition. One of the jettisoned planes landed on her fan tail and a fire started but it was quickly put out. This ship was not steady and the Hudson was caught against the gun tubs and catwalks and received damage to her superstructure. At 2025H unable to establish any communications the captain and remaining personnel left the bridge and took up station on the flight deck, forward of the fire. The pressure was removed from both catapults and all magazines, torpedo and bomb storage were flooded. Two fire fighter *LCI'S* (Landing Craft Infantry) were dispatched from KERAMA RETTO and they arrived at 2100H. *LCI- 13* came along side to starboard and received considerable damage to his superstructure from gun tubs. *LCI- 61* came along side to port and aided in fighting the hangar deck fire. He was also damaged along side. At 2126H all engines stopped. By 2200H all fires were reported under control. The fire in the forward end of the hangar deck was still burning. The only communications were by megaphone and flash light signals. The *USS FULLAM* had been keeping CTU 52.1.3 informed of the situation and at 2240H relayed orders that the *SANGAMON* was to join TU 52.1.3 at dawn. By 2300H all fires were out and by 2310H all vessels had cleared outside. There were several vessels at this time still engaged in picking up personnel from the water. At 2333H, *SANGAMON* was underway at 12 knots on a course of 135 degrees-True, escorted by the *USS FULLAM* and the *USS DENNIS* in route to rendezvous with TU 52.1.3. All radar and external communications were out. ComDesRon 45 in the *USS FULLAM* steered all contacts clear of this vessel and performed the necessary navigation. Ship control was at Battle II with auxiliary steering and a combination of magnetic

compass and a phone connection to the after gyro for steering. All of the gyro repeaters were out. The damage to the ship was extensive and would require being worked on in a Navy Yard for a period of time. The hangar was gutted by fire and had several holes in the bulkheads from the explosion. There was a large hole in the flight deck where the plane crashed, and the flight deck between the elevators was bulged upward by the explosion. Both elevators were blown out with the after one being turned over on its end in the well with one corner sticking 20 feet above the deck. Reported casualties were: 17 dead (11 identified, 6 unidentified), 39 missing and 116 wounded.

Note: More than one sighting of the Japanese suicide plane seen diving into the SANGAMON'S deck has reported that once the "NICK" was over the carrier on its final glide and only seconds before it crashed into the deck, the pilot released what was thought to be a 500# bomb that penetrated the deck and exploded inside the hangar. This explosion among other things caused the ships deck to buckle and the two elevators to be blown out of their positions. After the strike on the carrier and all fires were out. There was one airplane left on deck. The airplane was shattered but its radio still worked. This plane's radio served for awhile as the only means of communications the ship had with other ships around. A very likely factor that the SANGAMON suffered a hit by a suicide plane while leaving KERAMA RETTO can be contributed to a late delivery of a supply of Aircraft lubricating oil that caused a delay in the ship getting underway from KERAMA. Otherwise if the oil had been delivered on time the carrier would have been on her way earlier and this may have just been another routine day for the crew on the USS SANGAMON. The first Japanese airplane that attacked the SANGAMON was the "Tony". It was a single engine army fighter known as a Kawasaki-KI-61Hien with a top speed of 368 mph. The second airplane that was successful in crashing into the SANGAMON was the "NICK". It was a two engine Army attack fighter built by Kawasaki and named the KI-45 Toryu. Its top speed was 336 mph.

When the British returned on the 4th of May after replenishing at San Pedro Bay, Admiral Rawlings called for ship bombardment of MIYAKO JIMA. While his ships were being screened by his destroyers and overhead CAP fighter planes, battle ships *KING GEORGE V* and *HOWE* pulled close to MIYAKO JIMA and shelled HIRARA Airfield and nearby radar and communication installations with 200 rounds of 14 inch. Cruisers *SWIFTSURE*, *GAMBIA*, *BLACK PRINCE* and *EURYALUS* shelled the NOBARA runways, while *UGANDA* shelled the SUKAMA runway.

The whole island shook from the British bombardment. The people on the island were sure that this was the precursor for the landing of enemy troops on the island and the Island's army was ready, although the gunfire was trained onto the airfields. Later in the day it was reported that there were no troop transport ships among the enemy ships. This helped to lower the tension among the soldiers. Finally, the attacking ships and their airplanes retreated, but too late to protect their carriers, for the Japanese Special Forces took advantage of the island bombardment. They had anticipated that the British Aircraft Carriers were now less protected, for their fighter aircraft, battle ships and cruisers had left them and were some distance away from the carriers at this time. So the Kamikazes came in waves and attacked the less-protected carriers. One suicide plane dove into the deck of the FORMIDABLE exploding its bomb, destroying planes spotted on the deck and making a sizeable hole in the ships deck. Men were killed and injured and fire broke out. Another Kamikaze came close to hitting the INDOMITABLE as it fell near the forward port side of the carrier. Seafires and Corsairs flying local Combat Air Patrol splashed 14 enemy planes with a loss of four British planes. (It was thought that the Kamikazes in this group were from the Japanese 17th Righteousness unit from Ilan Formosa). FORMIDABLE was up and running the next day. The hole in the deck had been patched and her airplanes that had to land on the other carriers were now able to return.

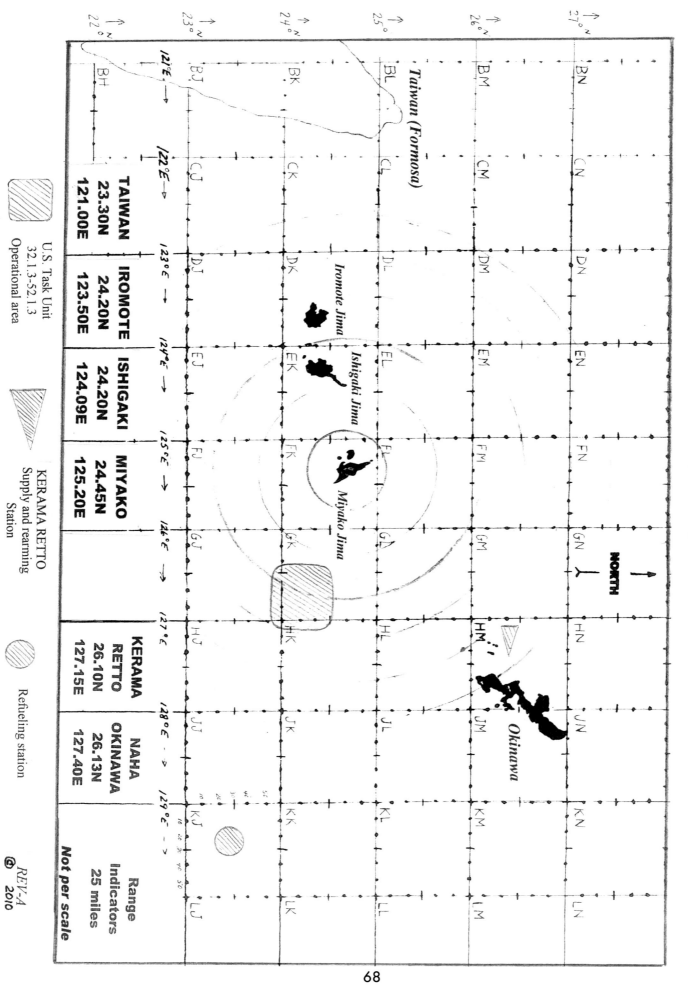

Author's area position map.

Drawn by Fredio Samples

TAIWAN 23.30N 121.00E	**IROMOTE** 24.20N 123.50E	**ISHIGAKI** 24.20N 124.09E	**MIYAKO** 24.45N 125.20E	**KERAMA RETTO** 26.10N 127.15E	**NAHA OKINAWA** 26.13N 127.40E	

U.S. Task Unit
32.1.3-52.1.3
Operational area

KERAMA RETTO
Supply and rearming
Station

Refueling station

Range
Indicators
25 miles

Not per scale

Taiwan (Formosa)

Iromote Jima

Ishigaki Jima

Miyako Jima

Okinawa

NORTH

REV-A
2010

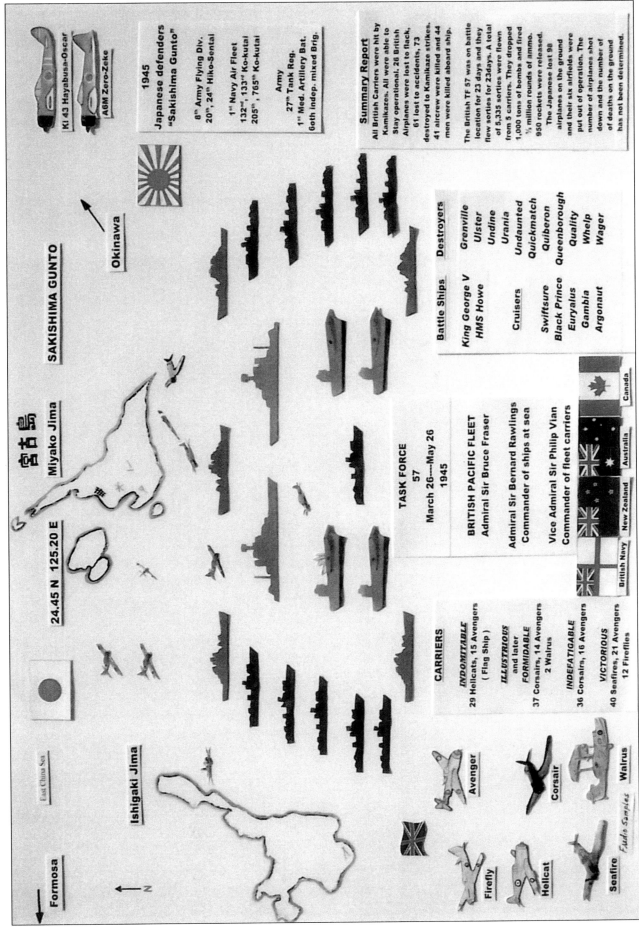

KI 43 Hayabusa-Oscar

A6M Zero-Zeke

**1945
Japanese defenders
"Sakishima Gunto"**

8th Army Flying Div.
20th, 24th Hiko-Sentai

1st Navy Air Fleet
132nd, 133rd Ko-kutai
205th, 765th Ko-kutai

Army
27th Tank Reg.
1st Med. Artillery Bat.
60th Indep. mixed Brig.

Summary Report

All British Carriers were hit by Kamikazes. All were able to Stay operational. 26 British Airplanes were lost to flack, 61 lost to accidents, 73 destroyed to Kamikaze strikes. 41 aircrew were killed and 44 men were killed aboard ship.

The British TF 57 was on battle location for 23 days and they flew sorties for 23days. A total of 5,335 sorties were flown from 5 carriers. They dropped 1,000 tons of bombs and fired ½ million rounds of ammo. 950 rockets were released. The Japanese lost 98 airplanes on the ground and their six airfields were put out of operation. The number of airplanes shot down and the number of deaths on the ground has not been determined.

Okinawa

SAKISHIMA GUNTO

宮古島

Miyako Jima

24.45 N 125,20 E

East China Sea

Ishigaki Jima

Formosa

N

	Destroyers
	Grenville
	Ulster
	Undine
	Urania
Battle Ships	Undaunted
King George V	Quickmatch
HMS Howe	Quiberon
	Queenborough
Cruisers	Quality
	Whelp
Swiftsure	Wager
Black Prince	
Euryalus	
Gambia	
Argonaut	

**TASK FORCE
57**

March 26—May 26
1945

BRITISH PACIFIC FLEET
Admiral Sir Bruce Fraser

Admiral Sir Bernard Rawlings
Commander of ships at sea

Vice Admiral Sir Philip Vian
Commander of fleet carriers

Canada Australia New Zealand British Navy

CARRIERS

INDOMITABLE
29 Helicats, 15 Avengers
(Flag Ship)

ILLUSTRIOUS
and later
FORMIDABLE
37 Corsairs, 14 Avengers
2 Walrus

INDEFATIGABLE
36 Corsairs, 16 Avengers

VICTORIOUS
40 Seafires, 21 Avengers
12 Fireflies

Avenger

Corsair

Walrus

Firefly   Hellcat   Seafire   *Radio Samples*

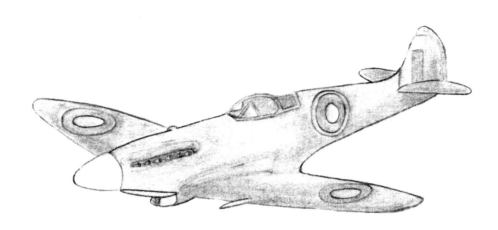

Supermarine Seafire

British Naval Carrier Fighter Bomber
Single seat folding wings
Engine 1600hp (1193kw) Rolls-Royce Merlin 55M
12 cylinder Vee engine
Maximum speed 560km/h (348mph)
Service ceiling 7315m (24,000ft)
Range 890km (553miles)
Two 20mm fixed forward firing cannons and four 303in Browing fixed
forward firing machine guns in the leading edge of the wings
Can be fitted with a bomb and rockets

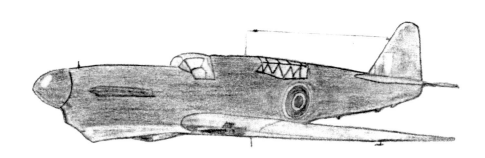

The Fairey Firefly

Two seat British Naval fighter with folding wings
Engine 2000 Rolls-Royce Griffon II 12 cylinder vee
Maximum speed 386 mph (618 km/h)
Normal range 740 miles (1185km)
Four 20mm cannons /Two in the leading edge of each wing

Chapter 7
AMERICAN TASK UNIT 52.1.3/32.1.3
SAKISHIMA GUNTO

**5 May (L-plus-34) 1945**   British planes struck targets at ISHIGAKI, MIYAKO JIMA and NOBARA Airfield. _USS BLOCK ISLAND II, CVE 106 joined TU 52.1.3. She replaced the USS SANGAMAN who was in bad need of repairs after the ship was hit by a suicide plane near KERAMA RETTO on 4 May 1945. The USS BLOCK ISLAND took her place along side the USS SUWANNEE, USS SANTEE and the USS CHENANGO at SAKISHIMA GUNTO. BLOCK ISLAND was built by the TODD Pacific Shipyards in TACOMA WA on 5 July 1944. A CVE being built at these shipyards having the name of USS SUNSET BAY number 106, was officially changed to the USS BLOCK ISLAND CVE 106. The changing of the name of this new carrier was made in honor of the first USS BLOCK ISLAND CVE 21 that was sunk on 29 May 1944. USS BLOCK ISLAND II, CVE 106 was commissioned as a "COMMENCEMENT BAY class Carrier" on 30 December 1944. She was a few feet longer and a bit faster than the four older SANGAMON class CVE's and she carried more crewmembers and her guns and radar were of the latest designs. The US Naval engineers had added into the design of the "Commencement Bay Class Carriers" all of the good and successful things that had been learned from the previous fighting Escort Carriers up till this time. For the first time to be stationed on a CVE, the air group's fighter pilots and bomber pilots along with the bomber crewmembers were US Marines. Under the title of: "Marine Carrier Air Group one", the Marines flew F4U Corsairs and F6 Hellcats from their VMF-511 Squadron and TBM Avengers from their VMTB-233 Squadron. Also there was a Marine staffed aircraft service detachment to care for the airplanes aboard the ship._

6 May 1945 (L-plus-35) The British Pacific Fleet pulled away from its SAKISHIMA battle station position and went for replenishments. The American Task Unit 52.1.3 with Rear/Admiral Sample and carriers: _USS SUWANNEE, CHENANGO and BLOCK ISLAND_ replaced the British on the SAKISHIMA GUNTO station. The fourth carrier of TU 52.1.3, the USS _SANTEE_ reported to KERAMA RETTO to pick up her supplies and would later report back to the task unit. _CHENANGO_ planes from _Air Group 25_ attacked SAKISHIMA airfields and preformed photo coverage today and reported that the Japanese had discharged smoke bombs at the airfields and they thought this was done to keep the Americans from seeing and photographing any damage done by previous attacks to the airfield's runways. Forty fighters and 27 bomber sorties were flown against ISHIGAKI JIMA targets. Damaged on this run were the ISHIGAKI and MIYARA Airfield runways and also some barracks. Thirty two planes flew CAP and ASP. Expended were 68-500# G.P. bombs, 74-100# G.P. bombs and 316 HVA rockets The _USS SUWANNEE_ never let up on her attacks. Her planes flew 52 sorties. This included 8 Hellcats that flew Target Combat Air Patrol, one Hellcat that flew a photo mission and one TBM that was assigned to making a message drop. Twenty three Hellcats and 19 Avengers then struck targets of opportunity on MIYAKO JIMA, dropping 75-500# General Purpose Bombs, 74-100# G.P. bombs and firing 300-5 inch High Explosive rockets. The _USS BLOCK ISLAND_, the new CVE on station with TU 52.1.3 was standing by, while her ship's company and air group members were getting themselves acquainted with operations. Her air squadrons would get their attack orders for SAKISHIMA GUNTO on the 10th of May.

7 May (L-plus-36) The *USS SANTEE* was now back on the SAKISHIMA GUNTO station after being replenished with supplies and ammunition. She launched 4 Avengers and 28 Hellcats for strikes on ISHIGAKI Airfield. Runways were cratered and dispersals and barracks were damaged. One single engine airplane was destroyed on the ground. Expended from the *AG-24* planes were 20-500# bombs, 80-100# bombs and 129-H.E. rockets. Four Hellcats from *SANTEE* preformed Local Combat Air Patrol while the *USS SUWANNEE'S* eight Hellcats swept SAKISHIMA. Sixteen more Hellcats and 16 Avengers from *SUWANNEE* split into two groups and hit the airfields, AA positions and dispersal areas on MIYAKO JIMA, destroying one Japanese aircraft on the ground. From *AG-40*, the *SUWANNEE* planes expended 71-500# General Purpose bombs, 101-100# G.P. bombs and 107 High Explosive five inch rockets. *CHENANGO'S Air Group- 25* planes resumed their action against SAKISHIMA, hitting airfields at ISHIGAKI and MIYAKO. Runways were cratered at ISHIGAKI and HIRARA Airfield along with damage to nearby dispersal areas and buildings near HIRARA Airfield. Expended were 39-500# G.P. bombs, 136-100# G.P. bombs and 283 rockets. After today's action the four American CVE carriers prepared to leave the SAKISHIMA station for refueling and ship gun practice southeast of OKINAWA SHIMA. The British fleet will relieve the American task force.

8 May (L-plus-37) The British Pacific Fleet were on station at SAKISHIMA GUNTO. Bad weather had moved in and forced all their planes to remain on their carriers. A "Stand Down" was the order of the day.
Word reached the Pacific that Germany had surrendered on the 7th of May.

9 May (L-plus-38) The British sent bomber strikes against MIYAKO and ISHIGAKI. Two planes found on the ground at MIYAKO were destroyed in this strike. Two Kamikazes attacked the *HMS VICTORIOUS* and one of them crashed into the carrier's deck causing a fire. She was hit again and the enemy's plane bounced over the side of the carrier. Reported casualties were three and twenty men were wounded. Luckily there was little damage caused to the ship from the two hits. Ten minutes later a Kamikaze crashed into *HMS FORMIDABLE*, destroying several of her planes and causing a fire. Both *VICTORIOUS* and *FORMIDABLE* went for repairs.

10 May (L-plus-39) The *USS CHENANGO* located southeast of OKINAWA was given orders to strike targets at ISHIGAKI JIMA. She sent 8 Hellcats and 8 Avengers to bomb and strafe. When they arrived the planes had only ten minutes over their target before having to return to base. Bombed and rocketed with eight 100# bombs and 48 rockets were runways and dispersal areas at ISHIGAKI and MIYARA airfields. *AIR GROUP 25* had 20 of their planes on CAP and ASP. *USS SANTEE* whose planes were originally assigned for strikes on OKINAWA targets were reassigned to carry out missions at SAKISHIMA GUNTO. Eight fighters were launched from *SANTEE'S* deck at 1400H for a strike on MIYAKO airfields. Thirty two rockets were fired into airfield dispersals and one single engine plane was destroyed on the ground. Four *SANTEE* planes flew tactical combat air patrol and 20 flew LCAP and LASP. Targets hit by *BLOCK ISLAND'S* fighter and bombers were HIRARA and NOBARA airfields on MIYAKO JIMA. The Marines had to fly 175 miles over water to make their first strike against HIRARA and NOBARA airfields. Launched were 8 fighters and 8 Avengers. The Avengers were armed with 10 each 100# G.P. bombs and eight 5-inch rockets. The F4U Corsairs and the F6F-5 Hellcats were armed with one each, 500# G.P. bomb and eight 5 inch rockets. One Hellcat on a photo mission was armed only with a machine gun. The fighters started their sweep with a high speed dive, dropping their bombs on the runway, strafing; and then they return to rendezvous with the Avengers who proceeded to make a glide bombing attack on the airstrips while surrounded by a section of fighters who strafed and rocketed the AA positions. With some rockets remaining, the flight then broke up into divisions to attack planes in revetments, repair shops, storage areas and targets of opportunity. Spotty AA fire was encountered and no tracers were seen. Because of the sustained volume of fire encountered, the planes found it necessary to pull out of their bombing attack at 2,500 feet although the fighters often went lower than that while in a steep high speed dive. In the first strike an Avenger, TBM-3 Bureau 68706 was lost over NOBARA Airfield, presumably being hit by AA while in its last rocket run on the area. It was not seen to crash, but a large fire was observed in the area. The TBM was piloted by 2nd Lieutenant Douglas Henry Merrin, 035081 USMCR. The two crew members were: Sgt. Joseph Lawrence Butehorn, 473293 USMCR and Sgt. Edward Thomas Gunning, 395254 USMCR. All three belonged to squadron *VMTB-233*. Another Avenger was so severely damaged by a medium caliber shell in the landing gear and hydraulic system that it was forced to ditch alongside an escort ship upon return. The pilot and crew were picked up uninjured by the *USS BUTLER*. Several other planes suffered light damage from AA.

11 May (L-plus-40) *USS SUWANNEE* sent 8 Hellcats and 8 Avengers to strike NOBARA Airfields on MIYAKO JIMA. Expended were 19-500# G.P. and 74-100# General Purpose bombs against runways and installations and 103-5 inch rockets were fired against AA positions. Hellcats and Avengers totaling 14 planes flew TCAP, LCAP, LASP and photo coverage. *CHENANGO'S* planes struck ISHIGAKI and MIYARA Airfield runways. One "*Kate*" and a twin engine airplane were damaged at the ISHIGAKI Airfield and fires were started in the dispersal areas. Twenty six 500# bombs, 140-100# bombs and 124 rockets were expended. CAP and ASP was handled by 22 planes. The *USS SANTEE* launched two photo planes, Sixteen Hellcats and 15 Avengers for strikes against MIYAKO JIMA airfields. Runways were cratered and dispersals were damaged. One single engine plane was destroyed and 4 more were damaged on the ground. Expended on these strikes were 150-100# bombs, 8-500# bombs and 70-H.E. rockets. Twenty of *SANTEE'S* planes were assigned Local CAP and ASP duty. One Hellcat crashed at sea after being hit by AA fire while attacking MIYAKO JIMA. The pilot landed his plane in the water about 2 miles off the N.E. shore of MIYAKO where he got into his raft. He was later rescued by a patrol plane. *BLOCK ISLAND* launched three sweeps against ISHIGAKI JIMA airfields and installations. Sixteen fighters, Hellcats and Corsairs and 7 Avenger Torpedo Bombers made the sweep. One fighter served as a photo plane. Twelve 500# bombs were expended. Two Avengers were later launched to join fighters from other carriers for Target Combat Air Patrol. Enemy AA damaged 2

Corsairs, 2 Avengers and one Hellcat but these all safely returned to the carrier. One Avenger with a loose 100# bomb in its bomb bay was sent to land at KADENA Airfield at OKINAWA.

12-13 May (L-plus-41-42) The British took over the bombing and strafing of the airfields at SAKISHIMA while the US Task Unit 52.1.3 moved near OKINAWA and flew sorties there. For two days the British planes poured bombs and rockets on MIYAKO and ISHIGAKI JIMA hitting airfields, barracks and small vessels at sea. Two torpedo bomber airplanes were shot down by enemy fire. The two bomber crews were rescued by *USS BLUEFISH* an American Submarine.

14 May (L-plus-43) The US Task Unit 52.1.3 took over the SAKISHIMA GUNTO station from the British. *USS SUWANNEE* launched 2 TBM Avengers for a photo mission and one for a message drop. Four Hellcats were launched for Local Combat Air Patrol and 8 more flew a sweep mission over the NOBARA Airfield at MIYAKO. These planes expended 8-500# general purpose bombs and 48-5 inch high explosive rockets hitting the two runways and rocketing and strafing small boats on the northeast coast of MIYAKO. Another afternoon strike was made against NOBARA by eleven Hellcats and fourteen Avengers from the *SUWANNEE*. These planes struck the runways with 11-500# G.P. bombs, 134-100# G.P. bombs and 167-H.E. rockets. The *USS SANTEE* launched 28 planes for a strike on MIYAKO airfields and 32 planes for LCAP and LASP. AT MIYAKO, airfield runways were cratered, dispersals, and buildings were hit. One "Tony" and one single engine plane was destroyed on the ground. Nineteen 500# bombs and 80-100# bombs were dropped. 204-H.E. rockets were fired at enemy positions. *USS CHENANGO* launched *AG-25* planes for strikes at ISHIGAKI and MIYARA airfields. Bad weather in the area caused some problems. Runways were cratered and a 50 foot boat was sunk. Expended were 8-500# G.P. bombs and 50-100# G.P. bombs and 79 rockets. Enemy AA guns found their target and hit three of the *CHENANGO'S* Avengers, One was shot down. Ensign Rice and his two crewmen were rescued by a Dumbo rescue plane after 90 minutes in their raft, just one mile south of ISHIGAKI town. *CHENANGO* planes provided constant cover and strafed the beaches during the rescue as the enemy gunners on the ground continued to fire their AA guns. *BLOCK ISLAND* launched 8 fighters including a photo plane and 4 Avengers for a sweep on ISHIGAKI JIMA. Expended were 12-500# bombs and 62 rockets. At 1040H, two more fighters were launched to support the escorting of a Dumbo rescue plane from KERAMA to pick up survivors of *CHENANGO'S* Avenger which had been shot down and had made a water landing just off the shores of ISHIGAKI JIMA. The fighters covered the rescue site.

15 May 1945 (L-plus-44) *USS SUWANNEE* Hellcats and Avengers flew Local Combat Air Patrol and Local Anti Submarine Patrol and one Avenger flew a message drop to the *USS MAKIN ISLAND*. Eight more Hellcats fighters flew a sweep over MIYAKO, dropping 8-500# G.P. bombs and expending 47-5 inch rockets, hitting NOBARA and HIRARA airfields and dispersal areas. The fighters were followed by 4 Avengers that dropped 17-100# G.P. bombs and fired 47-5 inch rockets hitting the same airfields. Two divisions of Hellcats flew Tactical Combat Air Patrol, one over MIYAKO and the other over ISHIGAKI JIMA. They expended 8-500# G.P. bombs and 24-5 inch High Explosive rockets. At 1845H a division of Hellcats flying LCAP were vectored, 000 degrees true, and a few minutes later they "Tally Hoed" and "Splashed" 3 "*Vals*" 45 miles from the formation. *("Tally Hoed" and "Splashed" This is fighter pilots jargon for reporting that he has sight of an enemy plane and has shot it down.)* Planes from the *USS CHENANGO* made a run on ISHIGAKI Airfield and spotted 3 enemy planes landing. One a biplane, probably a "*SPRUCE*" was exploded on the ground and another, a "*ZEKE*" burst into flames after being hit on the second pass. This same air group paid a visit to MIYAKO JIMA and dropped bombs that cratered the HIRARA runways. Bombs and rockets expended by *AG-25* were 10-500# G.P.bombs, 60-100# G.P. bombs and 2 rockets. *USS BLOCK ISLAND* launched 4 Avengers and 4 fighters including one photo fighter for an early morning strike on ISHIGAKI. During the strike, an Avenger was hit with AA, but managed to make it back to the carrier. One fighter was hit with a medium caliber shell and several machine gun hits, so the plane was vectored to KADENA Airfield with an Avenger flying along as an escort. *BLOCK ISLAND* planes were again launched in the afternoon. Three Avengers and 4 fighters struck HIRARA Airfield on MIYAKO. One Avenger was damaged by AA and one other was struck in the canopy by AA fire. Exploding fragments blinded the pilot in his left eye; nevertheless he pressed home his rocket attack, then with another fighter for escort, with part of his left eye hanging from his cheek, he flew 100 miles back to the carrier and landed safely aboard. Expended were 12-500# bombs, 85- 100# bombs and 98 rockets. Two more planes were launched for Combat Air Patrol.

16-17 May (L-plus-45-46) The British fleet relieved the American Escort carriers at SAKASHIMA and they sent planes to pound MIYAKO and ISHIGAKI. Enemy aircraft on the ground was bombed and strafed, runways were cratered and small sea vessels were strafed and left sinking. Trucks carrying soldiers was strafed and left burning. One British fighter crashed at sea near MIYAKO and its pilot was rescued by an American submarine. Foul weather on the 17th caused limited operations.

18 May (L-plus-47) The British TF 57 refueled. American Escorts TU 52.1.3 was near OKINAWA. *USS SUWANNEE* was at KERAMA RETTO, tied to berth K-99. She was being replenished with supplies.

19-22 May (L-plus -48-51) On the 20th, the British ran into foul weather and thick fog and a destroyer and a carrier collided. The destroyer had to be towed for repairs. The British was only able to make one strike on MIYAKO. The next day three successful strikes were flown against MIYAKO and two against ISHIGAKI. Fighters from the *INDOMITABLE* intercepted a Japanese airplane and shot it down. The four US Escort carriers of TU 52.1.3 were 50-60 miles south of Okinawa except for the *CHENANGO* who was replenishing at KERAMA on the 20th and then the *SANTEE* took on her supplies at KERAMA on the 21st. Thunderstorms moved in over SAKISHIMA and on the 22nd, the cloud ceiling was reported from 2,000 to 800 feet. *CHENANGO'S* planes were able to bomb the airfield at NOBARA dropping a total of 8-500# bombs from their 8 Hellcat fighters. *SANTEE* managed to launch 16 fighters and 15 Avenger torpedo bombers for a strike on airfields at MIYAKO. Runways were cratered and storage facilities were strafed and rocketed. Twenty five 500# bombs were dropped and 14 H.E. rockets were fired. Limited air support was given to SAKISHIMA due to low cloud cover.

23 May (L-plus-52) R/Admiral Sample, commander of TU 52.1.3 and his four Escort Carriers returned to station at SAKISHIMA GUNTO for one day and resumed the duties of neutralizing the Airfields. *SUWANNEE* launched 29 airplanes. Twelve of these planes struck the NOBARA Airfield at MIYAKO JIMA, expending 12-500# and 70-100# General purpose bombs. Also expended were 54-5 inch rockets. Other planes that were launched from this carrier flew TCAP and LCAP with one plane having a message drop and another having been assigned a photo mission. *USS SANTEE* launched 24 planes for strikes on ISHIGAKI and launched 10 planes for LCAP and LASP. Airfield runways were bombed with 15-500# bombs and 80-100# bombs. Two single engine planes were destroyed on the ground. One 50 foot lugger and one 50 foot tug was damaged in the water. *CHENANGO'S* planes made only one sweep over MIYAKO JIMA due to low visibility, rain and a low cloud ceiling. NOBARA Airfield was bombed with eight 500# bombs. Twenty planes from the *CHENANGO AG-25* were assigned Combat Air Patrol and Anti-Submarine Patrol. *BLOCK ISLAND* launched 8 fighters and 4 TBM Avengers for a strike on ISHIGAKI. The fighters made the regular attack on the Airfields and installations, while the Avengers attacked and destroyed a cable station at Target area 7657 on the eastern peninsula of the island. At 1300H, four fighters were launched for Target Combat Air Patrol over ISHIGAKI. Undesirable flying weather prevented further flights during the day. Planes from *BLOCK ISLAND* expended 12-500# bombs, 40-100# bombs and 96 rockets.

24-25 May (L-plus- 53-54) The British once again and for their final two days at SAKISHIMA took over the bombing and strafing of the SAKISHIMA GUNTO and then the fleet withdrew from SAKISHIMA and set sail for AUSTRALIA.
TF-57 had flown near 5,000 flights and they had dropped near 9,000 tons of bombs and fired an undetermined amount of rockets and ammunition. Over 100 enemy airplanes were destroyed and many others put out of commission. Even with all of this pounding the Japanese continued to repair their cratered runways and broken airplanes.

26 May (L-plus-55) *USS BLOCK ISLAND* at 0359H launched 4 night fighters for a heckler mission at SAKISHIMA. Airfields and a radar station were bombed and strafed on MIYAKO and ISHIGAKI. AA fire was reported to be meager to moderate. Two of the fighters were hit but sustained only minor damage. At 1201H eight fighters and eight Avenger torpedo bombers were launched to strike ISHIGAKI. On arrival over ISHIGAKI, a solid overcast obscured the entire target area and the strike planes proceeded to an alternate target, that being MIYAKO JIMA. Weather conditions were found to be even worse there. Four 500# bombs, 24 rockets and 4 flares were expended. The planes were ordered to return to base. On the way all remaining bombs and rockets were jettisoned at sea before landing on the carrier. Four more fighters and 2 torpedo bombers were launched from this carrier for LCAP and LASP duty. The *USS SUWANNEE* planes flew 53 sorties. Twenty hellcats flew Local Combat Air Patrol, 6

Avengers flew Local Anti Submarine Patrol and one Avenger flew the photo mission. Eight Hellcat fighters flew Tactical Combat Air Patrol and 1 flew a message drop. Eight Hellcats flew a morning sweep over MIYAKO JIMA, HIRARA and SUKAMA Airfields, expending 8-500# G.P. bombs and 48-5 inch H.E. rockets. Three F6F Hellcats and 6 TBM Avengers struck MIYAKO, hitting HIRARA and SUKAMA airfields again, expending 3- 500# G.P. bombs, 30-100# G.P. bombs and 47-5 inch H.E. rockets. Eight fighters flying TCAP over MIYAKO expended 8-500# G.P. bombs and 47-5inch H.E. rockets on the same Airfields. *USS SANTEE* planes flew 44 strike sorties. Ten planes were assigned LCAP and LASP. Strikes were made on runways, buildings and dispersals. At ISHIGAKI, boats were strafed. Damaged were one 50 ft. lugger, One 20 ft. boat and two Sampans. Expended at ISHIGAKI were 22-500# bombs, 80-100# bombs and 216-H.E. rockets. At MIYAKO 7-500# bombs and 70-100# bombs and 84 H.E. rockets were expended. *CHENANGO* sent her planes to ISHIGAKI and MIYAKO to strike targets at HIRARA, NOBARA and HEGINA airfields and disposal areas. Twenty six fighters and 15 Avengers expended 25-500# G.P. bombs, 148-100# G.P. bombs, 45 rockets and 204-HVA rockets at targets.

27 May (L-plus-56) *BLOCK ISLAND* planes made an early morning launch of 3 night fighters for a heckler mission over MIYAKO. The planes attacked the airfields and targets of opportunity. At 1515H four fighters were launched, led by Major R.C. Maze the Squadron commander. While making an attack on a boat yard and small craft at ISHIGAKI Town, Major Maze's plane, an FG-1D Corsair was not observed to come out of its dive and was seen to crash in the shallow water off shore. It was believed that his plane was hit with AA. The submerged plane was seen in later photographs taken of the area. At 0730H four fighters and eight torpedo bombers were launched for a strike at ISHIGAKI Airfield. However, due to fowl weather at ISHIGAKI a secondary target at MIYAKO JIMA was chosen. For the second time at 1130H the attack planned for ISHIGAKI was launched consisting of four fighters and eight bombers. This strike was accomplished under adverse weather conditions. While making a dive bombing attack on enemy shipping about ½ mile from the location of a previous attack, another fighter was lost. An explosion observed nearby in the surf at about this time is believed to have been the crash of this plane. 2nd Lieutenant Robert Aaron Goldberg of VMF-511 Squadron was later listed as missing in action when no trace of him or his Corsair could be seen after the run. Three additional fighters were launched at 1400H for a sweep over ISHIGAKI. Upon finding the target obscured. The flight then attacked the island of TAKETOMI. *(TAKETOME Island is located approximately 8 km southwest of the southwest shore of ISHIGAKI JIMA.) BLOCK ISLAND* planes expended 16-500# bombs, 127-100# bombs and 184-5 inch rockets. *USS SUWANNEE:* Fifteen of her Hellcats and 11 Avengers struck ISHIGAKI Airfield and MIYARA Airfield and barracks on ISHIGAKI. They dropped 27-500# G.P. bombs and 40-100# G.P. bombs. Eight fighters performing a sweep dropped 8-500# G.P. bombs on HIRARA Airfield and strafed luggers at the dock at IKEMA SHIMA. *USS CHENANGO* airplanes bombed and strafed HIRARA, ISHIGAKI, MIYARA and NOBARA runways and also damaged dispersal areas. Hellcats and Avengers totaling 35 planes on this strike expended 27-500# bombs, 80-100# bombs and 205 rockets. Twenty one planes flew CAP and ASP. *USS SANTEE* is being replenished with supplies and ammunition at KERAMA RETTO on this day.

May 28. The US third fleet now takes over and relieves the 5th fleet at Okinawa. Admiral Halsey relieves Admiral Spruance. Task Force 58 is now Task Force 38, making R/Admiral Sample's Task Unit at SAKISHIMA: 32.1.3.This change of command meant very little to the way the carrier battle units operated at SAKISHIMA. It was merely a number change on the paperwork for them. A sailor aboard a carrier or a fighter pilot may have not known of the change for days afterwards. But it was a nightmare for the supply depot. Those supply organizations that had to move the supplies to the war ships and keep the records. All of the provisions that hadn't arrived at the front that were labeled for the 5th fleet's Task Force 58, were held up until they could be relabeled and routed to the 3rd fleet's Task Force 38. One could imagine what would happen to any shipments to their home if one number of their house number or zip code were changed

May 28 (L-plus-57) Business was as usual on the 28th of May at SAKISHIMA as the Escort carrier *USS BLOCK ISLAND* at 0300H launched 3 night fighter for a heckler mission and had them return before reaching their target because of mechanical troubles found in two of the three airplanes. At 0830H eight fighters and two torpedo bomber planes were launched for local combat air patrol and local anti submarine patrol. Four Avengers and 3 fighters were launched at 1530H for a strike on ISHIGAKI. It was necessary to conduct the attack through the overcast. Expended on targets were 40-100# bombs and 24 rockets. *USS SUWANNEE* planes made a morning sweep over NOBARA Airfield. They expended 8-500# G.P. bombs and 16-5 inch H.E. rockets. Seven Hellcats and eight Avenger torpedo bombers struck the same airfield some hours later damaging revetment areas, AA positions and barracks. They expended 7-500# G.P. bombs, 79-100# G.P. bombs and 104-5 inch H.E. rockets. 4 F6F Hellcats flying TCAP dropped 4-500# G.P. bombs on the NOBARA Airfield. One F6F Hellcat, piloted by Lieutenant (jg) M.F. Denman was hit by enemy AA fire. The pilot was seen to bail out over NOBARA Town on MIYAKO ISLAND. He was not seen after hitting the ground. (*More is written about this pilot, as he tells his own story elsewhere in this book.*) *USS SUWANNEE* left the formation at 1950H for KERAMA RETTO. *USS SANTEE* launched 31 planes for strikes on ISHIGAKI airfields and 15 planes for LCAP and LASP. Striking planes cratered the airfield runways and damaged dispersals with 15-500# bombs, 160-100# bombs and 200-H.E. rockets. *USS CHENAGO* received R/Admiral Sample and his flag aboard. Twenty two fighters and bombers from this carrier cratered the runways at MIYARA, ISHIGAKI and HIRARA Airfield at MIYAKO with 11-500# bombs, 80-100# bombs and 123 rockets. Ten planes flew CAP and ASP.

29 May (L-plus-58) *BLOCK ISLAND* sent 4 Avengers and 7 fighters for local ASP and local CAP at 0510H. At 0833H, she launched 8 Avengers and 3 fighters including a photo plane for a strike on ISHIGAKI Airfield. During this attack, *BLOCK ISLAND* pilots observed a *SANTEE* plane crash and explode on the runway at ISHIGAKI. At 1530H, 4 Avengers and 3 fighters were sent to strike HIRARA and NOBARA runways at MIYAKO. Clouds prevented observation of the results. One fighter was damaged by AA on this strike. Seven TBM Avengers were launched at 1330H for a strike on ISHIGAKI Island. This group formed up with a group from CHENANGO and formed a single strike group. BLOCK ISLAND planes were directed to make a rocket attack against barracks in the western edge of ISHIGAKI town. While making this run in the face of heavy AA, one BLOCK ISLAND TBM Avenger was observed to lose the port wing and crash nearby. A column of black smoke from this area observed in photographs at this time was believed to be the plane burning on the ground. The pilot of this plane was 2nd Lieutenant Jack Marconi. The two crewmen aboard were: Staff Sgt. Joe F. Surovy and Staff Sgt. Ben D. Cannan Jr. All three were attached to VMTB-233 squadron. BLOCK ISLAND planes expended 7-500# bombs, 156-100# bombs and 161-5 inch rockets. USS SANTEE planes flew 38 strike sorties against the airfields at ISHIGAKI and MIYAKO. Ten planes were launched for LCAP and LASP. The airfield runways were well cratered, buildings and a radio station were damaged. At ISHIGAKI, three single engine planes were destroyed on the ground. Expended on targets were 24-500# bombs, 140-100# bombs and 148 rockets. At 1030H, Lieutenant John Frank Gray from AG-24 flying off the SANTEE, piloting a F6F-5 fighter airplane failed to pull out of a dive and crashed on ISHIGAKI Airfield runway. The plane exploded on ground impact. There was no sighting of the pilot after the crash. The plane was believed to have been hit by AA. USS CHENANGO planes from AG-25 ran two strikes against MIYAKO airfields. Twenty three planes bombed and strafed HIRARA and NOBARA runways and storage facilities. Four 40 foot boats were strafed. Sixteen 500# bombs, 70-100# bombs and 80 rockets were expended on targets. Twenty four planes were assigned CAP and ASP. The USS SPIKEFISH SS-404, an American submarine joins in lifeguard duty at SAKISHIMA.

30 May 1945 (L-plus-59) BLOCK ISLAND launched 8 Avengers and 9 fighters including one fighter for photo operations against ISHIGAKI. Heavy clouds obscured the target but attacks were made through the overcast. Expended were 8-500# bombs, 73-100# bombs and 106-5 inch rockets. Local flights of 5 fighters and 2 Avengers were flown on LASP and LCAP. SUWANNEE sent her Avenger torpedo bombers and Hellcat fighters to strike NOBARA and HIRARA airfields, dispersal areas, buildings and AA positions. These planes expended 16- 500# G.P. bombs, 137-100# G. P. bombs and 198-5 inch rockets. Also 4 Hellcats that were on TCAP dropped 4-500# G.P. bombs and fired 16-5 inch rockets. A total of 21 planes from SUWANNEE flew LCAP and LASP. USS SANTEE planes flew 56 strike sorties against MIYAKO and ISHIGAKI Airfield runways. Ten planes were launched for LCAP and LASP. At MIYAKO and ISHIGAKI, runways, storage facilities and dispersals were damaged. One single engine plane was destroyed on the ground at ISHIGAKI and one 70 foot boat was damaged off the islands shore. Expended on targets at MIYAKO were 15-500# bombs, 80-100# bombs and 112 H.E. rockets. Expended at ISHIGAKI were 16-500# bombs, 80-100# bombs and 112 H.E. rockets. USS CHENANGO planes hit MIYAKO at NOBARA with 3 strikes. Runways were cratered, storage areas were damaged, and small boats were strafed. One strike was made against ISHIGAKI where an AA position and an amphibious tank base were hit. A total of 23 fighters and 16 bombers were involved in these strikes. Nine fighters and two Avengers flew CAP and ASP.

31 May (L-plus-60) *USS BLOCK ISLAND* between 0526H and 1640H launched 25 fighters and 18 Avenger torpedo bombers for strikes against ISHIGAKI JIMA and HIRARA Airfield at MIYAKO JIMA. Bombing was accomplished through the overcast at ISHIGAKI. One of the fighters was a photo plane and eight fighters flew Local Combat Air Patrol. *BLOCK ISLAND* planes expended 33-500# bombs and 18 rockets at ISHIGAKI and 22-500# bombs and 12 rockets at MIYAKO. *USS SUWANNEE* had 19 of her Hellcats flying TCAP and LCAP with 2 Avengers covering the ASP and one Avenger flying a message drop. Sixteen of her fighters and 16 of her Avengers hit NOBARA, HIRARA and SUKUMA airfields and the town of NOBARA, all on MIYAKO Island. These fighters and bombers expended 16-500# G.P. bombs, 107-100# G.P. bombs and 66-5 inch H.E. rockets. Twelve Hellcats flying TCAP loaded each with a 500# G.P. bomb and a total of sixty six rockets split into two groups of eight, four hitting MIYAKO and four hitting ISHIGAKI. One AVENGER crashed before returning to base. The pilot, Ensign V.C. Calo was rescued by a Dumbo plane. Crewmembers: R.S. Baird and J.D. Christmas were not found. The *USS SANTEE* planes flew 31 strike sorties at ISHIGAKI and MIYAKO. Twenty four planes were launched to fly LCAP and LASP. Runways and storage facilities were bombed on MIYAKO and ISHIGAKI. At an Amphibious base, 3 boats and storage facilities were hit with 2-500# bombs, 30-100# bombs and 48-rockets. *USS CHENANGO* is taking on supplies at KERAMA RETTO.

Over the month of May, planes came daily and bombed, rocketed, and strafed SAKISHIMA GUNTO. It didn't seem that anything was going to escape being hit. First Aid stations were set up in tents through out the island of MIYAKO and hospitals were set up using caves for shelter. One of these hospitals was in a cave dug into the side of NOBARADAKE, close to the Army Division Headquarters where young local high school girls worked as nurses. What was not ruled out by the Japanese Army was the thought that the American soldiers might assault the island by parachuting from airplanes. The local Japanese soldiers were given some instructions and training on how to fight this type of an assault from the air.

On 1 June 1945, USS GILBERT ISLANDS CVE 107 a COMMENCEMENT BAY class CVE Carrier having US Marine Carrier Air Group 2 aboard was detached from Task Unit 32.1.1 late on the 31st of May while operating near OKINAWA and ordered to report to R/Admiral Sample's Task Unit 32.1.3 near SAKISHIMA GUNTO. This will now be the second COMMENCEMENT BAY class carrier having a US Marine air group assigned to TU 32.1.3. She took her place next to her sister; USS BLOCK ISLAND and her planes will join in with the bombing and strafing of the SAKISHIMA airfields. Marine pilots from Air Squadrons VMF512 will be flying the F4U Corsairs and the F6F Hellcats fighters and Marine pilots assigned to VMTB143 Squadron with their Marine crewmen will be operating the TBM-3 Avenger torpedo bombers.

1 June 1945 (L-plus-61) *USS BLOCK ISLAND* at 0515H launched 7 fighters and 8 Avenger torpedo bombers for a strike against ISHIGAKI JIMA. Three fighters and two Avengers were launched at 1029H to fly LCAP and LASP. Fourteen planes, a mixture of fighters and bombers were launched at 1613H. Repair shops were struck and left burning east of ISHIGAKI Airfield. Expended were 64-500# bombs and 64 rockets. At 2107H this carrier took departure from the Task Unit for KERAMA RETTO in company with *USS FARENHOLT (DD-491)* and *USS HEMMINGER (DE-746). USS SUWANNEE* Hellcats and Avengers totaling 21 planes in two different strikes hit MIYAKO Island. They bombed rocketed and strafed NOBARA and HIRARA airfields, HIRARA town and AA positions. *Air group 40* expended 24-500# G.P. bombs, 100-100# G.P. bombs and 314-5 inch H.E. rockets. *USS GILBERT ISLANDS CVE 107* on her first day of operations with the SAKISHIMA carrier formation provided planes for Local Combat Air Patrol and Local Anti-Submarine Patrol for the Task Unit. *USS SANTEE* sent 24 Avengers and 32 Hellcats against airfields and installations at MIYAKO and ISHIGAKI islands. Three 80 foot boats and six 30 foot boats were damaged and one single engine airplane on the ground was destroyed. Expended were a total of 32-500# bombs, 160-100# bombs and 178 H.E. rockets. Twenty planes from *USS CHENANGO* struck ISHIGAKI and MIYARA runways and dispersal areas and one amphibious tank base in two sweeps. Damaged by strafing were about 13 boats that were 40-50 feet long. One enemy *"DINAH"* airplane was destroyed by Local Combat Air patrol near MIYAKO. Twenty-two planes covered CAP and ASP. Eleven 500# bombs, 67-100# G.P. bombs and 183 rockets were expended on targets. An F6F-5 Hellcat was hit by AA over ISHIGAKI and the pilot attempted to return to the carrier. With the engine smoking he was forced to make a water landing 55 miles west of the formation. The pilot was able to get into his life raft and was rescued by a Dumbo.

2 June (L-plus-62) Planes from the *USS GILBERT ISLANDS* provided Local Combat Air and Anti-Submarine Patrols for the Task Unit. Her planes bombed MIYARA Airfield and rocketed military installations in the vicinity of the airfield at ISHIGAKI JIMA. *SUWANNEE'S* planes flew 43 sorties including 16 F6F for LCAP, 6 TBM for LASP, 4 F6F for TCAP, one TBM for a photo mission and 1 TBM for a message drop. Eight F6F Hellcats and 7 Avengers were sent for strikes at NOBARA and HIRARA airfields on MIYAKO JIMA. Expended were 8-500# G.P. bombs, 70-100# G.P. bombs and 104-5 inch H.E. rockets. The 4 F6F Hellcats on TCAP expended 4-500# G.P. bombs and 24-5 inch H.E. rockets on NOBARA Airfield. The *SANTEE* planes flew a total of 28 strike sorties over ISHIGAKI. Airfields runways were cratered and five 50 foot and four 30 foot boats were damaged. A total of 51-500# bombs were dropped on targets. Four planes from the *SANTEE* flew TCAP and 10 more flew LCAP and LASP. *CHENANGO* planes struck MIYAKO'S NOBARA Airfield runways and dispersal areas in two strikes. Expended were 15-500# bombs, 74-100# bombs and 98 rockets. Ten planes flew CAP and ASP.

3 June (L-plus-63) While *BLOCK ISLAND* was rejoining the SAKISHIMA formation from her return from KERAMA RETTO, she launched 2 Avengers for Local Anti-Submarine Patrol and she recovered two F4U Corsairs replacement aircraft from the *USS GILBERT ISLANDS*. At 1235H, nine fighters, including a photo plane, and 8 Avengers were launched for a strike on ISHIGAKI JIMA. When they arrived at the target it was found to be completely closed in by weather, so this division decided to strike MIYAKO instead and dropped their bombs and fired their rockets on the MIYAKO airfields just as the airfields were about to be closed by weather. Expended on MIYAKO were 4-500# bombs, 76-100# bombs and 82-5 inch rockets. Planes from *GILBERT ISLANDS* bombed the East-West and the North-Southwest runways at ISHIGAKI Airfield and also strafed and rocketed AA installations in the vicinity of the field, damaging what was thought to be an AA Director, and set fire to the town. One TBM Avenger was hit and seen smoking and then it landed in the water after leaving its target. The pilot and one of the crewmen were rescued by a PBY rescue plane. The other crewman, Radioman Sgt. William C. Boyd Jr. attached to *VMTB 143* squadron was lost with the plane. *SUWANNEE* sent 8 Hellcats for a morning sweep over HIRARA Airfield at MIYAKO. Later, 12 Hellcats and 16 Avengers in two groups struck the same airfield. Strafing destroyed 5 aircraft on the ground and bombs were dropped on the runways and AA positions were strafed and rocketed. Fifteen 500# G.P. bombs, 147-100# G.P. bombs and 150-5 inch H.E. rockets were expended. *SANTEE* launched 20 planes for bombing and rocket strikes at ISHIGAKI JIMA. Runways on airfields were cratered, buildings were burned and AA positions were hit. Four 35 foot boats were damaged. Expended were 8-500# bombs and 16 H.E. rockets. 4 fighters were launched to fly Tactical Combat Air Patrol and 22 others flew Local Combat Air patrol and Local Anti-submarine Patrol. Later in the day after recovering her planes, the *SANTEE* left the formation, in route for KERAMA RETTO for supplies and ammunition. *CHENANGO* planes struck HIRARA and NOBARA runways on their first of two strikes at MIYAKO. Runways at NOBARA Airfield, AA positions, dispersal areas and storage buildings were the targets on their second strike. Thirty one Hellcat fighters and Avenger torpedo bombers dropped 15-500# G.P. bombs, 140-100# bombs and fired 136 rockets. Nine planes flew CAP and ASP.

4 June 1945 (L-plus-64) USS BLOCK ISLAND at 0505H launched 8 fighters and 7 Avenger torpedo bombers for a strike on the two runways at NOBARA at MIYAKO. Seven 500# bombs, 67-100# bombs and 98-5 inch rockets were expended on the targets. One Corsair fighter was damaged by AA. When it was discovered that the pilot couldn't lower the plane's flaps, he was vectored to KADENA with an Avenger escort. Six planes were launched at 1830H for LCAP and LASP. Due to the report of a typhoon, all flight operations were shut down on this carrier. Planes from the *USS SUWANNEE*, 8 Hellcats and 6 Avengers struck HIRARA Airfield and repair center expending 14-500# G.P. bombs, 50-100# G.P. bombs and 40-5 inch H.E. rockets. Twelve planes were launched to fly LCAP and LASP. Later *SUWANNEEE* prepared the ship for heavy weather. Planes from the *USS GILBERT ISLANDS* bombed HIRARA Airfield, rocketed and strafed houses and dispersal areas and started a fire 400 yards north of the field. Light and inaccurate anti-aircraft fire of moderate intensity was encountered over the target. Weather prevented completion of the assigned mission. A low pressure trough existed over the local area and a typhoon was reported to the south-southwest. Eight of *USS CHENANGO'S Air Group-25* fighters made an early sweep over MIYAKO JIMA striking AA positions and boats near the island with 8-500# G.P. bombs and 48 HVA rockets. *Air Group-25* Avenger Torpedo bombers and fighters made a second strike on the NOBARA runways, parked aircraft and nearby buildings. Expended on this strike were 6-500# bombs, 78-100# bombs, 58 rockets and 24 H.V. rockets.

5 June (L-plus-65) *BLOCK ISLAND, SUWANNEE* and *GILBERT ISLANDS* suspended their flight operations due to typhoon disturbance. *SANTEE* put 6 airplanes in the air to fly Local Anti- Submarine Patrol and Local Combat Patrol. *CHENANGO* launched 4

Hellcats for Combat Air Patrol and 2 TBM Avengers for Anti-Submarine Patrol. The US life guard Submarine, *SPIKEFISH (SS-404)* operating near SAKISHIMA, bombarded the MIYARA airstrip at ISHIGAKI JIMA with her 5-inch gun.

6 June (L-plus-66) BLOCK ISLAND launched 2 Avengers and 8 fighters at 0638H to fly LASP and LCAP and at 1240H she launched 9 fighters, 1 photo plane and 7 Avenger torpedo bombers for a strike on the east-west runway at ISHIGAKI Airfield. Expended were: 60-100# bombs, 8-500# bombs and 88-5 inch rockets. One F4U Corsair fighter was hit in the canopy by a 20 mm shell. *USS SUWANNEE* launched 23 Hellcats and 15 Avengers of Air group 40 for a strike on HIRARA and NOBARA airfields on MIYAKO JIMA. They also launched 12 planes for LCAP and TCAP and 1 photo plane. They expended 51-500# G.P. bombs, 17-350# depth bombs, 60-100# G.P. bombs and 69-5 inch H.E. rockets. Planes from *GILBERT ISLANDS* flew 49 sorties over targets at SAKISHIMA GUNTO firing 196-5 inch rockets and dropping 73-500# bombs. ISHIGAKI and MIYARA airfields were bombed and the runways received 21 observed hits. At ISHIGAKI field, buildings, a grounded plane, and revetments were strafed, and buildings at the eastern end of the Northeast-Southwest runway were strafed and rocketed. A fishing boat in the bay to the east of ISHIGAKI was strafed. A bridge on the road running from the west coast of ISHIGAKI near NAGASHI SAKI northeast into the hilly wooded area was strafed and fired, and 3 loaded trucks were burned. Explosions and fire were caused by a strafed unidentified target in the wooded area to the north of YAEYAMA SUGAR REFINERY, and 4 fires were set in the towns of HIRAGE and OHOMA. *USS SANTEE* launched 8 Hellcats and 8 Avengers at 0630H for strikes at ISHIGAKI. Runways were cratered, damaged were bridges, boats, trucks and AA positions. 8-500# bombs, 8-100# bombs were expended and 96 rockets were fired into targets. At 1230H, 4 fighters were launched for a strike at MIYAKO airfields. Runways were cratered; warehouses and two 60 foot luggers were damaged. Twenty two planes from *SANTEE* flew LCAP and LASP. General quarters sounded on *BLOCK ISLAND* at 1510H. Combat Air Patrol planes by visual sighting reported a bogie approaching from the north to within 23 miles of the ship. Combat Air Patrol from other ships which was covering the unit failed to intercept the bogie. It was thought to have been a high flying single engine plane. After a while the bogie retired on an erratic course to the north. *CHENANGO* launched planes for strikes on the two NOBARA runways at MIYAKO. In addition to bombing runways and dispersal areas, also strafed were AA positions and boats near the island. A second strike was made on the runways at nearby ISHIGAKI and MIYARA. These runways were cratered and an Administration building was damaged. Hellcats and Avengers flew 39 sorties, expending 23-500# G.P. bombs, 144-100# G.P. bombs and 243 rockets.

7 June (L-plus-67) *USS SUWANNEE* is at KERAMA RETTO replenishing her supplies. *USS GILBERT ISLANDS* got in some AA gunnery practice, received some fuel and provided Local Combat Air Patrol and Anti-submarine Patrols for the Task Unit. *USS SANTEE* now east of the SAKISHIMA formation commenced fueling from *USS ESCAMBIA* at 0925H and at 1147H received Rear Admiral W.D. Sample, Commander of Task Unit 32.1.3 and his staff from the *USS SUWANNEE*. The *SANTEE* conducted gunnery drills and proceeded to KERAMA RETTO to rearm. At 1335H, *USS*

CHENANGO CVE 28 was detached from task unit 32.1.3 and preceded on duty assigned. *USS NATOMA BAY CVE 62,* a *CASABLANCA* class jeep carrier assigned and cruising with Task Unit 32.1.1, a sister unit to T/U 32.1.3 was at a point approximately 58 miles east of MIYAKO SHIMA with other jeep carriers when her *VC-9* planes struck HIRARA Airfield on MIYAKO JIMA. At 0635H a *"Zeke"* was observed on *NATOMA BAY'S* port quarter a distance of about 700-800 yards and at an altitude of about 500 feet headed toward the ship. The plane made a sharp left turn and came in strafing over the stern in about a 20 degrees glide along the axis of the ship and directly over it. The strafing was incendiary ammo which damaged the SK radar antenna and the flight deck. When about breast of the bridge, and at the level, the plane pushed over sharply and crashed into the forward end of the flight deck just aft of the ramp and between the centerline and the catapult track. The plane disintegrated upon impact, the wings and fuselage going over the bow while the engine, propeller and bomb continued through to the forecastle. The bomb apparently exploded in the open space between flight and the forecastle decks. The blast and debris from the impact on the flight deck punctured the starboard gas tanks on an FM2 Wildcat fighter which was spotted on the catapult and set it afire. The plane was quickly disposed of by catapulting it into the sea. The attack left a hole in the flight deck plating 12 feet wide, beginning two feet to port of the center line of the deck and extending to port, and 20 feet in depth from a point just aft of the forward end of the deck. This hole was decked over semi-permanently and the flight deck shored up and braced across its entire forward section sufficiently so that it could be used for flyaway and catapult-launches. These repairs were completed by 1500H while the regular operating schedule was resumed two hours after the attack. One officer from the ship's company was killed, an officer pilot was seriously injured and three men received minor wounds. From recovered fragments, it is believed that the bomb type carried by the enemy plane was a type 99 Navy SAP 63 kg bomb. A third *"Zeke"* was spotted at 1014H at about 12-15 thousand feet. The plane circled and was out of gun range. The 40 mm guns were fired for spotting the planes position to the other ships. The plane flew into a cloud and left the area. *VC9's* Air operations for the day consisted of 55 sorties, 32 FM2 Wildcat fighters and 23 TBM Avenger torpedo bombers were launched in four strikes. The target for all the strikes was HIRARA Airfield at MIYAKO JIMA with its surrounding buildings and installations, together with any boats or shipping encountered. In bombing, rocketing and strafing attacks, a radio station was destroyed, 4 barracks buildings were destroyed and two others left ablaze, 6 metal landing type boats and 5 wooden fishing boats were strafed with unobserved results, HIRARA Town was strafed and fired, a light house was strafed and rocketed, the NE-SW runway was hit with 12-500# bombs, the E-W runway was hit with 40-100# bombs, the N-S runway with 12-500# bombs, and the intersection of the runways with 4-500# bombs and 30-100# bombs. All runways were believed to be left inoperative at the conclusion of the day's attacks. *USS LUNGA POINT CVE 94* another of the seven jeep carriers in formation near SAKISHIMA who watched the *NATOMA BAY* get hit and watched as the enemy plane barely missed the *USS HOGGATT BAY* near by, reported that she could maintain station in the units formation and provided 56 sorties for LCAP and LASP. The *USS SARGENT BAY CVE 83* watched as the third plane to penetrate the screen headed toward them. The *"Zeke"* attacked from the astern, approaching at an angle of about 20 degrees from an altitude of about 2,000 feet, strafing with machine guns and 20 mm cannon, at 2,500-

3,000 yards, the ship's batteries opened fire, scoring repeated hits which diverted the plane. With pieces from the shattered plane falling to the flight deck as it passed overhead, it splashed 100 yards dead ahead. Six of the ship's personnel were slightly injured from the strafing and two torpedo bombers were hit. Thirty six fighters and 24 torpedo bombers were flown on strikes from *VC-83* Air Composite squadron. Their primary mission was destruction of operational aircraft and neutralization of two airfields assigned this ship, MIYARA and HEGINA, on ISHIGAKI JIMA. Twenty two of the sorties flown selected targets of opportunity at ISHIGAKI. Five single engine and two twin engine airplanes on the ground were damaged by bombing, rocketing and strafing. Revetments and dispersal areas with planes were further damaged. Both Airfields were cratered with bombs. Stock piles and fuel tanks and at least two gun emplacements were hit, extent of damage was undetermined. Various buildings in SHIRAHO town were hit by rockets and strafing attacks, many left burning. Buildings of a radar station and a lighthouse were damaged. One 20mm gun emplacement and undetermined number of machine guns, two trucks and a 100 foot x 25 foot frame building were destroyed. Bomb, rocket and strafing hits were made on many caves reported to contain enemy equipment and activity. At 1225H a FM-2 was forced to make a water landing because of engine failure three miles from the east coast of ISHIGAKI. The pilot was able to get into his life raft and he was picked up by the life guard submarine *USS SPIKEFISH SS404*. *USS WAKE ISLAND CVE 65*, her *VOC1* squadron flew 40 sorties for Tactical Combat Air Patrol using their own and visiting planes. Seventeen fighters and 4 Avengers from shore base operations at YONTAN Field at Okinawa landed on this carrier. *USS SHAMROCK BAY CVE 84*, steaming on base course 010 degrees True in company with Task Unit 32.1.1, zigzagging in accordance with plan #6. At 0528H commenced flight operations and *VC96* managed to fly 63 sorties at SAKISHIMA GUNTO.*USS NEHENTA BAY CVE 74* with *VC8* aboard at 0550H launched their first strike of five coordinated strikes for this day by launching 8 fighters and 6 Avenger torpedo bombers to attack SUKAMA Airfield on MIYAKO JIMA. The single runway, taxi strip, ammo storage and airfield's control tower were bombed, rocketed and strafed with .30 and .50 caliber. The ammo did not explode or burn in the storage when hit and this might have meant that the storage was empty. The airstrip was left cratered. The control tower showed that it had been heavily hit by previous machine gun fire. One well riddled single engine plane was seen on the airfield. No enemy AA was observed during this strike. All through the day planes from the *USS NEHENTA BAY'S VC8* Squadron struck targets at SUKAMA. During the remaining four hops made to SUKAMA Airfield on MIYAKO JIMA, targets hit in addition to the runway were small buildings near the runway, a wooded area north of the runway thought to be a hiding place for supplies, a large ammo revetment, a nearby cave near the beach and a possible radar position. A radar antenna was spotted on the small nearby island of KURIMA (target #0691). All planes in the division went into a flying circle formation and fired their rockets and guns at the radar screened antenna destroying it. On *VC8s* last strike for the day, the runway was left cratered by 500# bombs and buildings were left burning near the runway area. No enemy AA was encountered throughout the strikes during the day. Some pilots reported what they thought to be rifle fire as they attacked. The five hops to SUKAMA this day consisted of a total of 27 TBM Avengers and 32 FM-2 Wildcat fighters making a total of 59 sorties dispensing 166-100# G.P. bombs, 24-500# bombs, 336 HVA rockets, 38,000 rounds of .50 and 4,000 rounds of .30 caliber ammo. Later the *NEHENTA BAY* was detached and ordered to KERAMA RETTO for replenishing. *USS HOGGATT BAY* planes from *VC99* squadron flew 56 sorties over the target area and 4 LCAP sorties. 152-100# bombs and 20-500# bombs were dropped on ISHIGAKI Airfield. It was reported that a radar station was bombed. Gun positions were rocketed and strafed. During the attacks, Window *(a form of jamming)* was used against enemy radar. The only damage to the *HOGGATT BAY* planes was one small hole in the stabilizer of one Torpedo bomber. Expended on targets were: 40,000 rounds of .50 caliber ammo, 231-5 inch rockets, 44-500# bombs and 156-100# bombs. After returning from fueling, *BLOCK ISLAND'S* C.I.C. (*Combat Information Center*) made an interception of a bogie by Combat Air Patrol planes from other carriers, resulting in the splashing of one "*Dinah*" at 1858H, sixty eight miles from base.

8 June 1945 (L-plus-68) *USS BLOCK ISLAND* launched 7 fighters for a sweep over MIYAKO at 0500H. Besides bombing runways, the planes rocketed a power station at Target # 1395-R and hit other targets of opportunity. At 0700H four fighters and seven torpedo bombers were launched for a strike on ISHIGAKI, damaging a shop area east of ISHIGAKI Airfield. Seven planes were launched at 1000H for LCAP and LASP. Between 1300H and 1608H nineteen more planes were launched for strikes at ISHIGAKI JIMA'S airfields. Runways were attacked and assistance was given to other carrier planes for the destruction of small ships at the island of IRIOMOTE. Later a sweep was made on targets of opportunity at ISHIGAKI JIMA. One fighter took some light hits from machine gun fire, but returned safely aboard. Twenty 500# bombs, 134-100# bombs and 158-5 inch rockets were expended. Planes from *GILBERT ISLANDS* were over targets at SAKISHIMA GUNTO firing 116-5 inch HVA rockets and dropping 40-500# bombs. Nine 500# bomb hits were observed on the Northeast-Southwest runway at ISHIGAKI Airfield, 23-500# bomb hits were observed on the Northeast-Southwest runway at HIRARA Airfield. Rockets were fired at a Radar station on ISHIGAKI JIMA, a dispersal area on MIYAKO JIMA, a building on IRABU SHIMA, a bridge on IRABU SHIMA and installation at the south end of ISHIGAKI Airfield. AA Installations northwest of ISHIGAKI Airfield were strafed, as was a village on MIYAKO. Five or six camouflaged ships in the bay on the west coast of IRIOMOTE SHIMA, estimated 100 to 150 feet in length, were strafed and left burning and emitting black smoke. One FG-1D Corsair piloted by 2nd Lieutenant T. Logan Millard White Jr. was shot down over the target. Planes from *GILBERT ISLANDS* provided Local Combat Air Patrol and Local Anti-Submarine Patrol for the task unit. The *SANTEE* launched 16 planes for strikes on ISHIGAKI at 0700H. Airfield runways were cratered, dispersals were hit and one "*ZEKE*" was destroyed on the ground. Eight 500#, 80-100# bombs were dropped and 96 rockets were fired on ISHIGAKI targets. Twenty four planes were launched between 1000H and 1600H for strikes against targets at MIYAKO JIMA. Runways were cratered; buildings and storage facilities were hit. Twenty five fighters and 6 torpedo bombers flew LCAP and LASP. One plane flew as a courier.

9 June 1945 (L-plus-69) *USS BLOCK ISLAND* went to General Quarters at 0213H after a "Bogie" came within 37 miles range at a bearing of 333 degrees from the ship. The bogie retired out of range later and the ship secured from General Quarters at 0220H. A tired crew at 0500H launched 8 fighters and 7 torpedo bombers for a strike on ISHIGAKI

JIMA. Solid cloud cover was over the target on arrival and the bombers had to bomb through the overcast by aid of radar. The fighters did a sweep of IRIOMOTO Island and located a probable radar station on the western tip of the island at target area 3044. At 0730H, 4 fighters were launched for a sweep over MIYAKO. Runways and buildings were attacked at HIRARA Airfield through the overcast. 4-500# bombs and 25 rockets were expended on the E-W runway. At 1030H eight fighters and eight Avengers delivered 66-100# G.P. bombs and 88-5 inch rockets on the East-West runway strip at NOBARA. At 1330H, three fighters were sent for a target sweep over ISHIGAKI where they dropped 3-500# bombs and fired 16-5 inch HVA rockets while attacking the airfield and a radio station. ASP and CAP were flown by 8 fighters and two Avengers from this ship. Four Hellcats fighters from the *USS SUWANNEE* flew TCAP over MIYAKO JIMA and expended 4-500# bombs and 25-5 inch rockets on NOBARA Airfield. Eight more fighters along with 8 Avengers attacked the NOBARA Airfield and dispersal areas. They expended 8-500# bombs, 80-100# G.P. bombs and 105-5 inch H.E. rockets. *USS GILBERT ISLANDS* reported that her planes had flown 20 sorties over targets on SAKISHIMA GUNTO, dropping 8.4 tons of bombs and firing 66 rockets. Forty eight 5 inch HVA rockets were fired on the eastern boundary of ISHIGAKI Airfield and 32-500# bombs were dropped there. Three 500# bombs were dropped and 18-5 inch HVA rockets were fired on a bridge on ISHIGAKI SHIMA. Barges were strafed south of OBAMA SHIMA and in the bay on the west coast of IRIOMOTE Island, and a radio or radar installations were strafed on the most westerly point of IRIOMOTE SHIMA. The planes also provided Local Combat Air and Submarine patrol for the task unit. *USS SANTEE* launched 12 fighters and 8 torpedo bombers for two strikes against targets on MIYAKO and ISHIGAKI JIMA. Because of low cloud cover, bombing the runways at the airfields were made through the overcast and results were not observed. Expended were 12-500# bombs, 80-100#bombs and 12 H.E. rockets.

10 June (L-plus-70) *USS BLOCK ISLAND* started this day by launching 4 F6F Hellcat night fighters at 0303H for a heckling mission over ISHIGAKI and MIYAKO airfields. Two fighters struck ISHIGAKI with 2-500# bombs and 10 rockets and two struck MIYAKO with the same ordnance. The runway and landing lights were attacked at the ISHIGAKI Airfield. A burning green beacon was seen to come on during the bombing approach to HIRARA Airfield at MIYAKO and was attacked near the shoreline at MIYAKO. After daylight these four fighters struck targets of opportunity. At 0500H eight Avenger torpedo bombers and four fighters were launched for a strike at ISHIGAKI which was conducted through a heavy overcast and a boat base at target # 9161 was attacked. Expended were four 500# bombs, 76-100# bombs and 58-5 inch high velocity rockets. At 1302H four fighters were launched for a sweep over ISHIGAKI. The planes found some small watercraft around the island and attacked them in addition to bombing the runways. Expended were 4-500# bombs, 76-100# bombs and 58-5 inch rockets. At 1608H seven fighter and eight bombers were launched for a strike at ISHIGAKI JIMA. As they bombed through the overcast, heavy, accurate AA burst was encountered through the clouds indicating possible enemy radar controlled fire. Eleven 500# bombs, 58-100# bombs and 68-5 inch H.V. rockets were expended on the airfield. Between 0500H and 1014H, twelve fighters and two bombers were launched for LCAP and LASP.

USS SUWANNEE CVE-27, AG-40, sent sixteen fighters and sixteen bombers to strike NOBARA and ISHIGAKI airfields. Twenty fighters and four bombers were launched for LCAP, TCAP and LASP. The unit of sixteen fighters and bombers expended 16-500# G.P. bombs, 160-100# G.P. bombs and 200-5 inch H.E. rockets on NOBARA and ISHIGAKI airfields. Four fighters assigned to TCAP expended 4-500# G.P. bombs and 24-5 inch rockets on ISHIGAKI Airfield. USS *GILBERT ISLANDS* was taking on supplies and ammunition at KERAMA RETTO on this day. While at KERAMA, two men, 1st. Lieutenant Robert B. Cromwell USMCR, and Corp. Robert L. Wood USMCR belonging to *VMTB-143*, shot down in their Avenger on 3 June and rescued were returned aboard. The *USS SANTEE* launched 19 planes for strike sorties against targets at MIYAKO between 0700H and 1000H. These planes expended 12-500# bombs, 70-100# bombs and 96-H.E. rockets on airfield runways and boats. One camouflaged plane was destroyed. Twenty four planes were launched between 1000H and 1600H for strikes against ISHIGAKI JIMA. Runways there were cratered; the town and storage facilities were hit. Expended were 12-500# bombs, 120-100# bombs and 112 H.E. rockets. Twenty two planes from the *SANTEE* flew LCAP and LASP.

11 June 1945 (L-plus-71) *USS BLOCK ISLAND* at 0526H launched 8 fighters and 7 torpedo bombers. Their target was ISHIGAKI and MIYAKO JIMA. Foul weather obscured most of ISHIGAKI but the attack was delivered over airfields on the southern tip. Thirty 500# bombs and 36-5 inch H.V. rockets were expended. At 0934H, another launch of 6 fighters and 8 bombers was made. These planes struck ISHIGAKI Airfield and repair shops with 37-500# bombs and 24-5 inch H.V. rockets. At 1430H four Avenger bombers were launched for a strike on NOBARA Airfield at MIYAKO. Also 2 Avengers and 7 fighters were launched to fly local combat patrol. Four 500# bombs and 16-5 inch rockets were expended on target 1396 at NOBARA Airfield. The ship received reports of a typhoon in the Luzon Straits moving north northeastward. Air operations were suspended and the ship was secured for heavy weather. *SUWANNEE* launched 8 F6F fighters for a morning sweep over MIYAKO JIMA hitting airfields with 8-500# bombs and 29-5 inch H.E. rockets. Sixteen Hellcat fighters and 14 TBM Avengers were launched for a strike on NOBARA runways, dispersal areas, buildings and AA positions. Expended on these were 16-500# G.P. bombs and 127-100# G.P. bombs and 193-5 inch H.E. rockets. Planes from *USS GILBERT ISLANDS* made 40 sorties over targets on SAKISHIMA GUNTO, dropping bombs and depth charges and firing 5-inch HVA rockets. Dropped on ISHIGAKI Airfield were 19-500# bombs, 120-100# bombs, 11 depth charges and 52 rockets. Eighty four rockets were fired and 3 depth charges were dropped on the towns located in ISHIGAKI, MIYAKO and IKEMA SHIMA. Sixteen rockets were fired at emplacements, 28 rockets were fired at shops and bridges, and 24 rockets were fired at storage facilities and other installations on ISHIGAKI SHIMA. All towns and installations were strafed. Six rockets were fired at barracks on IRABU JIMA, 5 rockets were fired at barracks on IRIOMOTE SHIMA, 5 rockets were fired at barracks on a small island just west of IRIOMOTE SHIMA and 2-500# bombs were dropped on barracks on IRIOMOTE SHIMA. Three direct hits were observed on barracks. The planes also provided local combat air and anti-submarine patrol for the task unit. This ship readied for an on coming typhoon that was reported to be centered northwest of FORMOSA. USS *SANTEE* launched planes for strikes on ISHIGAKI and MIYAKO

JIMA. Launches were made at 0500H, 0700H and 1400H for strikes at ISHIGAKI and at 1200H planes were launched for a strike at MIYAKO. At ISHIGAKI, airfield runways were bombed and cratered and strikes were made against storage facilities. Near the island of IRIOMOTE, 19 boats, 13-20 feet in length were strafed and damaged. Expended were 23-500# bombs, 150-100# bombs and 128-H.E. rockets. At MIYAKO JIMA, airfield runways were cratered by bombs. Expended were 7-500# bombs, 70-100# bombs and 58 H.E. rockets. One fighter pilot from the *SANTEE* experienced the loss of oil pressure in his engine and had to land his plane in the water about 2 miles east of MIYAKO JIMA where he was picked up about one hour and a half later.

12 June 1945 (L-plus-72) *During the night, Task Unit 32.1.3 moved 65 miles east to avoid the effects of a typhoon that passed north between ISHIGAKI and FORMOSA and the unit returned in time for dawn air operations.* USS BLOCK ISLAND at 0520H launched 4 Marine fighters for early morning local Combat Air patrol. At 0800H, 4 fighters and 7 torpedo bombers struck ISHIGAKI Airfield with 21-500# bombs, 10-100# bombs and 20 rockets. At 1100H four fighters were launched for a strike on the East-West runway at ISHIGAKI Airfield. After attacking the airfield, targets of opportunity was attacked on IRIOMOTE SHIMA. Expended were 4-500# bombs and 16-5 inch HVA rockets. Launched at 1400H were two Avenger torpedo bombers for local patrol and 4 fighters and one photo plane to sweep ISHIGAKI and IRIOMOTE. Two 500# bombs, 2-350# depth bombs were dropped and 20-5 inch HVA rockets were fired. Two Avengers were launched at 1600H to sweep targets on ISHIGAKI and IRIOMOTE and 2 were launched for local patrol. Expended on the E-W runway at ISHIGAKI were 4-350# depth bombs. Because of exhausted supply of General Purpose bombs these planes were loaded with depth bombs. *BLOCK ISLAND* later in the evening departed with 3 escorts: *USS FARENHOLT, USS LANDSDOWNE* and *USS HALL* for KERAMA RETTO. *USS SUWANNEE* launched 24 Hellcats and 18 Avengers for strikes on NOBARA and SUKAMA airfields at MIYAKO expending 24-500# G.P. bombs, 166-100# G.P. bombs and 266-5 inch H.E. rockets. Two Japanese *"Frances"* bombers were destroyed on the ground on KOBI SHO SHIMA by strafing. *USS GILBERT ISLANDS* planes made 36 sorties over targets on SAKISHIMA GUNTO, dropping 20.5 tons of bombs and firing 48-5-inch rockets. 24-500# bombs were dropped on the E-W runway at ISHIGAKI Airfield and 8-500# bombs on the Northeast-Southwest runway. Nineteen hits were observed on the East-West runway and five on the Northeast-Southwest runway. Twenty three-500# bombs were dropped on the East-West runway at NOBARA Airfield with 18 hits being observed. Four 500# bombs were dropped on the North-South runway at HIRARA Airfield AA installations on MIYAKO JIMA, IRABU SHIMA, and ISHIGAKI JIMA was strafed. Fourteen rockets were fired at AA installations and 10 rockets were fired at revetments and a bridge in the western part of ISHIGAKI. Planes also provided local combat air patrol and Anti-submarine patrol for the Task unit. One fighter who couldn't get but one wheel to retract for landing was ordered to proceed to OKINAWA for a forced landing ashore. At 1425H a report was received that one TBM, Bureau No. 69026, which was launched at 1106H and scheduled to return at 1400H, had been shot down by enemy AA fire over NOBARA Field at MIYAKO JIMA, at (Lat. 24-45N, Long.125-20E). The plane was observed to have lost its right wing and then crashed on the runway, whereupon the bombs exploded. The pilot, 1st Lieutenant Kelvern

O. Misamore, USMCR, and crew members, Sgt. Otto R. Schaefer USMCR and Sgt. Chancel A. Hall USMCR were reported killed in the crash and explosion. *(See elsewhere in this book, Lieutenant Fritz Liebich's account of the loss of Lieutenant Misamore's plane on 12 June.)* USS SANTEE launched a total of 16 F6F Hellcat fighters and 8 TBM Avenger torpedo bombers for two strikes against ISHIGAKI JIMA. Runways were bombed and cratered, storage facilities and one twin engine plane was destroyed on the ground and one 50 foot lugger was damaged. Expended were 15-500# bombs, 80-100# bombs and 30-rockets. At MIYAKO, runways were cratered, dispersals and storage facilities were damaged and one camouflaged plane was destroyed. Eighteen planes from the *USS SANTEE* flew LCAP and LASP.

13 June (L-plus-73 Planes from *USS GILBERT ISLANDS* struck targets at SAKISHIMA GUNTO dropping 15.5 tons of bombs and firing 182-5 inch rockets. Thirty two 500# bombs were dropped on the NE-SW runway at ISHIGAKI Airfield and 5-500# bombs were dropped on the E-W runway there. Fourteen hits were observed on the Northeast-Southwest runway and 5 on the E-W runway. Twenty one 500# bombs were dropped on the North-South runway at NOBARA FIELD on MIYAKO and 3-500# bombs were dropped on the East-West runway there. Seven hits were observed on the N-S runway and one on the E-W runway. Eighteen rockets were fired at the NE-SW runway at ISHIGAKI Airfield. Twenty eight rockets were fired at buildings on ISHIGAKI JIMA and MIYAKO JIMA, 18 rockets were fired at barges west of IRIOMOTE SHIMA and east of IRABU SHIMA, 12 rockets were fired at storage facilities on ISHIGAKI JIMA, MIYAKO JIMA and IRABU SHIMA, 16 were fired at towns on ISHIGAKI JIMA, 46 fired on AA emplacements on ISHIGAKI JIMA and MIYAKO JIMA, 8 fired at a bridge and two were fired at caves on MIYAKO JIMA and 4 at revetments on ISHIGAKI JIMA. One Japanese Ki-46 "*DINAH*" airplane was strafed and destroyed at the north end of HIRARA Airfield's NE-SW runway at MIYAKO. Planes from the *USS SUWANNEE* flew 55 sorties including 4 fighters for TCAP, 8 fighters for LCAP, 2 TBM Avengers flew LASP, one message drop was flown and one F6F Hellcat flew a photo mission at SAKISHIMA GUNTO. Eight fighters flew a morning sweep over IRIOMOTE Island, hitting an amphibious training center there. These planes expended 8-500# G.P. bombs and 48-5 inch H.E. rockets. Fifteen Hellcat fighters and 16 Avenger torpedo bombers struck NOBARA and ISHIGAKI airfields, expending 28-500# bombs and 130-100# bombs and 72-5 inch H.E. rockets. *USS FANSHAW BAY CVE-70* with Air Squadron *VOC-2*, reporting to the task unit on the 12th of June, launched 22 planes for LCAP and ASAP. Sixteen Wildcats and 3 Avengers were released for strikes against targets. One Avenger was sent on a ferry flight. The striking group bombed the runways at NOBARA Airfield and fired rockets into the dispersal areas with unobserved results expending 26-100# G.P. bombs and 66-5 inch H.E. rockets. *USS SANTEE* launched between 0800H and 1300H, sixteen Hellcat fighters and thirteen Avenger torpedo bombers for two strikes on airfield runways and buildings at MIYAKO JIMA. The runways were left cratered and buildings damaged. Expended were 34-500# bombs, 84-100# bombs and 110 rockets. Twenty planes from Air group *24* from the *SANTEE* flew LCAP and LASP.

14 June (L-plus-74) *USS BLOCK ISLAND* launched 4 Avengers at 0827H for a strike on ISHIGAKI Airfields. Under the directions of a flight leader from another carrier, *BLOCK*

ISLAND planes bombed and rocketed the E-W runway, expended 35-100# bombs and 16-5-inch H.V. rockets. Eight fighters were launched at 1105H for a sweep of ISHIGAKI Airfield and IRIOMOTE SHIMA, expending 7-500# bombs and 28-5-inch HVA rockets. Planes from the *USS GILBERT ISLANDS* attacked targets on SAKISHIMA. Eleven 500# bombs and 183-100# bombs were dropped and 42 rockets were fired on the East-West runway at ISHIGAKI Airfield and 7-500# bombs were dropped and 28 rockets were fired on the NE-SW runway there. *USS SUWANNEE* launched 24 Hellcats and 15 Avengers for a strike on MIYAKO, ISHIGAKI and IRIOMOTE Islands. These planes expended 43-500# bombs, 41-100# bombs and 6-250# fragmentation bombs on targets. *USS SANTEE* launched 40 planes in three launches for strikes at MIYAKO JIMA. Targeted were runways, repair shops and boat pens where large fires were set. One single engine plane was destroyed on the ground at HIRARA Airfield. Four boats, 60-70 feet in length were destroyed near the small island of IKEMA SHIMA, located north of MIYAKO. A total of 88-500# bombs were dropped on the three strikes. *(At the end of this strike the USS SANTEE conducted its last air operations over SAKISHIMA GUNTO and was routed to SAN PEDRO BAY at LEYTE in the PHILLIPINEE ISLANDS.)* USS FANSHAW BAY launched 24 Wildcats, 14 Avenger bombers for strikes and 8 fighters for TCAP. Destroyed were 3 fishing boats, one barracks building, and one small gun boat. The runways were bombed at HIRARA and ISHIGAKI airfields. Expended were 140-100# G.P. bombs and 266-5-inch H.E. rockets. *The USS SHIPLEY Bay CVE-85* launched 8 Wildcats at 0705H. Each plane was armed with 1,600 rounds of .50 caliber ammo for Tactical Combat Air Patrol at MIYAKO JIMA. Once they arrived the flight leader requested and received permission to attack targets of opportunity. Two unidentified enemy twin engine planes were strafed while parked in a revetment to the Northeast of HIRARA Airfield. Also strafed was an *"Oscar"* and *"Val"* parked in a revetment to the west of the center of the field. Two more single engine planes in the southern tip of the North-South runway were strafed. On another run, enemy planes were strafed on the N-S runway and two single engine planes on the east side of the northern tip of the NE-SE runway. Three planes were strafed on the westerly side of the NE-SW runway. A building on the southern end of the NE-SW runway and two aircraft on the NE-SW runway were hit. All eight fighters then strafed what was thought to be an Oil Refinery located about 1000 yards south of KAWAMITSU and succeeded in starting fires. In all, 7,200 rounds of .50 caliber ammo were used on targets. VC-97 airplanes were again launched from the *SHIPLEY BAY* at 0930H and this time 8 Avenger Torpedo bombers were launched along with 8 Wildcat fighters. The Avenger torpedo bombers were armed each with 10-100# G.P. bombs, 8-5 inch H.E. rockets, 1000 rounds of .50 caliber ammo and 400 rounds of .30 caliber ammo. The Wildcat fighters were armed each with 1,600 rounds of ammo, 6-5 inch H.E. rockets and one 100# G.P. bomb. The Wildcats and Avengers flew to ISHIGAKI JIMA and joined planes from the *USS SUWANNEE* for an attack on airfields, roads, AA installations and other targets. The torpedo bombers each dropped 10 of their 100# bombs on the E-W runway at ISHIGAKI Airfield and four Avengers fired a total of 30 air rockets into the western most part of the runway. Roads south of the town of MIYARA were hit with 30 rockets and strafed by the torpedo planes. At least 7 of the rockets hit the town of MIYARA. Seven Wildcat fighters strafed and fired 42 rockets into suspected AA positions in HIRAE town. Three fighters strafed and damaged 4 single engine planes parked at the southern end of the North-South runway at ISHIGAKI Airfield. At 1430H, 8 fighters armed each with 6-5 inch H.E. rockets and ammo and 2 TBM-3 Avenger Torpedo bombers, each armed with 10-100# G.P. bombs and 8-5 inch H.E. rockets were to join planes from the *USS FANSHAW BAY* for a strike on HIRARA Airfield at MIYAKO JIMA. Two torpedo planes attacked HIRARA Airfield, each dropping 10-100# bombs and each firing 7 rockets at the N-S runway. One fighter division fired 20 rockets at the N-S runway and the other division of fighters and bombers dropped 2-100# bombs and fired 16 rockets at the E-W runway. The fighter divisions strafed boats and buildings along the western coast of MIYAKO, setting fire to one building located about 2,000 yards south of SUKAMA Airfield.

15 June 1945 (L-plus-75) *USS BLOCK ISLAND* launched 4 TBM Avengers at 0827H for a strike on ISHIGAKI airfields. Under the direction of a flight leader from another carrier, they bombed and rocketed the east-west runway and targets at IRIOMOTE JIMA. Expended were 35-100# bombs, 7-500# bombs and 44-5 inch HVA. rockets. *USS GILBERT ISLANDS* planes flew 7 sorties over SAKISHIMA GUNTO, dropping 7-500# bombs on runways at HIRARA Airfield. The planes also strafed trucks, installations near the runways, and AA installations. The trucks were observed to be set on fire and the personnel manning them killed. Planes from *USS STEAMER BAY CVE-87* made 44 strike sorties at SAKISHIMA. VC-93 pilots found low ceiling of 400-800 feet over the target at MIYAKO that made the strikes very difficult. The first strike group damaged revetments and field artillery pieces. The extent of the damage couldn't be observed. The midday striking group from this squadron found the same low ceilings, but struck aircraft facilities with unobserved results. Intense, accurate medium and light AA fire was encountered, and all but five planes of the group of 16 were damaged. Three were seriously damaged. At 1300H the flight leader reported that FM-2 Wildcat fighter, Bureau number-74118 flown by Ensign George J. Vigeant Jr., A1, USNR 363776 had been badly hit by light AA fire over the target. The pilot had been able to fly his plane well clear of the island but at about 300 feet altitude the plane was seen to break up, crash, burn and sink. The flight leader orbited the spot of the crash but couldn't find the pilot. Only a gas tank remained floating. At 1612H, FM2 Wildcat, Bureau number-73930 with pilot Lieutenant (jg) Robert H. Allison, A1, USNR 346998 on fly away take-off crashed about 150 yards dead ahead of the ship's bow when the engine failed. The plane sank, but the pilot was picked up at 1618H by *USS LANDER* and returned to the carrier unhurt. Another Wildcat flown by Lieutenant (jg) Donald H. Sherlock landed in a skid and crashed through the barriers after the landing hook pulled out. The airplane was reduced to a dud after it somersaulted. A later strike by planes from this carrier damaged two airplanes on the ground, sank a Harbor Lighter and damaged unidentified military installations. *(A Harbor Lighter is a vessel assigned to move passengers or freight in and around the harbor.)* USS FANSHAW BAY CVE-70 commenced flight operations by launching 8 Wildcat fighters for a sweep of SAKISHIMA GUNTO, 8 more Wildcats for target combat patrol, 16 Wildcat fighters, and 4 Avenger torpedo bombers for a strike group and 8 for local combat patrol sorties. *VOC-2* squadron airplanes sank one 40 foot boat and damaged one 40 foot boat, two 30 foot boats, one 100 foot Harbor Lighter, two single engine planes on the ground and one radio station. Expended were 56-100# G.P. bombs and 223-5 inch H.E. Rockets. *USS MANILA BAY CVE-61*, planes from this carrier's *VC-71* air squadron made two strikes on ISHIGAKI JIMA. Eight FM-2 Wildcats were launched at 0900H for targets at ISHIGAKI Airfield that included the rocketing of the runways and strafing of two parked single engine airplanes and airfield installations. Later at 1300H, 8 Wildcats and 4 TBM Avenger bombers were launched for a strike at the Northwest part of OHAMA town near the ISHIGAKI Airfield where enemy AA positions were earlier reported. Here, bombs were dropped on buildings and installations. More bombs were dropped and rockets were fired onto the nearby NE-SW ISHIGAKI Airfield runway and parked airplanes that were thought to be *"Nicks and Irvings"*. Expended bombs and rockets were forty 100# G.P. bombs and 96 rockets. Ammo expended was 4,500 rounds of .50 cal. *USS SHIPLEY BAY CV-8* at 0500H launched Air Squadron VC-97's TBM Torpedo bombers armed each with 10-100# G.P. bombs, 8-5 inch rockets, 1000 rounds of .50 caliber and 400 rounds of .30 caliber ammunition. Also launched were 8 FM-2 Wildcat fighters having each 1,600 rounds of .50 caliber ammo, 6-5 inch rockets and one 100# general purpose bomb. The first attack by these planes was HIRARA Airfield at MIYAKO JIMA. Thirty nine bombs were released from 2,000 feet onto the runways leaving them cratered. Afterwards, a Japanese merchant ship located in a large cove, N-NE of HIRARA town was seen and fired on with rockets. Two rockets hit this ship at its waterline and the vessel was last seen smoking. Just north of MIYAKO JIMA on the small island of IKEMA, five small boats anchored in a harbor on the north coast were strafed as well as the island's light house and surrounding buildings. Back on MIYAKO JIMA, at the southeast edge of HIRARA town a warehouse and transformer installations were rocketed and strafed. At 0800H *SHIPLEY BAY* launched 6 TBM Torpedo bombers and 8 FM-2 fighters. These planes joined planes from the *FANSHAW BAY* for a strike on MIYARA Airfield at ISHIGAKI JIMA, where they left the runway well cratered. On the return flight from ISHIGAKI, two fighters dropped their 100 pound bombs on SUKAMA Airfield located on the western side of MIYAKO JIMA. At 1300H, 5 TBM Avengers and 8 FM-2 Wildcats were launched for targets at ISHIGAKI and MIYARA airfields, AA positions in the town of OHAMA and AA positions seen earlier in a ravine about 1,200 yards north of the northern end of the NE-SW runway of ISHIGAKI Airfield. Lieutenant (jg) William F. Waters flying a FM-2 fighter was hit by AA fire coming from the ravine or the town of OHAMA. His plane burst into flames and was seen to crash into buildings and trees, approximately 2,500 yards north of the E-W runway. He was not seen leaving the airplane before the plane made ground impact. Following this strike, the striking group turned their attention to the AA positions in OHAMA town, where they dropped 30 bombs and fired 30 rockets at these positions. Fighters strafed a radio station on the eastern side of the town of ISHIGAKI and AA positions in the town of MIYARA. Eleven planes were launched from the *SHIPLEY BAY* at 1600H for a strike on HIRARA and SUKAMA airfields at MIYAKO JIMA. Bombs dropped from these planes cratered the runways of both airfields. Also damaged near the SUKAMA Airfield was an Administration building.

16 June (L-plus-76) *USS BLOCK ISLAND* sent 4 of her Marine fighters for a sweep at MIYAKO JIMA. HIRARA Airfield was bombed with four 500# bombs and 16-5 inch rockets. Targets were strafed at target: 1199-0616-L and 0995-2893. *(This is the last strike at SAKISHIMA for planes from BLOCK ISLAND and she was detached from Task Unit 32.1.3.)* USS GILBERT ISLANDS launched 3 planes for strikes at HIRARA Airfield. The E-W runway was hit with 3-500# bombs and 18 rockets were fired at boats. The planes also strafed towns and barracks on the island. *(Like her sister carrier, the BLOCK ISLAND, GILBERT ISLANDS was detached from Task Unit 32.1.3 and sailed to LEYTE ISLAND. Other CVE carriers leaving TU 32.1.3 and sailing to LEYTE were the USS SUWANNEE and the USS SANTEE escorted by the USS FARENHOLT, USS HELM, USS LANDER and USS LANDSDOWNE.)* USS STEAMER BAY planes flew 43 sorties against MIYAKO and ISHIGAKI. The weather was better than the previous day. Targets destroyed by *VC-93* squadron planes were three aircraft service buildings, a small supply dump, two small boats and an unidentified beach installation. Targets damaged were airfield runways and 8 boats and several barracks. One plane completed a photo mission. R/ Admiral E.W Litch USN in the *FANSHAW BAY* took over as Task Commander of TU 32.1.3 from Admiral W.D. Sample who is sailing for LEYTE on the *USS SUWANNEE*. *FANSHAW BAY* launched planes at 0459H for LCAP, ASP, TCAP and 20 planes for a sweep on SAKISHIMA GUNTO. They struck and damaged two 30 foot lighters, one building, and starting fires at both targets. One twin and three single engine planes on the ground were attacked with unobserved results. Expended on these strikes were 44-100# bombs and 174-5 inch rockets. *USS MANILA BAY* launched 8 FM-2 Wildcats at 0500H for a fighter sweep at MIYAKO. *VC-71* fighters made their first strike with 16 HVA-rockets on the HIRARA runways causing considerable damage. After the strike all planes rendezvoused and then they flew to IKEMA island located at the northern tip of MIYAKO and there they strafed a lighthouse at the north end and small boats in the harbor at the southern end of the island. Planes launched from *MANILA BAY* at 0730H were eight Wildcats and 4 TBM Avengers that rendezvoused near MIYAKO with planes from the *USS STEAMER BAY* and they struck HIRARA Airfield. Approximately 35-100# G.P. bombs and 23 rockets were expended on the E-W runway and the intersection of the three runways. The runway disposal areas were strafed with .50 caliber ammo. Following this attack, *VC-71* planes attacked targets of opportunity in other sections of the island. Some small boats were strafed in an inlet at IKEMA SHIMA and several barracks buildings were strafed at SHIMAJIRI town. Eight more *VC-71* fighters from *MINILA BAY* were launched at 1300H. Their target was NOBARA Airfield runways. Both runways were hit with High Velocity rockets. Also enemy AA emplacements and dispersal areas were strafed near the runways. Following this attack the fighters attacked some small boats and buildings with rockets and .50 caliber ammunition. Some light inaccurate enemy AA fire was encountered over IKEMA. *SHIPLEY BAY* launched her first planes for strikes on ISHIGAKI JIMA at 0500H. Four TBM Avengers, each armed with 10-100# bombs, 8 rockets, .50 and .30 caliber ammunition and 8 FM-2 Wildcat fighters armed with rockets and ammo struck AA positions at ISHIGAKI JIMA with 29 bombs along a ravine about 1,200 yards northeast of the northern end of the N-S runway of ISHIGAKI Airfield and AA positions in the town of OHAMA. Also attacked were probable storage facilities in a town located at the eastern coast of ISHI-ZAKI Peninsula. Two fighter divisions dropped 5-100# bombs and fired a total of 26 rockets into AA positions at OHAMA. A coordinated bombing and strafing attack was made against the town of ISHI-ZAKI Peninsula. *SHIPLEY BAY* launched *VC-97* planes again at 1030H. Six TBM Avengers each armed with 10-100# bombs, 8 rockets, 1000 rounds of .50 caliber and 400 rounds of .30 caliber ammo. Also launched were 8 FM-2 fighters, each having 1-100# bomb, 6 rockets and 1,600 rounds of .50 caliber ammo. These 14 planes joined other allied planes for a strike against enemy installations on ISHIGAKI JIMA.

Struck were AA positions in OHAMA town, storage facilities in a town on the eastern coast of ISHI-ZAKI Peninsula and AA installations along a ravine about 1,200 yards NE of the northern end of the NE-SW runway of ISHIGAKI Airfield. A combined bombing and rocket attack was made on the town of OHAMA. Six 500# bombs, 12-100# bombs and 22 rockets were expended on the town. A radio station on the northern tip of ISHIGAKI SHIMA was strafed. Four Fighters from *VC-97* was launched at 1330H for Combat Air Patrol over ISHIGAKI SHIMA. Later into their patrol the leader ask for and received permission to attack targets of opportunity. An unidentified town was strafed and a Sampan type boat was strafed and sank while underway between IRIOMOTE SHIMA and KOHAMA SHIMA. Also three large buildings were strafed on the eastern coast of IRIOMOTE. Planes launched at 1600H from *SHIPLEY BAY* were 7 Torpedo bombers and 8 fighters for a strike on MIYAKO JIMA. Their prime target was to bomb and strafe a ship that had been beached in a cove, located north-northeast of HIRARA town. One hundred and 500 pound bombs were dropped and rockets were fired and seen to hit at amidships right above its water line. Rockets were also fired at storage facilities and warehouses around HIRARA Airfield and HIRARA town, starting large fires. Rocket attacks were made on a possible radar station installation that was floating on a 15 X 15 foot raft off the eastern coast of MIYAKO. A similar type of raft had been reported earlier, seen off the coast of IKEMA SHIMA. IKEMA town and the islands lighthouse was strafed and bombed. A nearby building to the lighthouse was also damaged. The NE-SW runway at HIRARA Airfield on MIYAKO was strafed before the planes returned to their carrier.

17 June (L-plus-77) USS *HOGGATT Bay* CVE-75 and her *VC-99* Squadron started their air operations against ISHIGAKI Airfield. Ten tons of bombs and 151 rockets were expended on the airfield and 16 rockets were fired on gun positions at the north of ISHIGAKI's MIYARA Airfield. One of *HOGGATT BAY'S* airplanes completed a photo mission. USS *NATOMA BAY* CVE- 62 commenced launching her *VC-9* Wildcat fighters at 0445H for Combat Air Patrol and strikes against MIYAKO JIMA. Twenty four FM2 Wildcat fighters, 16 TBM Avengers were launched for strikes and 12 Wildcats were launched for CAP with one Avenger to fly a photo mission. The strikes damaged one twin engine plane on the ground at HIRARA Airfield, one boat north of MIYAKO and five boats on the southeast coast of IRABU JIMA. A barracks was set afire north of HIRARA Airfield and another barracks was fired south of NOBARA Airfield. Gun positions and buildings were strafed southwest of HIRARA Airfield. Bombs were dropped on the HIRARA runways leaving them inoperative. Expended were 158-100# G.P. bombs, 237-5 inch High Explosive rockets and 16,200 rounds of .50 caliber ammunition. One returning plane had to make an emergency landing at YONTAN Airfield at OKINAWA due to a landing gear problem. USS *NEHENTA BAY* CVE-74, *VC-8* squadron sent six TBM Avengers to strike MIYARA Airfield at ISHIGAKI JIMA. Four FM-2 Wildcats from *SARGENT BAY'S* VC-83 and eight Wildcats from *HOGGATT BAY'S VC-99* joined the attack and conducted a fighter sweep and then escorted the Avengers on their strike. One rocket and two bombing runs were made plus strafing on each run with an addition of one extra strafing run. Thirteen single engine airplanes were observed in the revetments. These were bombed, rocketed and strafed. The planes seen appeared to have been previously riddled and none were believed to have been operational. The airfield had been hit many times previously and the runway was badly cratered. Enemy AA could be located by muzzle flashes and these were strafed. The six *NEHENTA BAY* Avengers expended a total of 59-100# G.P. bombs, 42-HVA rockets, 1,050 rounds of .50 and 470 rounds of .30 caliber Ammo.

NOTE See elsewhere in this book. "I was a TBM Torpedo/Bomber pilot at Okinawa and Sakishima" by Lieutenant (jg) Marvin W. Ray Rachal and also see Stewart Wasoba's drawings for this day.

18 June (L-plus-78) *USS STEAMER BAY* sent 32 planes to attack targets at MIYAKO JIMA. Targets destroyed were 9 buildings, 2 trucks and 1 small boat. Targets damaged were a radar station, AA positions, caves, vehicle revetments, 2 landing craft and 2 barracks. Twelve planes were assigned LCAP and 8 planes were assigned LASP. *USS FANSHAW BAY* commenced her air operations at SAKISHIMA GUNTO at 0512H consisting of 12 planes assigned LCAP, 8 planes for TCAP. Sixteen fighters and 8 Avenger bombers flew strike sorties. The strike airplanes destroyed one building and damaged one fishing boat, two small boats, one radar station and one boat yard. ISHIGAKI Airfield runways were bombed and rocketed. Expended were 80-100# General Purpose bombs and 192-5 inch High Explosive rockets. Planes launched from the *USS SHIPLEY BAY* AT 1410H made a direct attack against HIRARA Airfield and nearby Anti-Aircraft gun positions and hangers a short distance away in the taxi area between the two runways at NOBARA Airfield. Two divisions of fighters fired their rockets into AA positions located along a ridge about 100 yards north of the northern end of the runway and strafed along the sides of the runway. Avengers made a bombing attack on the NE-SW runway at HIRARA Airfield. Each of the five Avengers dropped 2-500# bombs and 4-100# bombs, spaced 130-150 feet apart. The next target attacked by the Avengers was hangers situated in the taxi area between the runways at NOBARA Airfield. Also fighters joined in with their guns with a strafing attack along the sides of the runways. One pilot flying an Avenger made a bombing attack on the E-W runway at NOBARA Airfield and scored hits with 2-500# and 4-100# bombs. This same pilot fired his rockets into the camouflaged positions just off the western end of the E-W runway. At 1630H, 3 TBM Avengers from *VC-97* flying from *SHIPLEY BAY* armed with 2-500# G.P. bombs, 4-100# bombs, rockets and ammo and one Avenger armed with 10-100# bombs, rockets and ammo, attacked AA positions on a ridge running 100 yards North of the NE-SW runway at HIRARA Airfield. Bombs were dropped on the first attack run and the second run was made firing rockets into the ridge resulting in four fires. *USS LUNGA POINT CVE-94* launched 8 fighters and 8 TBM-3 Avenger torpedo bombers at 0815H for a strike at ISHIGAKI. *VC-98* planes made a bombing run on ISHIGAKI and MIYARA airfields and both fields were well hit with 80-100# bombs rendering the runways inoperative. The fighters made strafing and rocketing runs on the revetments, buildings and parked planes. All planes on the ground were thought to be dummies since they didn't burn during and after the strike. A lugger was attacked in NAGURA WAN and left sinking. Light and moderate AA fire was experience during these attacks. Launched again from *LUNGA POINT* at 1415H were 8 Wildcats and 8 Avengers for a strike against ISHIGAKI and MIYARA Airfields. One bombing run was made on each airfield from 8,000 feet in a 40 degree glide. Bombs were released over the runway at 4,000 feet having good results. The fighters strafed and rocketed buildings and barracks

adjacent to the runway. Damaged seriously were 5 building that appeared to be a small factory complex and another building that appeared to be an administration building. Several fires were started. Upon leaving the island, 4 luggers were spotted off the island's southern coast and they were strafed and rocketed and left seriously damaged. The 8 Avengers on these strikes expended a total of 80-100# bombs and 64 rockets. The fighters fired a total of 48 rockets and 7,500 rounds of ammunition. *VC-98* fighters and TBM-3 bombers took to the air again from *LUNGA POINT* at 1630H for a strike to neutralize the ISHIGAKI Airfield runway. The Avengers dropped 40-100# G.P. bombs on the runway and the Wildcat fighters and Avengers together fired 80 rocket.
Lt. GENERAL SIMON B. BUCKNER JR., COMMANDER OF THE 10th US ARMY WAS REPORTED KILLED THIS DAY ON OKINAWA SHIMA.

19 June 1945 (L-plus-79) At 0458H, *USS FANSHAW BAY* launched 8 fighters for LCAP, 4 Avengers for LASP, 8 fighters to fly a sweep and 16 fighters and 3 bombers for a strike group at SAKISHIMA GUNTO. Ground targets damaged during this strike were five 30 foot barges and one radar station. Also bombed and rocketed were ISHIGAKI and HIRARA airfields, where 30-100# G.P. bombs, 142-5 inch High Explosive rockets and 12 High Velocity rockets were expended by planes from *VOC-2*. *USS STEAMER BAY* commenced flight operations at 0506H and provided 47 sorties during the day of which 31 of these were strikes against targets at MIYAKO JIMA. Targets destroyed were four buildings and one truck. Targets damaged were airfield runways and dispersal areas.
At 0500H, *USS MANILA BAY* launched 8 FM-2 Wildcat fighters armed with a total of 32 rockets and guns loaded with .50 caliber ammunition for a sweep at ISHIGAKI Airfield. The main target selected was the NE-SW runway. Here, twenty one rockets were fired. During this attack it was noticed that enemy AA was coming from the nearby OHARU town and this was countered by the fighters firing eight rockets into the AA positions and neutralizing them. In subsequent strikes against AA positions the fighters fired two rockets and strafed these AA positions and small shacks with .50 cal. ammunition before returning to base. At 1015H, eight fighters were again launched having been armed with rockets and .50 cal. ammo. This fighter sweep first attacked the North-South 4,800x175 foot runway at NOBARA at MIYAKO JIMA. Fourteen rockets were fired and 10 hits were confirmed. Following this attack the formation flew to the nearby HIRARA Airfield, where a similarly executed attack was made on the 4,830x300 foot runway. Nine out of 14 rockets fired struck the target. Five single engine aircraft parked in revetments at the eastern end of the E-W runway were strafed with .50 cal. After completion of the attack at HIRARA the fighters few to SUKAMA Airfield located two miles southwest of NOBARA where the single runway was found to be inoperative. One airplane on the ground concealed in the brush was strafed as were several buildings seen to the north of the airfield. In addition to the rockets expended on this sweep, a total of 4,900 rounds of .50 caliber ammunition were fired on targets. *USS SHIPLEY BAY CVE-85* launched her 8 Avengers and 8 Wildcats planes at 0745H for targets at ISHIGAKI SHIMA. The first run was a bombing and rocket attack on the E-W runway and installations at ISHIGAKI Airfield and then another run was a bomb, rocket and a strafing of the same runway using an instrument approach due to a 9/10 overcast over the airfield. Wildcats from this group made a rocket and strafing attack on the towns of OHAMA and SHIRAHO damaging four or five buildings and AA positions in OHAMA

town. Before returning to the carrier the pilots of the planes engaged into a combined rocket and strafing attack against a reservoir and barracks at TARAMA SHIMA. Again at 1010H, *SHIPLEY BAY* launched eight Wildcat fighters for a sweep over ISHIGAKI JIMA. Once they arrived over the airfield the fighters strafed and rocketed parked airplanes between the E-W runway and the southern coast of the island and strafed 20-30 parked planes that were parked along the east side of the N-S runway. Later it was determined that all of these parked airplanes had been previously damaged in earlier attacks. A combined rocket and strafing attack was made on two heavy AA guns located near the road junction about 300 yards northeast of ISHIGAKI town. Ten rockets were fired into AA positions in the town of HIRAE. At 1300H four TBM Avengers were launched, each armed with 2-500# G.P. bombs, 4-100# G.P. bombs, 8-rockets and ammo. The Avengers made a rocket attack against AA positions in OHAMA town and a bombing attack against the North-South runway at ISHIGAKI Airfield leaving the runway cratered. *VC-97* fighter from *SHIPLEY BAY* took to the air in the afternoon at 1530H, for their last strike on this day. Each of the FM-2 Wildcats was armed with 6-5 inch rockets and .50 caliber ammo for a strike at NOBARA Airfield on MIYAKO JIMA. The Wildcats fired their rockets and strafed along the E-W runway and the disposal areas nearby. Then they turned the planes and strafed and fired their rockets at AA positions along a ridge running north and south across the island, about 3,000 yards east of NOBARA'S North-South runway. (*This ridge is presently marked on Miyako maps as "Nobarudake" and became the sight for a US radar station after 1945.*) A strafing run was made by the leader of the 2nd division of fighters against AA positions in the town of FUKUZATO before the planes returned to their base carrier. *USS LUNGA POINT CVE 94* launched 4 of *VC-98's* FM-2 Wildcat fighters at 0730H for a strike on SHIRAHA town at ISHIGAKI. The Wildcats were armed with a total of 24 rockets and 6,400 rounds of .50 caliber ammunition. The target runs were started from 9,000 feet at a dive angle of 20 degrees. Since the cloud cover was .9 with a base of 1,500 feet it was necessary to find holes in the cover to dive through. The town was well strafed and rocketed and several buildings were thought to have been damaged. At 1530H, *LUNGA POINT* again launched 8 Wildcats and 4 Avengers for an attack on two airfields at ISHIGAKI SHIMA. The Avengers made glide bombing runs on the two airfields dropping 100 pound and 500 pound bombs on the runways. The fighters strafed and rocketed adjacent revetments to the fields hitting parked planes. All of the planes were believed to have been duds, except one that caught on fire and was destroyed. Following this run fighters attacked buildings and barracks. Three buildings were left burning. One Wildcat was hit with light AA in both wing leading edges, the windshield and two places in the engine. The pilot of this plane was able to fly safely back to the carrier.

20 June 1945 (L-plus-80) *USS FANSHAW BAY* launched twelve planes at 0454H for LASP and LCAP. Launched for strike sorties were twenty four Wildcat fighters and 4 Avenger torpedo bombers. The strikes from these planes damaged one single engine plane on the ground, one AA position, one barracks building and runways at ISHIGAKI Airfield. Expended on targets were 30-100# G.P. bombs, 8 Napalm bombs and 112-5 inch H.V. rockets. *USS STEAMER BAY* commenced flight operations at 0503H under average to good flying conditions. Aircraft sorties provided were 42, of which 14 were strikes against MIYAKO JIMA. Targets destroyed were two aircraft service buildings and one small ammunition dump. Targets damaged were airfield runways and dispersal areas. *USS MANILA BAY* launched planes at 0600H for a strike on MIYAKO JIMA. Four FM-2 fighters from *VC-71* armed with a total of 16-5 inch rockets headed to NOBARA Airfield. The attack was to be on the North-South runway. However, the airfield was impaired by a thick cloud layer. The fighter pilots picked an area to place their rockets. This area was immediately adjacent to the south end of the North-South runway and to the west end of the East-West runway, an area about 400 square yards containing several small buildings and one ammunition dump. Six rockets were fired into this area. Another fighter pilot fired 4 of his rockets into the nearby south end of the North-South runway. Another run was executed and again the area adjacent to the runways first picked for attack was rocketed with six rockets and strafed with .50 caliber gun ammo. Besides the rockets fired, 4,500 rounds of ammunition were expended. Another launch was executed at 1430H. Eight Wildcat fighters were sent from the *MANILA BAY* for another strike on MIYAKO JIMA. These planes were armed with a total of 48 rockets and loaded with .50 caliber ammo. Upon arrival over MIYAKO JIMA, the flight leader from the group selected the camouflaged and wooded disposal area to the south of the west end of the East-West runway at NOBARA. At least thirty two rockets were fired at Installations. Meager inaccurate medium AA was observed coming from NOBARA - NOBARU town. The flight then rendezvoused over a reef off the northeast shore and went into a dive attack on the North-South runway at HIRARA Airfield. Thirteen rockets were released into the intersection point of the three runways. Planes observed parked in revetments off the east end of the East-West runway were strafed with gun fire. During the pull out from the attack, pilots noticed what appeared to be cement structured "Pill Boxes", numerous AA installations and low well constructed buildings, all well camouflaged. These were 2-3 miles east of HIRARA Airfield. The fighters flew on to the small island of IKEMA SHIMA at the north tip of MIYAKO JIMA were they strafed two small boats and fired two rockets at buildings. While returning along the NE coast of MIYAKO, barracks near KARIMATA town were strafed and the last rocket was fired into the barracks causing a large bright fire.

ON THIS DAY TASK UNIT 32.1.3 IS DISSOLVED. ALL CARRIERS IN SUPPORT OF THE SAKISHIMA OPERATIONS WERE TO REPORT TO TASK UNIT 32.1.1.

21 June (L-plus-81) *USS STEAMER BAY, VC-93* airplane sorties provided for this day totaled 34, of which 28 were strikes against ISHIGAKI airfields. Targets destroyed were 7 buildings, one small ammunition dump and one light AA position. Targets damaged were airfield runways and dispersal areas. Aircraft from *USS FANSHAW BAY'S VOC-2* squadron destroyed one building, damaged two AA batteries and bombed HIRARA Airfield and NOBARA Airfield, expending forty 100# G.P. bombs, 12-500# G.P. bombs and 95-5 inch HVA rockets. *USS NEHENTA BAY CVE-74* launched 12 TBM Avengers and 16 FM-2 Wildcats from *VC-8* Squadron for 2 morning hops to strike SUKAMA Airfield at MIYAKO and one afternoon hop to strike HEGINA Airfield at ISHIGAKI. On the two morning attacks, the runway and taxi strip was bombed and strafed leaving approximately 45 craters. Some small buildings located in tree clumps that were seen on the first strike of the morning were bombed, rocketed and strafed along with the same action taken against airfield revetments. Some light AA fire was seen coming from the village of SUKAMA. (*known also as SUGAMA.*) On the second morning hop while making a run on the airfield, Lieutenant (jg) Roger I. Melvin leading a division of fighters noticed a fuel dump containing oil drums at a position northeast of the field. He organized the group and because of the small amount of AA and low clouds organized a traffic circle of individual attacks. While attacking this fuel dump, 28-100# G.P. bombs, 50-HVA Rockets and 9,000 rounds of .50 caliber ammo was expended, resulting in the dump exploding, sending flames 200 feet into the air and heavy black smoke up to 2,000 feet. Some nearby buildings, where AA fire was noticed were rocketed and strafed setting them on fire. Expended armament on the two morning hops was: 120-100# bombs, 180-rockets and 25,000 rounds of .50 caliber ammunition. *NEHENTA BAY* planes made an afternoon attack on HEGINA and MIYARA airfields at ISHIGAKI JIMA with 6 TBM Avengers and 8 Wildcats. The runways were bombed and MIYARA revetments were rocketed and strafed. Stores expended on this attack were 58-100# bombs, 87 HVA rockets and 8,000 rounds of .50 caliber ammunition. Fifteen of the 58 bombs dropped had 2 hour delay fuses and 15 had 12 hour delay fuses. An enemy airplane was reported by Combat Air Patrol closing on NEHENTA BAY within 19 miles. CAP planes closed to within 3 miles of the enemy plane, but due to the lack of sufficient fuel were forced to break off the pursuit. Aircraft from *USS HOGGATT BAY, VC-99* flew 41 sorties over the target area and one photographic run was made over ISHIGAKI and MIYARA Airfield. Seven tons of bombs and 164-5 inch rockets were expended with the following results: A bridge on the northeast part of ISHIGAKI Airfield was destroyed. AA positions, storage dumps, radio stations in HIRAE town were attacked and damaged, as well as oil and gas storage dumps north of the airfield. *USS SHIPLEY BAY* launched fighters and torpedo bombers at 0530H. These eight planes made a combined run, dropping 39-100# bombs along the E-W runway of HIRARA Airfield at MIYAKO. A separate rocket run was made against revetments and installations along the NE-SW runway. AA installations were rocketed that were situated just to the north and east of HIRARA Airfield. The second division of fighters attacked AA positions, revetments and buildings in the vicinity of the airfield. Upon leaving the area two rockets were fired at AA positions in the town of MATSUBARA causing fires. Planes were again launched from *SHIPLEY BAY* at 1530H. The flight leader of these VC-97 airplanes led six Avengers and 8 Wildcats against HIRARA Airfield and nearby installations. A combined bombing, rocket and strafing attack was made. Thirty seconds before entering into their glide bombing of the NE-SW runway they began to drop "Window" and continued dropping it until well clear of the target. *"Window", also called chaff is a British name for a form of thin metallic material much like narrow strips of aluminum foil that is released into the air by the attacking aircraft for the purpose of radar jamming and confusing the radar operator. The results of dropping window are that these metal strips will be detected by the enemy radar, resulting in target saturation on the radar scopes, further making it extremely difficult for the radar operator to identify the actual location, true altitude and correct number of attacking targets.* Following this attack and radar jamming the Avengers made a rocket attack against AA positions about 1000 yards due east of the northern end of the SUKAMA airstrip. Two of the Wildcats fired a total of 12 rockets into AA positions in HIRARA town, destroying three houses and setting small fires. The same two fighters strafed AA positions in YONAHA town. The second section of Wildcats fired a total of 12 rockets into KAWAMITSU town and strafed AA positions about 1,500 yards south of NOBARA Airfield and the town of YONAHA. Another division leader led his fighters on a rocket attack against a ridge having AA placements just north of the northern end of the NE-SW runway of HIRARA Airfield. Planes from *USS SHAMROCK BAY* were launched from her deck at 0530H. These were 8 Wildcats armed each with 6 rockets. Launched also were 6 Avenger torpedo bombers each armed with 8 rockets and 10-100# G.P. bombs. These planes rendezvoused with Avengers and Wildcats from *VC-99* planes from *HOGGATT BAY* to strike airfields at ISHIGAKI. *SHAMROCK BAY'S VC-96* planes attacked HEGINA and MIYARA Airfield and the other group attacked ISHIGAKI Airfield. On their first run at MIYARA Airfield each Avengers dropped 5-100# bombs on the wooded areas and runway. The Wildcats strafed and rocketed the dispersal areas starting several fires. On their second run on HEGINA Airfield each Avengers dropped 5-100# bombs and the Wildcats fired rockets into buildings. The Avengers made a third run, firing their rockets into the wooded area. Another strike was launched from the *SHAMROCK BAY* at 1130H for HEGINA and MIYARA Airfields consisting of 8 fighters and 6 torpedo bombers. At MIYARA the run was made from north to south with the fighters preceded the bombers strafing the area and the bombers followed, each dropping 5-100# bombs on barracks and gun positions south of the runway. The fighters followed up this action by firing their rockets into gun positions in the wooded areas. The next run was made on HEGINA Airfield. This run was made from northwest to southeast. The Wildcats strafed and rocketed and each Avenger dropped 5-100# bombs on the wooded areas north of the field starting two fires. A third rocket attack was made into the wooded area north of the field. *VC-96* planes flying from *SHAMROCK BAY* made their last strike for this day at MIYAKO JIMA. Launched at 1530H were 8 fighters each armed with 6 rockets, 8,300 rounds of .50 caliber ammo and 6 Avengers each armed with 4-500# bombs. The weather was clear over the target with a visibility of 13 miles. The Avengers made four runs from south to north over the SUKAMA runway each dropping 1-500# bomb onto the runway surface. The fighters made 7 strafing and rocketing runs on gun positions and the villages of YONAHA and SUKAMA. One gun position was knocked out at target number-1095. Two large fires were started in the villages and the wooded areas at the field. Three small boats were strafed in the bay near KAWAMITSU. Moderate, light AA was encountered but no damage was reported to the attacking planes. Each of the Wildcat fighters was fueled with 226 gallons of gasoline before launching. Total fuel consumed by each fighter plane on this 3 hour mission was 160 gallons. The Avenger Torpedo Bombers at launching each carried 328 gallons of gasoline and in 3 hours flying time they each used 190 gallons of fuel.

22 June 1945 (L-plus-82) *USS STEAMER BAY* reported that Lieutenant Commander C.P. Smith, the CO for Air Squadron VC-93 was forced down 20 miles east of ISHIGAKI due to engine failure after his engine had been hit with flak over the target. He was rescued by the submarine *HACKLEBACK SS-295* that was on life guard duty. LCAP airplanes from this carrier were vectored in pursuit of a bogey that passed 20 miles south of the formation. The bogey was never sighted by interceptors as it climbed to 23,000 feet and took a retirement course of 250 degrees and faded at 250 miles. Twenty eight sorties of 34 flown were strike groups attacking ISHIGAKI airfields. Targets destroyed were 7 buildings, one small ammunition dump and one light AA position.

Targets damaged were airfield runways and dispersal areas. *USS FANSHAW BAY* at 0458H commenced flight operations. Twelve planes were launched for LCAP, 4 for LASP, 17 fighters and 8 torpedo bombers for strike group sorties. Destroyed were one repair shop and one building. Damaged were two AA positions and runways were bombed at HIRARA Airfield at MIYAKO JIMA. Expended were 40-100# G.P. bombs, 12-500# G.P. bombs, 30-5 inch HVA rockets and 64-5 inch H.E. rockets. *USS HOGGATT BAY'S* air operations for the day included 25 sorties over MIYAKO targets and 12 LCAP sorties. Eight 500# bombs were dropped on the North-South runway at HIRARA. Two small boats were burned on the south end of the island, eight more 500# bombs were dropped on the field at NOBARA and rocket hits were made on buildings north of the field. One photographic run was made that covered HIRARA, NOBARA and SUKAMA Airfield. It was noticed that the radar was fouled at 70 miles from target indicating the use of radar jamming. *USS NEHENTA BAY'S VC-8* planes launched 6 Avengers and 8 FM-2 Wildcat fighters against SUKAMA Airfield. When the planes arrived another fuel dump was located only 100 yards east of the one that was destroyed the day before. Lieutenant Norman D. Hodson set up a traffic circle from the east against the fuel dump and the planes released their bombs at 2,500 feet. Lieutenant (jg) Albert R. Leroy ignited the dump causing a very large oil fire. Other planes attack this target with bombs, rockets and machine gun bullets. During this raid a bombing run was made against the runway further damaging it. A total of 70-100# General Purpose bombs, 90 HVA rockets and 7,000 rounds of .50 caliber ammunition were used against targets. Meager and light enemy machine fire was encountered during the attack on targets. *NEHENTA BAY* again launched planes for an afternoon strike against MIYAKO. This time it would be HIRARA, NOBARA, and SUKAMA airfields. Six Avengers and 8 Wildcat fighters from *VC-8* were launched and they rendezvous with planes from three other carriers mentioned in this day's raid for a coordinated strike on the three airfields at MIYAKO JIMA. Two Avengers and eight Wildcat fighters from *VC-8* along with other planes from other carriers bombed HIRARA, NOBARA and SUKAMA airfields in three separate coordinated runs. Fifteen 100# bombs landed in the intersection of the three runways at HIRARA Airfield, Enemy AA opened up during this bombing run but they were immediately taken under fire by eight fighters and two Avengers who silenced the fire with rockets and machine gun fire. On the bombing raid at NOBARA Airfield, 5-100# bombs landed on the eastern runway and 7-100# bombs landed on the western runway. Twenty 100# bombs landed on the single runway at SUKAMA Airfield. (Bombs dropped by *VC-8* planes were equipped with delayed fuses). In addition to the number of bombs dropped on this afternoon raid against the three airfields, 91 HVA rockets and 11,000 rounds of .50 caliber ammunition were fired on enemy targets. *USS SHIPLEY BAY CVE 85* launched her 6 Avengers and 8 Wildcats at 1025 hours, 93 miles from the target. The Avengers made a bombing run along the E-W runway at ISHIGAKI Airfield. One parked plane at the intersection of the NE-SW and E-W runway was destroyed. The Wildcats and Avengers made a rocket run on a ravine just north of the NE-SW runway causing several fires. "Widow" was dropped during each of the above attacks. Expended during the above strikes were 60-100# bombs, 90 rockets and 4,000 rounds of .50 caliber ammo. At 1530H, *VC-97* planes from *SHIPLEY BAY*, *VC-98* planes from *LUNGA POINT* and *VC-93* planes from *STEAMER BAY* with a combined attack, struck targets at ISHIGAKI Airfield. Bombs with long delay fuses were dropped along the N-S runway.

Rockets were fired into AA installations in OHAMA town and HIRAE town. Others dropped their bombs on HEGINA Airfield and fired rockets at buildings north of the field. Two of the Avengers dropped their bombs along the NE-SW runway at MIYARA Airfield. Rockets were fired into revetments containing AA guns along the eastern side of the above runway. "Window" was dropped by all of the Avengers during the attacks and until well clear of the target. The Wildcats made a combined rocket attack against AA positions in a ravine just north of the NE-SW runway of ISHIGAKI Airfield, AA positions around the field and in the town of HIRAE were fires were reported to be seen burning after the attacks. Expended were 60-100# bombs, 79-rockets, 4,500 rounds of .50 caliber and 800 rounds of 30 caliber ammo. *USS SHAMROCK BAY CVE 84* launched *VC-96* planes at 1030H for an attack on NOBARU Airfield on MIYAKO JIMA. The 8 Wildcats and 6 Avengers set their course at 272 degrees and flew 90 miles to the target. The first run on the field was from the north to south against the N-S runway and adjacent areas. Five of the Avengers dropped a total of 25-100# bombs and one Avenger dropped 2-500# bombs while the Wildcats were firing their rockets at a wooded area nearby. A second run was made from east to west on the E-W runway with five of the Avengers dropping 25-100# bombs and one Avenger dropping 2-500# bombs. The Wildcats fired their rockets into the nearby buildings and barracks. The Avengers and the Wildcats formed up and made two runs firing their rockets into a wooded ridge located east of the NOBARU Airfield, causing three fires. (This ridge would have been NOBARU DAKE.) After these runs against the ridge, Ensign R.E. Weeks piloting an Avenger failed to join up with the rest of the planes. Although, 3-4 burst of AA was observed, no one from the other planes heard any messages or seen any evidence of a plane going down. The two crewmen aboard the missing Avenger torpedo bomber were AMM3c G.G. Kaylor and ACM2c H.J. Gericke. At 1530H *SHAMROCK BAY* launched 8 fighters and 6 Avengers for an attack at MIYAKO. The Avengers made a bombing run from north to south against SUKAMA Airfield located on the west side of MIYAKO. Four Avengers dropped a total of 8-500# bombs and 20-100# bombs. The other two Avengers attacked the HIRARA Airfield, dropping 8-500# bombs on the runways. The fighters made three, east to west runs against the SUKAMA Airfield, firing their rockets on each run into buildings and the wooded area nearby. *USS LUNGA POINT CVE 94* launched 28 *VC-98* planes while in route to join the carrier formation after taking on supplies at KERAMA RETTO.

23 June 1945 (L-plus-83)   No known strikes.

24 June 1945 (L-plus-84) *On 24 JUNE 1945, the OKINAWA campaign for the US Navy, TASK UNIT 32.1.1 ended. US ARMY AIR FORCES took over the neutralizing of the airfields and other targets at SAKISHIMA GUNTO. US 20th ARMY AIR FORCE P47 Thunderbolt fighter bombers from IE-SHIMA attacked targets of opportunity at SAKISHIMA GUNTO. On the 27th and 28th of June, there were strikes at SAKISHIMA GUNTO by the US 7th AIR FORCE P-47's and on July 31, ARMY AIR FORCE P-51 Mustangs attacked the airstrips at SAKISHIMA GUNTO.*

It now seemed to the people at SAKISHIMA GUNTO, near the end of June that the Americans might skip an all out assault on MIYAKO JIMA and her neighboring islands. They had captured airfields on OKINAWA SHIMA, closer to Japan's homeland and were operating land based fighters and bombers from these bases. This eased some of the tension felt by the Japanese soldiers and sailors who were defending MIYAKO. However, there was now another major problem. The island was cut off from any supplies reaching them. They were completely isolated. The 32nd Army at Okinawa was in a serious situation for they had been driven from their SHURI strong hold, east of NAHA and were making a stand on the southern end of OKINAWA with their backs to the sea. There were no longer any communications between the MIYAKO JIMA army division headquarters and the OKINAWA 32nd army. Their closest contact with another army of their own was at TAIWAN (FORMOSA). There were approximately 80,000 people, that includes the military people who had to be fed each day at MIYAKO JIMA and there were no means for transporting food supplies to them. This meant that they would starve or have to go to work planting and growing their own food and the fishermen would have to brave going back out onto the sea. Many able bodied civilians had been conscripted into the Army and were expected to defend the island in case the enemy tried to land. Many of these were local farmers and now that food was scarce, their help was needed to grow sweet potatoes, soy beans and tend to animals, so they were given time away from their military assignments. The regular Japanese Army and Navy troops also pitched in and helped. After the battle of OKINAWA and the bombing of HIROSHIMA and NAGASAKI, the Japanese decided to lay down their arms and accept the Potsdam Declaration. Some planes flew over SAKISHIMA GUNTO and dropped some leaflets onto the islands. These were informing the Army and Navy troops that they should surrender. However, the troops who had been cut off from any official communications from Japan declined to act without official notice. So they continued to maintain their readiness to defend the islands. Later on the MIYAKO JIMA 28th Division Army made contact with the Japanese Army at Taiwan and learned that the surrender made by Japan was official and it was to be honored by SAKISHIMA forces. A hand picked delegation was sent to OKINAWA to meet with the US tenth army personnel for talks about disarming and then they returned to MIYAKO JIMA and explained the procedures to Lieutenant General Noumi the 28th Army Division Commander. After this General Noumi and his staff flew to OKINAWA and he signed a cease fire agreement. Because there were no surviving commanders of the OKINAWA battle, General Noumi again traveled to OKINAWA from MIYAKO and signed the surrender for the RYUKYU ISLANDS at the US 10th ARMY headquarters on the 7th of September1945.

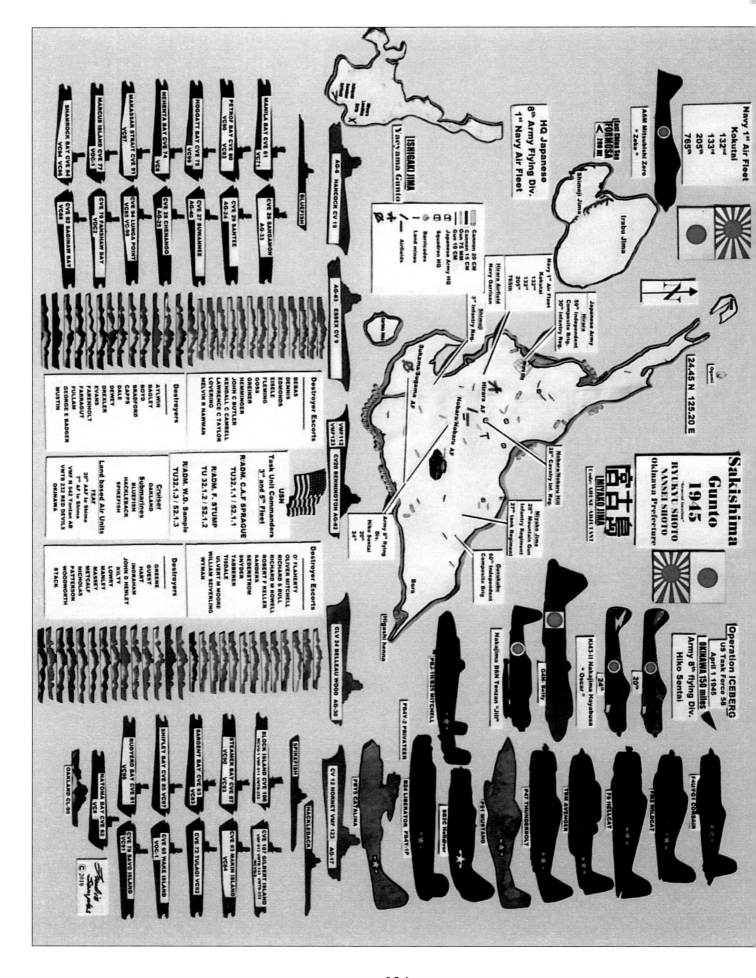

Rear/Admiral William Dodge Sample
9 March 1898 - 3 October 1946
Photo: National Archives

Commander of Carrier Division 22, Task Unit 32.1.3 and 52.1.3 at
SAKISHIMA GUNTO

W.D. Sample graduated from the United States Naval Academy in 1918 and served in
the Navy for the remainder of World War I

During World War II, he was the Commander on the USS Santee (CVE-29) and
participated in the invasion of North Africa

As a Captain he commanded the USS Intrepid (CV-ll) and the USS Hornet
(CV-12)
As R/Admiral he was the Commander of Carrier Divisions 27 and 22.

On 2 October 1945, an airplane that Admiral Sample was listed as a passenger, was
declared missing near Wakayama Japan after it didn't return to base

Admiral Sample was officially declared dead one year later

Sangamon Class Escort Carrier

USS Suwannee CVE-27 shown. *Photo: National Archives*

All four of the Sangamon Class Escort Carriers with their Air Groups seen action at Sakishima Gunto. They were: USS Sangamon CVE-26, USS Suwannee CVE-27, USS Chenango CVE-28 and USS Santee CVE-29.

These Carriers each had a crew of 800+ and up to 30 planes per ship. Airplanes mostly used from these carriers against the airfields at Sakishima Gunto were the F6F Hellcats and the TBM Avengers.

The USS Sangamon CVE-26 suffered extensive damage and loss of life after being hit by a Kamikaze on 4 May 1945 near Okinawa.

Casablanca Class Escort Carrier
USS Tulagi CVE-72 shown. *Photo: National Archives*

Twenty of these Casablanca Class Escort Carriers and their Air Composite Squadrons participated in action against Sakishima Gunto airfields. The names of the ships are listed in the daily action section of this book. The Escort Carriers were shifted back and forth where needed between the action on the island of Okinawa and the air war being fought against the S-West airfields of Sakishima Gunto.

These Escort Carriers each had a crew of 800+ and 25-28 planes per ship. The airplanes mostly used to neutralize Sakishima Gunto airfields that were launched from these carriers were the FM-2 Wildcats, a Grumman design, General motors built airplane that replaced the F-4 Wildcat and the TBM Avenger torpedo bombers that was the replacement for the earlier TBF Avenger torpedo bombers.

Commencement Bay Class Escort Carrier
USS Gilbert Islands CVE-l07 shown. *Photo: National Archives*

Two Commencement Bay Class Escort Carriers with their Marine Air squadrons seen action at Sakishima Gunto. They were USS Block Island CVE-I06 and USS Gilbert Islands CVE 107.

These Carriers each had a crew of 1000+ and up to 35 planes per ship. From the decks of these carriers were flown the F4U/FG1 Corsairs, F6F Hellcats and TBM Avengers that struck the Sakishima Gunto airfields.

Fletcher Class Destroyer
USS Fullman DD-474 shown *Photo: National Archives*

Destroyers were nicknamed "Tin Cans" because of their thin skin.
Several classes (designs) were built before and during WWII and several of
these different designed Destroyers operated at Okinawa and Sakishima
Gunto.

The Fletcher class Destroyer was 376 feet 5 inches long and its beam was 39
feet 7 inches. Its speed was 38 knots. The crew size was approximately 275.
(The ship dimensions, engines, crew size, and guns varied some what
between the classes).

Destroyers were a fast ship, armed well and very maneuverable, therefore
they were used for many tasks. Some of the important tasks that they
performed well at Okinawa and Sakishima Gunto were:
Picket Duty, Screening Aircraft Carriers, Rescuing downed pilots and air
crewmen, delivering wounded to hospital ships, delivering mail and
supplies, escorting other ships to and from battle stations, Mine sweeping,
Submarine hunting, Shooting down enemy planes with their AA guns and
many more duties.

John C. Butler Class Destroyer Escort

USS Dennis DE-405 shown *Photo: National Archives*

Destroyer Escorts were originally built and used early on in WWII to protect
Supply ship convoys in route to Europe against enemy Submarine attacks.
Later they were used in the Pacific to protect and escort other ships along
with performing radar picket duty and Anti-submarine patrols.

They were smaller and slower than the Destroyers but more maneuverable.
Several classes (designs) were built and their dimensions and engines varied.
The length of the John C. Butler class of Destroyer Escorts was 306 feet and
their beam was 36 foot 6 inches. Their speed was approximately 24 knots
and they carried a crew of 215.

The Destroyer Escorts carried a number of depth charges aboard as offensive
weapons against enemy submarines. They were armed with torpedoes and
had a variety of machine guns to defend their ship and others from surface
and air attack. On the 4th of May 1945 the USS Dennis DE-405 came to the
aid of the USS Sangamon Escort carrier that was hit by a Kamikaze near
Okinawa. Sailors from the Dennis rescued 88 men from the stricken
Sangamon carrier.

FM2 Wildcat
Photo: National Archives

Single seat Naval Fighter
Grumman (General Motors Built)
Engine: Wright R-1820-56 Supercharged
HP 1,350
Maximum speed: 332 mph (534 km.h) at 28,000 ft (8,778 m)
Service ceiling 34,700 ft (10,577 m)
Range 900 mi (1,448 km)
Four or Six wing mounted .50 guns (12.7mm)
Two 250 lb or two 100 lb bombs
Optional: Six 5 inch rockets

TBM Avenger

Photo: Courtesy of John Lally via Adam Lewis

Torpedo Bomber
Grumman (General Motors Built)
Crew 3
Radar equipped
Engine Wright R-2600-20 Cyclone 1,900 hp (1417Kw)
Maximum speed 276 mph. (444km/h)
Service ceiling 30,100 ft (9,175m)
Range 1,920 miles (3090km)
Eight wing mounted 5 inch HVAR rockets
Two fwd firing wing mounted guns .50 calibers
Upper Turret gun .50 caliber (12.7mm)
Lower gun .30 caliber (7.62mm)
Bombs, Torpedoes and Depth charges
Maximum rocket, torpedo, depth charge and bomb load; 2,500
lbs. (1,134kg)

F6F Hellcat
Photo: National Archives

Single seat fighter with bombing capability
Mfg. Grumman
Engine: Pratt & Whitney R-2800-10w Double Wasp 18 Cylinder
2000 HP (1491KW)
Maximum Speed: 375 mph (605km h)
Service Ceiling: 37,398 ft (11,369m)
Range: 1,260 miles (2,028km)
Six .50 forward firing machine guns

Options
Two 20mm forward firing cannons with four forward firing .50
cal. machine guns, Six 5 inch (127mm) rockets
Two 1,000 lb (454kg) bombs
Radar and photographic equipment

FG1D Corsair
Photo: National Archives

Single seat naval fighter with bombing capability
Mfg. Chance Vought (Goodyear built)
Engine: Pratt &Whitney R- 2800 -8 Double .wasp Radial, 18
cylinders, water injected, 2,250 hp (1,678kW)
Maximum Speed: 425 mph (684 km h) @ 20,000 ft
Service Ceiling: 38,000 ft (11,582 m)
Range: 1,015 miles (1,633 km)
Six forward firing wings mounted .50 caliber machine guns
2,000 lb (907 kg) Bomb load
Eight 5 inch rocket
Extras: Radar Pod mounted on wing
External fuel tanks
Fuselage R&L Center line Rockets

PB4Y-1 (B24 LIBERATOR)
Photo: National Archives

10 crew US Naval Patrol Bomber and Reconnaissance
Manufacture by Consolidated Vultee and others
Engine 4 Pratt&Whitney *RI830-43/65
Maximum speed *279-297 mph
Service ceiling *28,000-31,000 feet
Range *1,900-2,960 miles
Armament 10x .50 caliber machine guns (see note below)
Gun placements. Nose turret-2 guns, Roof turret-2 guns, Tail turret-2 guns,
Aft of bomb bay retractable turret-2 guns and at waist position 2-guns.
Bomb load *5,400-8,000 lbs
Internal and external bomb racks

Note: On early models, some of the guns were .303 caliber.
* Several models of this airplane were made. Depending on the model, there
is a variation in its engine and other performances shown above.

PB4Y-2 (PRIVATEER)
Photo: National Archives

11 crew US Naval bomber and gun ship
Manufactured by Consolidated Vultee
Engines 4 Pratt&Whitney R1830-94 14 cyl radial type
Maximum speed 250 mph
Range 2,700 miles
Service ceiling 19,000
Armament 12x .50 caliber guns
Gun placements Nose turret-2 guns, forward top turret-2 guns, aft top turret-
2 guns, starboard waist-2 guns, port waist-2 guns, tail turret-2 guns.
Bomb load 12,800 1bs

Note: all gun positions were armor protected
Airplane was used in the Pacific in 1945

Bomb damaged Japanese Radar Set

Shown is what was left of Japanese radar at Nobara/Nobarudake- Miyako Jima after the island surrendered.
This appears to be a part of the radar antenna's rotating frame in an upside down position.

The US Air Force's 624th Aircraft Control and Warning Squadron opened up an Early Warning radar station here at Nobarudake in March 1950. Other than the US surrender party (shown elsewhere in this book) and clean up crews who arrived in late September 1945 and departed 23 days later, these were the first known Americans to permanently live and work on the island since the end of the war.

USS SANGAMON CVE 26
Hit by a Kamikaze on May 4 1945 just after departing
Kerama Retto in route to Sakishima Gunto

USS SANGAMON CVE 26

Top side deck damage

Damage to underside hanger

The only communications
left after the Kamikaze attack
was the radio in this airplane

"Sangy" CVE 26 Mascot

Inspecting the damage From
left- Cpt. Malstrom, R/Admiral
W.D. Sample and CMDR. O'Beirne

LOST OVER NOBARU/NOBARA AIRFIELD.

*Photo by
Doug Misamore
Adam Lewis*

VMTB-143, Marine Pilot USMCR 1st Lieutenant Kelvern O. Misamore (shown), USMCR Sgt. Otto R. Schaefer, and USMCR Sgt. Chancel A. Hall

Lieutenant George "Fritz" Liebich a TBM Avenger pilot's account of LT. Misamore's plane being hit by ground fire and crashing on 12 June 1945 at MIYAKO JIMA

*Photo by
John Lally
Via Adam Lewis*

Lt "Fritz" Liebich with his Avenger "FERTILE MYRTLE"

We were launched from the USS Gilbert ISLANDS CVE-107 with orders to bomb the runways at Nobara Airfield. Each of us was carrying 4-500# bombs. We were to peel off just before we made the run. Lt. Misamore was right ahead of me and I waited for him to peel off, instead he didn't. I motioned for him to peel off and he stared at me with a blank look. We were running out of time, so I went ahead of him and I noticed that he came in behind me. Then he took a hit in his wing root and the wing fell off. His TBM spun to the ground like a seed from a tree. The plane exploded when it hit the ground

Chapter 8
SURRENDER TERMS DELIVERED AND
ISLAND'S MILITARY DISARMAMENT

Lieutenant General Toshiro Noumi the Commander of the 28th Division Japanese Army with headquarters at Miyako Jima traveled to Okinawa and signed the surrender documents for Sakishima Gunto on the 7th of September 1945. On the 20th of September, the *USS Destroyer FARENHOLT DD 491* arrived at Naha Bay Okinawa with orders to standby for the arrival of 10th Army's Brigadier General Robert Milchrist Cannon and his staff. *(On the surrender documents the Japanese General's last name is spelled "Nomi".)*

The *USS FARENHOLT DD 491* was commissioned on April 2, 1942 in the Brooklyn N.Y. Navy yard. She was a 1,630 ton Destroyer (Tin can), known to her crewmembers as the "Fighting "F"". She was the flagship of "Destroyer Squadron 12" *(DESRON 12)* and would be awarded 13 operation and engagement stars between 7 August 1942 and 15 August 1945. She had recently participated in the battle of Okinawa and had escorted and screened the escort carriers with their air groups that were sent to neutralize the Kamikaze airfields at Sakishima Gunto. Now that Japan had surrendered the Ryukyu Islands, the *FARENHOLT'S* crew was to provide transportation for the US 10th Army General to Sakishima Gunto. General Cannon, aided by officers and sailors of the fighting "F", was taking the surrender terms to the Japanese Army and Navy on the islands and would be disarming them. On the 22nd of September, 10th Army General R. M. Cannon and his staff arrived and boarded the ship. Just before midnight on the 22nd of September the *FARENHOLT* got underway for the Sakishima Gunto, with its first stop to be Miyako Jima, located 150 miles southwest of Naha Okinawa. Accompanying the *FARENHOLT* was two LST'S and one LCT. The two LST'S with 10th Army troops aboard would accompany the *FARENHOLT*. These troops would go ashore to assure the islands were safe and participate in the disarming and oversee the removal of the weapons from the islands. According to a survey made early on the 22nd of September at Miyako Jima by the US Underwater Demolition team #6, the shores of the island were found to be very heavily mined. While in route to Sakishima Gunto the crew aboard the *FARENHOLT* enjoyed their first movie that had been shown on the fantail while the ship was underway. The *FARENHOLT* arrived off the shore of Miyako Jima the morning of the 24th of September in rain and gusty winds. Two Japanese barges constructed of wood with sailors and officers came to meet the destroyer and a Japanese General and one of his staff came aboard and met with General Cannon's staff to discuss the anchorage at the island's harbor. When the first boat with Americans reached shore, it was discovered that the island was infested with large black flies and they called for an airplane to spray the island with DDT before anyone landed and after this was completed the Japanese provided transportation for the men from the Destroyer and the two LSTs to shore. It surprised everyone to find out that a Japanese soldier who was the Japanese Army's interpreter had formally attended the University of Chicago and spoke excellent English. Another soldier had once lived in Ohio. The soldiers were dressed in shabby uniforms that bore many patches. They had been isolated on the island for over a year and they had been on half food rations for the past 6 months. Some of the Americans offered them cigarettes in which they gladly accepted. During the morning forty eight P47 fighter airplanes came over the island in a beautiful formation and wagged their wings and following them were thirty six B-25 bombers that were also flying in a formation. A B-17 and a PBY Catalina flew over and took pictures. The Army okayed the safety of a beach near a neat small village and some of the ship's sailors were allowed to go ashore for recreation, but they were not allowed into the village. At first the island's natives were afraid of the sailors. But they became friendly when offered cigarettes and treats and the sailors noticed that they acted so innocent. Some of the men ask the Japanese soldiers for souvenirs. They complied by tearing insignia patches from their uniforms and offered them to the sailors. On the 28th of September the *FARENHOLT* received typhoon warnings in the region and the ships prepared to ride it out. The ships were back at Miyako Jima on the 1st of October and the clean up resumed, continuing until the 5th of October. The crews departed Miyako Jima around 2000 hours on the 5th and got under way for Ishigaki Jima arriving there on the 6th. Once again they were met with a typhoon and the ships spent the next 4 days riding out the storm and arriving back at Ishigaki on the 11th of October. The next day, they got underway and stopped at Miyako, where General Cannon went ashore and paid his final visit. On the 14th the *FARENHOLT* got underway for Okinawa.

Photo (National Archives)

Lieutenant General Toshiro Nomi, representing Japanese forces in the Sakishima Gunto, signs the surrender document during ceremonies held at Tenth Army Headquarters on Okinawa, 7 September 1945.

Standing beside him is Colonel Philip H. Bethune, of the G-2 Section, and Major General Frank D. Merrill, Chief of Staff, Tenth Army.

Lieutenant General Joseph W. Stilwell, Commanding General, Tenth Army, and interpreter T/4 Robert H. Oda are standing opposite the table, at right. Other members of the Japanese delegation are standing behind the table, at left.

Note: The name Nomi is often spelled Noumi in Japanese records.

SURRENDER CEREMONY ON ISLAND OF MIYAKO SHIMA SEPTEMBER 29,1945
Lt. (jg) Walter Shackelford (far left) stands with other Naval officers, representing the US Navy, as Army General R. M. Cannon accepts surrenders from the Japanese forces commander. The island was a sea raiding base, containing infantry units, radar stations, shipping engineers, suicide boat units, and air landing fields.

Lt. (jg) Walter Shackelford's assessment of Miyako Shima 1945

During the period from 22 September to the 14th of October 1945 our ship; the USS FARENHOLT DD-491 participated in a very interesting operation—the surrender of a small group of Japanese Islands. I was fortunate in being able to join an inspection party which reviewed the troops and examined the installations on the island of Miyako Shima in the Sakishima Gunto group to the southwest of Okinawa. My squadron Commander was the senior Naval Officer present, so I was able to be on the spot when the Army General talked with the Japanese officers...through interpreters, of course...and discussed with them the training their men had had; where they had been activated; what fighting they had participated in; and general information about material, location of installations, and other confidential military dope.

We went from place to place on the island and inspected the troops. They looked well-fed and their uniforms were surprisingly well kept in view of the living conditions which I observed. When orders were given, the troops really "snapped to" and I didn't see an eye move after the Commander gave a horrible blood-curdling yell which brought them to attention.

(Continued)

I was especially interested in the facial expressions of a defeated foe. There were no smiles. Most of the numerous spectacled troops were expressionless; a few had a definite sneer of hatred, but whether the face was stupid or intelligent there was little display of emotion. However, I would not have cared to be left alone with any one of them.

As we rode through the small villages the natives would gather along the road sides to bow and salute as we passed. Even little babies who could hardly walk would give you a military salute or something vaguely similar to a "Heil Hitler" The women looked haggard, undernourished and overworked. We were told that women did most of the labor in the fields and around the houses; at the same time they must have raised huge families for the island was cluttered with babies and young children.

The food raised on the island consisted of sweet potatoes, sugar cane, and a small amount of rice, much of the latter is imported. There main diet is rice, sweet potatoes, and Bonita (a fish which they catch with nets.) The civilians, Army, and Navy each had their separate fields to grow their food.

The houses looked quite picturesque from a distance—typically Japanese with the sloping roofs of tile or grass. When one made a closer inspection, though, he noted that they were very poorly constructed. Most of them were weather- beaten, square wooden structures with sliding doors that opened into one or two room which were used for all household functions. No sanitary facilities were observed. As I passed the houses I could see the women and children inside sitting on floor mates doing their housework. There were signs that some more modern structures had stood on the island but most of them had been destroyed by constant bombings. A large amount of people had been forced to live in caves.

The people traveled mainly by foot, a few by horseback and bicycle. (For any bicycle rider: the bicycles had no brakes; in order to stop you had to jump off.) There were some horse- driven carts for the natives to use to carry their heavy loads. The horses, like people were very small...more like our Shetland pony. The Japanese Army had a handful of Chevrolet trucks. It might be interesting to note that the Japanese Army General guided us around in his very well polished 1940 Pontiac sedan. I was anxious to get a picture of the Pontiac leading a procession of Jeeps, U.S. Army trucks, and a Weasel and send it to General Motors to show them that their product really gets around. There were lots of...the Japanese pronounce it Die-hot-soo (small sailing craft.)..And a few Sampans which the Japanese used for inter- island traffic and fishing. I saw no war vessels but I did observe a lot of sunken ships in the harbor.

All of the officers that participated in this operation were given a Samurai Sword as a souvenir. This is the first souvenir I have had during the time I served out here. The Swords are quite valuable and play an important role in the Military Clique of Japan. They are handed down from generation and are a sacred symbol of the Japanese military families. The enlisted men had a choice of a field sword, pistol, or rifle and bayonet. Most of them chose the pistol.

USS FARENHOLT DD491

Brigadier General Robert M. Cannon
(holding the rail), aboard DD491.

The Japanese military officers drove
U.S. built cars, a Ford shown here, and
their Commander drove a Pontiac.

Japanese military helmets piled near
Hirara harbor, later to be dumped
at sea.

Farenholt Sailors examining Rifles and
other weapons removed from Miyako-
Jima soldiers.

Chapter 9
THE FATE OF AN AMERICAN POW

It was early in 1946 when the war crimes commission was being formed that the Americans learned from a reliable collaborator that a captured American pilot who survived bailing out of his Avenger Airplane after it had been hit with AA over MIYAKO JIMA was shot and killed by Japanese Army troops while being held captive.

Ensign Joseph Francis Florence, a US Navy TBM Avenger pilot, a member of Air Group-24, assigned to the USS SANTEE escort carrier was on a bombing run over the NOBARA/NOBARU middle Army Airfield on the 23rd of April 1945 when his Avenger bomber was hit with anti-aircraft fire and he bailed out of his crippled plane and landed near the Japanese 28th Army Division Headquarters at NOHARAGASHI. He was surrounded, captured and taken to the Army headquarters and turned over to the Japanese military police for interrogation.

During the War crimes investigation the Japanese that were questioned claimed that at the time the American was captured, there was no transportation available to send the American captive to the nearest POW camp, located at TAIWAN, so they held him as a prisoner near their quarters. According to investigation reports, the American pilot was ordered to de-fuse bombs that hadn't exploded, which he refused to do. His refusal to do this infuriated those to whom he was assigned, so they turned to Lieutenant General Noumi the 28th Army Division Commander for advice on how to handle the prisoner. It was known among the staff officers that before General Noumi was transferred to MIYAKO JIMA, he was once a police commander and he had experience handling prisoners.

According to the investigation, in June of 1945, the Japanese Army at MIYAKO thought it was highly probable that the Americans were going to assault MIYAKO by landing their troops on the island and everyone was preparing for the worst. They still could not move the prisoner to TAIWAN and didn't know what to do with the American pilot. On the night of 11 July, four Japanese soldiers arrived at the prisoner's cell and they told the American pilot that transportation was waiting at the local airfield to transport him to the POW camp at TAIWAN and they would walk him to the airplane.

The prisoner's hands were tied and they started out walking toward the airfield. Lieutenant Tonomura was walking in front of the prisoner and Sergeant Jiro Takeuchi, Corporal Kozo Hatano and Private Taira was behind the prisoner. When the group reached a selected spot, Lt. Tonomura jumped aside and Corporal Kozo Hatano stepped forward and fired point blank at the prisoners head. The prisoner fell and the others shot him on the ground. The ropes were removed from the prisoner's wrist and he was carried and placed into a grave that had been previously dug near the base of NOHARADAKE.

It was alleged by all involved during the investigation that General Noumi the MIYAKO 28th division commander, had ordered the killing of the American pilot and they were carrying out orders handed down to them. They claimed that Noumi issued a statement right after the pilot was killed that the prisoner was the victim of an airplane crash that killed all aboard while the airplane was taking off from MIYAKO for TAIWAN. They claimed he later made the air crash official by signing a crash report. However, nothing could be found in any records to support this claim.

Those questioned said that at the end of the war, a Japanese officer ordered the body of Ensign Joseph Florence to be removed from the grave and the remains burned. The ashes were then boxed and sent to TAIWAN. They felt that this was done to keep the Americans from finding the grave and the body when they disarmed the soldiers on the island.

After the results of the war crimes investigation in this case was completed. Four Japanese soldiers were arrested and accused of murder and accessory of murder. The four were found guilty and sentenced at the Yokohama Military Tribunal on July 26, 1948. Found guilty and sentenced were: Lt. Colonel Fujio Mutsuro, 28th division staff officer. He received 35 years hard labor. 1st Litieutenant. Okuji Tonomura, assistant to the 28th division headquarters received 9 years of hard labor. Corporal Kozo Hatano, received 3 years of hard labor and Sergeant Major Jiro Takeuchi received 3 years of hard labor.

Although General Noumi was charged with "B" and "C" class crimes after the war on matters that were involved while he was earlier serving in the war in China, it was never proven that General Noumi ordered the American pilot to be shot at MIYAKO for he ended his own life by taking poison shortly after he returned to MIYAKO from signing the surrendering documents for the Ryukyu Islands at the US 10th Army headquarters in OKINAWA in 1945.

Reference: Yokohama Japan war trials
National Archives

A note from the author about the death of Joseph Florence.
At Sakishima Gunto when one dies the body is returned to earth but ones spirit remains nearby to guide others along their way. I never met Joseph F. Florence in his life on earth, but after he died and was buried next to Noharadake near where I later lived. I believe his spirit delivered to me a message through a shocking dream that inspired me to want to know more about the war at Sakishima Gunto and eventually what I found inspired me to write this book.

Ensign Joseph Francis Florence USNR (New York City)
Air Group 24, Shot down and captured on 23 April 1945 at
Miyako Jima Japan. Killed by captures for no
apparent reason on 11 July 1945.

Pictures contributed by Harry Florence.

Ensign Florence (center)

130

Chapter 10
THOSE WHO FOUGHT AND LIVED
TO TELL THEIR STORY

Lt. (jg) Maxwell Franklin Denman from the US Navy's Air Group 40 stationed on the USS SUWANNEE CVE-27 took his Hellcat fighter off from the carrier early on Monday morning the 28th of May 1945 with 3 other Hellcat fighters for a sweep over Nobaru Airfield on Miyako Island. Max, a name his friends called him wouldn't be coming back with the other three today. His friends reported seeing his plane in trouble and watched as Max bailed out and descended to the island in his parachute landing near a shoreline village. His leader Earl Hartman sent his Hellcat whining low and fast over the spot where Max had landed. He saw the parachute and what he believed to be Max nearby. Again he flew back across the spot through intense AA and this time there was no sight of Max or his parachute. Bullet Lochridge climbed for sufficient altitude to contact the SUWANNEE. As soon as the word was received, Jack Longino led a fighter team to Miyako and continued the search. When Max landed he made a failed attempt to escape the island by diving into the ocean. 50 years later Max told about his attempt to escape and his capture and about being held as a prisoner.

In 1995 Lieutenant Max Denham wrote his story of his capture and experience as a POW in a Japanese prison in 1945 after being shot down on the Island of Miyako Jima. (Submitted by his daughter *Heidi Denman Hogan)*

After taking off at pre-dawn from the *USS SUWANNEE CVE 27*, rendezvous was accomplished as I joined on the wing of Lt. Monteau. Our four F6F's were led by Lt. Hartman. His wing man was E.S. Wiedeman, a recent replacement pilot. We were headed for Sakishima Gunto and the island of Miyako in particular that clear morning. We arrived in the area about 0530. Our first run was to drop our 500# bomb on the dirt runway, repaired nightly by the Japanese. We regrouped and prepared to make our rocket run. We had been doing this off and on during April and May. Anti-aircraft fire did not occur overtime but when it did, a target was struck over 50% of the time. We had lost several planes and pilots from VT 40. We pushed over and headed for Mother Earth. I had a target spotted in a revetment and put my nose on it. Suddenly fiery chain mail was coming up in my direction. My first reaction was to turn to starboard but Monte was there so I moved to portside. A jolt struck just behind the cockpit and both my feet hit the deck flat and the world began to spin crazily before me. Ground fire had blown my F6F out of the sky. I had no control, had to get out, hood back loose little ring make this chute open?! Ahaaa! That was a good feeling, now really floating on air. Oh! Oh! Someone is shooting at me. What am I doing here? This can't be happing to me. Look at that haystack! Plop on the ground, parachute all around me. Had to get clear, the ocean is only a short distance away, whoa, look at all those fellows between here and there. I had parachuted to the ground about 200 yards from the ocean. Got to move, pull out the 38 and run like hell! Headed for the beach, just have to dodge a couple of those guys and make it past them, there is a F6F flying over, a couple of canoes on the beach but one out a little ways. Go for it. I had made it to the beach and was about to dive in to the ocean to reach a canoe out in the ocean. There was this one big fellow who had kept close to me as I ran toward the beach. He was about 10 feet from me and moving slowly toward me. He knew I had my 38 cal. pistol in my hand. I decided that I had to stop him. I brought my 38 cal revolver to bear right between his eyes. As I began to squeeze the trigger a firm hand clasped my wrist and moved my arm slightly to the right. The traced bullet either clipped or went just over his left ear. Startled, I said "Where have you been?" I turned and dived into the ocean. I was into the ocean and swam out to a canoe that was a short ways off shore. When I pulled myself up into the canoe I found no paddles, just the empty canoe. I turned it crosswise to the shore, dived into the ocean again and began to swim. I pulled my Mae West to inflate and release the yellow dye. I was not 50 yards from the shore and a few bullets struck the water on either side of me. I had slim hopes that another F6F would make a pass and spot the situation but none came. I realized that I had on my flying boots and must be swimming almost perpendicular. Then I realized I did not hear anymore rifle fire and everything was very quiet. I glanced over my right shoulder and there was a boat full of mean (mad) looking fellows with spears, rifles, and two long poles high in the air about to swat me over the head. I turned in the water and bid goodbye to my folks and said I'm sorry that I could not make it. I was certain that death was very close. They hesitated as I tread in the water then they saw both of my hands paddling (they knew about my 38 revolver). I no longer had it I suppose I had dropped it in the canoe. Several arms reached me and pulled me into the small boat. I realized they were beating on me and I say it that way because I could feel no pain. Actually I'm sure I smiled because they shouted louder and soon had me ashore. They tied my hands behind me, blindfolded me and drug me not far from the shore. We seemed to arrive at some type of shelter and they began to remove my flying suite and boots and I was standing start naked. They left my arms untied and returned my flight suit but not my boots. Someone began to put my feet into some type slipper. I did my best making my feet not go into the slippers. It worked and they returned my boots. I was pushed to sit down with my back to some structure. Someone sit beside me and whispered in my right ear. "You go to Tokyo" I was not impressed at the time. Once again I was drug into some type underground cave and put in a sitting position and my blind fold removed. I was facing 3 quite mean looking Japanese officers. They asked me some questions and I answered them as truthfully as I could. This did not please them up to a point. Sometimes my answers did not please them and one would whack me on top of my head with the flat blade of his sword (we had been instructed to answer any questions except: 1. Ships position, 2. Radio Frequencies, and 3. Operational plans). After some time they seemed to blow their tops and they each took a whack at my head. I was blindfolded and a rope was put around my neck and we began to walk out of the structure we had been in then into the cave like feeling and now and then my head would bump into something. After quite sometime walking I felt wind in my face and could hear the ocean splash. The noose around my neck was tightened and suspended above me so that I had to stand straight or it would choke me. I ask myself "are they going to push me off this cliff and hang me?" So I thought. Then all was quiet and I stood that way for hours. Someone came and once again led me through the cave and out to the air and it was dark out. My mission this morning had us strike the island between 5:30 and 6:00 am. I realized I had stood the complete day perhaps until 8 or 9pm. anyhow back again to questioning. They asked many questions and wrote furiously. After a time I was put in a small cave with wooden slates across the entrance and a bowl of some kind of roots in it. I had not eaten nor did this morsel entice, I recall that I had some pancakes for breakfast aboard ship and had not eaten all of them. I thought of that particular event for many weeks. I decided if I got out of this situation I would not have pancakes for breakfast ever again. There were more questions. One particular question, which I could not answer (and they never believed me), was "how thick was the armor plate under the wood deck of our ship?" They had very complete blueprints of our carrier (which by the way was the Suwannee) marked top secret, also complete topographical plots of Okinawa with all sorts of initials. On May 30 I was taken at sun down out to an air strip which I recognized I had dropped 500# bombs hourly for almost two months. Shortly a DC-3 (*JapaneseL2D*) landed on that strip. I was hustled aboard along with many wounded Japanese sailors. I was blindfolded, handcuffed behind my back, feet tied together in the seat and then gagged. It was very tough. The plane bumped and bounced along the dirt runway and took off. I thought OH No! My own Navy will blow us out of the sky! But it didn't happen. We flew not very high and landed maybe two hours on which that time was called Formosa. I was put into a porch of a barracks still completely shackled. I awoke in early light feeling someone setting on me. He removed my blindfold and displayed the biggest hunting knife I had ever seen and made a motion as if he were going to cut my throat. I can still see his eyes. They were the largest hazel color eyes I had ever seen and are remembered that way. Again I thought I was gone. Suddenly he moved straight up and the largest Japanese sailor I still have ever seen tossed him across the porch. I didn't laugh. This petty officer said that he was assigned to me until I was flown out. A Japanese Admiral (who he named but I didn't remember) wanted to see me. This Admiral said that he hadn't spoken English in 20 years. We talked several hours and never came close to the present time. He told me things about America that I didn't know. He gave me a hot drink that had good taste to it. I had a feeling that there were other prisoners near the box which was the cell. I would yell out but never got an answer. Later the army captain that was there said they threatened him to make him quiet. After a couple days my CPO came and said we were to fly again and gagged, handcuffed, feet tied once again I feared being shot down by our own forces. We did not however. We flew to the coast of China and I managed to slip my blindfold off and saw a bit of war going on down below. We landed at what I was told later was Shanghhai and I was placed into a padded cell. Floor wall and ceiling all padded. My CPO had told me that "Smeesoo" meant water and when I saw a pair of eyes looking at me through a slot in the door, I said "Smeesoo Arogoto" (Thank you) this character opened the cell door, strode across the room and hit me over the head with the flat of his sword. I didn't ask again. We made a total of two landings in which I was placed in a cell. The 2nd also contained two Japanese prisoners and I didn't feel too good to be with them. Our last flight landed in central Japan not far from Tokyo. We were driven to a place called "OFUNA". I found out later and led into a building. No gag, no blindfold, no handcuffs, and I saw two other fellows with me. They were writing something on paper and I looked out of a window. I was sure startled. I saw two bodies walking from me and instead of a rump, there was nothing but bones. Then I noticed legs like tooth picks and that shook me. We were told no talking and led through a hall like and put into a small room 6 ft. by 10 ft. It was the best accommodations that I had seen since aboard the ship. I heard some slapping in a cell down the way and a mention of no shoes, I quickly removed my boots and placed them outside the door, and then I heard some real beating around in the cell next to me-like a body bouncing off a wall. I stood in about the middle of the cell and in walked a fellow about 5 ft. tall with a big scowl on his face and the words coming out of his mouth as if he expected me to know what he was saying. Then he drew back his fist and took a big swing up side my left jaw, amazing it did not hurt, it didn't even make me shift my feet. Then here came his left fist and still the same result. In my Naval career I made what is known as a stupid mistake and here came another. I smiled at him. He just about hit the roof. He ran out the cell door and stomped along and then I heard him stopping back and he entered my cell with what I learned is called the 'Bimko" in the Japanese Navy and is standard punishment for them. He proceeded to take my arm, move me over to the so called cot and motioned for me to stand upon, which I proceeded to do. There he introduced me to the Bimko making certain that he only hit me on my rump. It scared me more than it hurt and I realized it was June 8th, my birthday. It turned out that we were kept in solitary for 30 days or so. We received a small wooden bowl of boiled barley on the AM and another in the PM. Our cell doors were not locked but must remain closed unless we needed to use the head, which was down the hall to my left. It was about a 6 hole outhouse connected to our wooden cells. One evening I had to use the head and do proceeded. On my way back to my cell I was confronted by a guard. He blocked my way and loudly said something. Of course I did not know Japanese and he would thump me in the middle of the brow and shout again. This went on for several thumps then I heard a voice from a nearby cell saying" he wants you to respect what he is saying which is Benjo eurasee, hatizan. "The Bull" which I learned later was the tag the prisoners had put on him. I repeated the phrase and he stepped around me and left. Our food (the barley soup) was brought to our cell by a designated POW. These guys had not lost any weight. One of them was Pappy Boyinton, the famous marine. The other prisoners had no feelings about this good deal if you can get it. Sometime after 30 days I was released to the compound and visited with other POW's for the first time. One day I saw some tar on the side of a building and thought to myself it would help to chew some. I had to step up on a ledge to reach and when I did my foot broke through a board and I heard a guard holler from the other side and make movement to come out. It turned out to be the little fellow that first confronted me in my cell. He hauled back and hit me up beside my jaw and I fell back 10 feet or so. I thought he got stronger; fact was I didn't notice but I had gone from 160 lbs to about 120 and shortly to 112 lbs. Every prisoner weighed in that neighborhood, including those who started at 200 lbs and above. There wasn't any fat on any of us. This was an interrogation camp and I talked on and on. We had been advised to avoid 3 questions only, ships position, radio frequencies, and future operational info. My ship's position was on my plotting board in my airplane. radio frequencies I never could remember and the numbers on my radio were painted different colors for needed frequencies and as a Lt. 1st Class I never would hear about future operational plans. In those interrogation sessions I still smoked and the longer we answered questions the more time we could reach in the provided cigarette packages and take a couple drags and let them die, drop in a flight pocket and light up another. I got along very well except once. There were a few more officers in front and in answers to the question I thought I was asked, the more names of carriers I mentioned. I asked the interpreter why. He said you have named many carriers that we had known to have been struck by Kamikaze! I said no, no. I was just naming the names of carriers that I know. There are many other carriers whose name I do not know and I do not know if any specific carrier that had been hit by Kamikaze. That brought out many sailors and I don't think they all hit my head but it felt like it. We had different prisoners get ill and one time the little one who I had my personal events with slipped them milk of magnesia and it cleaned their systems and they got out of the sick room. Most who went to the sick room only came out to be buried. The little man told us that he had been involved in war since 1934 and had not seen any of his family in all this time. (11 years). He had been a baker by trade but was inducted into the Navy.

Lt. (jg) Maxwell Franklin Denman USNR
Stuttgart Arkansas

Air Group 40 USS SUWANNEE CVE 27
Shot down and captured on 28 May 1945 at Miyako Jima near Okinawa Japan
Sent to "OFUNA P.O.W. CAMP" near Tokyo and released after the war
Photo contributed by Heidi Denman Hogan

I was a TBM Torpedo/Bomber Pilot at Okinawa and Sakishima
By Marvin W. Rachal

I was a Lt.(jg) pilot of a TBM Avenger Torpedo/Bomber aircraft attached to US Navy Squadron VC8 aboard the aircraft carrier USS Nehenta Bay (CVE 74). Our complement consisted of 12 TBM's, 16 FM2's (Grumman Wildcat fighters), 42 pilots, approximately 24 air-crewmen plus ship's company. We joined the Fleet task force off Okinawa around the last week of May 1945 and begin operations there. I remember vividly the almost daily attacks by Japanese Kamikazes when we first arrived. Apparently it was determined by top Brass that they were using Miyako and Ishigaki Shima as a staging area for the attacks, and several carriers, including the Nehenta Bay were ordered down there to put those airfields out of commission. I made three flights on this campaign: June 7th against Miyako Shima, June 17th against Ishigaki Shima (Miyara Airfield), and June 21st against Miyako Shima- all targeting the airfields. I especially recall the June 17th strike. The unusual "Strike Force" consisted of 12 TBM's (3 from each of the 4 carriers) lead by the senior TBM pilot and 16 FM2's (4 from each of the same carriers). We would dive on the target from altitude in this order: 4 FM's leading with guns blazing, followed closely by the TBM's. The rest of the FM2's provided medium and top cover.

It seems we would hit the airfields during the daylight raids, and the very enterprising Japanese would repair the damage done to the airfield during the night hours and be operational against our fleet by daylight the next day. So we resorted to using 100# bombs with VT Fuses (set to explode at different intervals of from 2 to 12 hours in 2 hour increments) On this particular flight- a pre-dawn raid-my Avenger was loaded with eighteen of these, and my assignment was to spread-drop these down the Miyara airfield center- line from one end to the other. The aircraft was equipped with an automatic release switch which released bombs at set intervals. My job was to dive to the proper altitude, get lined up on the runway, hit the release switch and hold the altitude of the aircraft straight and level for the length of the runway. Hopefully, this would discourage the repairs, or least slow them down. Mission accomplished. Meanwhile, my turret gunner,
(Francis (RED) Campbell (17 years old out of California) used his 50 caliber turret gun to rake the perimeter of the runway as we moved along. On the other two flights my TBM carried four 500# bombs, in addition to the usual full load of eight 120# warhead forward-firing rockets under the wings, plus a full load of 50 caliber ammunition for the two forward firing wing guns and turret gun. Following the release of the bombs we expended the rockets and a large part of the 50 caliber ammo on "targets of opportunity" in the vicinity of the airstrips.

Stewart G. Wasoba joined the USNR in 1943 and served As a 1st Division-Deck Division sailor aboard the USS Nehenta Bay CVE-74 Escort Carrier while this ship's Air Squadron flew bombing and strafing missions against the Japanese Airfields at Sakishima Gunto. After the war Stewart Drew the following action scenes using wording from Air Action And Ship Deck Logs.

THE ACTION REPORTS, ARE PART OF MATERIAL FROM SHIPS LOG - SQDN. REPORTS - MY INPUT And 5 DIARIES (CHAMBERLAIN) "FORSYTHE" HOGUE" FOSS MCCLURE)

AFTER ALMOST 60 YRS, THE HISTORY OF CVE74- VC11- VC8- CAN BE TOLD, SO OUR GRAND CHILDREN, SHIPMATES, AND MANY NAVAL HISTORIANS - CAN GET A GENERAL IDEA OF DUTIES CVE TYPE SHIPS HAD IN WW II.

THE GOOD LORD, KEPT US AFLOAT THROUGH 3 MAJOR TYPHOONS - A TORPEDO ATTACK - SEVERAL JAP PLANES - AND SUBMARINES - WITH FLEET UNITS IN 13 ENGAGEMENTS - PACIFIC OPERATIONS I'M PROUD TO BE A PART OF CVE74 HISTORY AS A PLANK OWNER - AND GIVE A HEARTY THANKS TO THOSE WHO SUPPORT OUR REUNION ORGANIZATION And THE MEMORIES WE SHARED TOGETHER

S.G. WASOBA - USNR - 621-98-23

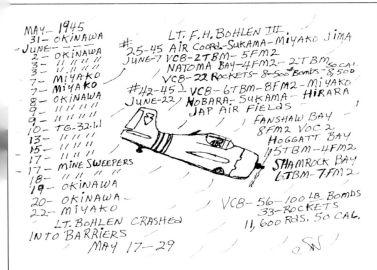

MAY- 1945
31- OKINAWA
-JUNE-
2- OKINAWA
3- " " "
3- " " "
7- MIYAKO
7- MIYAKO
8- OKINAWA
9- " " "
9- " " "
10- TG-32.1.1
13- " " "
15- " " "
17- " " "
17- MINE SWEEPERS
18- " " "
19- " " "
18- OKINAWA
19- " " "
20- OKINAWA
22- MIYAKO
LT. BOHLEN CRASHED
INTO BARRIERS
MAY 17-29

LT. F.H. BOHLEN III
#25-45 AIR COORD-SUKAMA-MIYAKO JIMA
JUNE 7 VCB-2TBM- 5FM2
NATOMA BAY-4FM2- 2TBM-50 CAL.
VC8-22 ROCKETS- 8-500# BOMBS- 8,500#
#42-45 VC8- 6TBM- 8FM2- MIYAKO
JUNE-22 NOBARA- SUKAMA- HIRARA
JAP AIR FIELDS
FANSHAW BAY
8FM2 VOC 2
HOGGATT BAY
15TBM-4FM2
SHAMROCK BAY
6TBM-7FM2

VCB- 56- 100 LB BOMBS
33-ROCKETS
11,600 RDS. 50 CAL.

JUNE 7- SAKI SHIMA GUNTO

OUT OF CLOUDS
5-OSCAR SUICIDE JAPS
PASS OVER FLEET UNIT
AND HEAD FOR CARRIERS

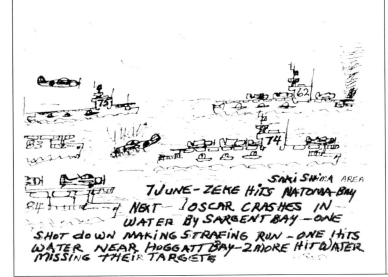

SAKI SHIMA AREA
7 JUNE- ZEKE HITS NATOMA BAY
NEXT 1 OSCAR CRASHES IN
WATER BY SARGENT BAY - ONE
SHOT DOWN MAKING STRAFING RUN - ONE HITS
WATER NEAR HOGGATT BAY - 2 MORE HIT WATER
MISSING THEIR TARGETS

ISHIGAKI- JUNE-17
NEH. BAY- SARG. BAY- HOGG. BAY- DESTROY BUILDINGS
A.A. POSITIONS- REVETMENTS AND RUNWAYS
52- 100LB BOMBS- 42 ROCKETS- 1,060 RDS.50- 470 RDS 30 CAL.
TWO BOMB- ONE ROCKET RUN MADE

June-21
ISHIGAKI SHIMA-MIYARA FIELD
6 TBMs WITH 10-100 LB. BOMBS EA
8 FM2 - MADE 3 ROCKET AND STRAFING RUNS
LT SMALL-SMITH-HANNA-ROSS-SEELEY
HOUSON-LEROY AND SQDN PILOTS PUT
AIRSTRIP AND HANGARS OUT OF ACTION

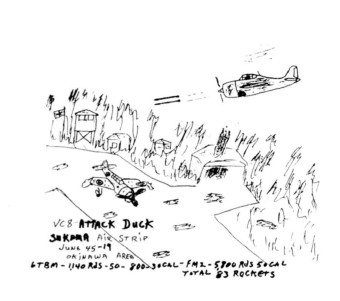

VC8 ATTACK DUCK
SUKOMA AIR STRIP
JUNE 45-19
OKINAWA AREA
6 TBM - 1140 RDS -50- 800 30 CAL - FM2- 5800 RDS 50 CAL
TOTAL 83 ROCKETS

LT ROGER MELVIN AND LT WICKWIRE HIT FUEL DUMP
8-FM2 FIRE 39 ROCKETS 4000 RDS 50 CAL
SUKOMA AIR BASE MIYAKA SHIMA RAID 1945
RAID 39-45

OKINAWA
RAID 20-45 SUKOMA AIR STRIP AND KUIEMA, IS.
FM2 SNAPS WELD ON WING TANK WHEN HE PULLED
UP OUT OF RUN — 5-TBM AND 4-FM2
TBMs- 600-30 CAL
1575 -50 CAL
49 -100 BOMBS
FM2- 3150 -50 CAL
TOTAL 56 ROCKETS
RUNWAYS-HANGARS
RADAR BLDG.

Drawings by Stewart G. Wasoba
USS Nehenta Bay CVE-74

TBM's returning from a raid on Miyako Jima
One of these planes is flown by Ensign Jeffreys
Note their squadron symbol on the tails.

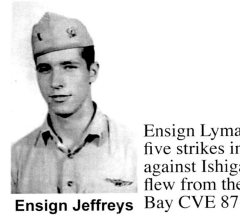

Ensign Jeffreys

Ensign Lyman W. Jeffreys from the US Navy Air Squadron VC-93 flew five strikes in his TBM Avenger against Miyako Jima and three strikes against Ishigaki Jima in conjunction with strikes against Okinawa. He flew from the escort carriers USS Petrof Bay CVE 80 and USS Steamer Bay CVE 87

On April 18 while he was striking Ishigaki Jima his airplane suffered a hit in the wing from what was believed to be from a 40mm shell. Shrapnel from this hit tore the skin off the wing, punched numerous holes in the fuselage and damaged the radio man's parachute.

On June 15 while VC-93 planes were striking Miyako Jima, Ensign George J. Vigents FM-2 fighter was hit by Anti-Aircraft fire. He made it to the east of the island several miles where he made a decent water landing. While circling above, others watched his plane slowly sink. George never opened the canopy. George is still there haunting Miyako.

Navigation skills and the airplanes of squadron VC-93

By Lyman W. Jeffreys

As a Cadet I had brief introduction to Celestial Navigation but never used it. Dead reckoning was the system we used. If you reckoned wrong, "You could be dead". For navigation out over the Pacific I had a plotting board about 10" X 18" that could be written on with a pencil. It had a grid under it that could be rotated. This fit under the TBM's instrument panel. I would plot the location, course and speed of the ship along with my course which was adjusted for wind. You could estimate surface wind by looking at the frequency and drift of white caps. Over open water the wind up to 1000 feet is much the same as on the surface. The aircraft had a magnetic and gyro compass. This gave me my heading which would be adjusted for wind drift. The craft had an auto pilot which held heading well but did nothing for altitude. You had to dicker with the elevator trim control frequently. Air speed held firm once RPM and manifold pressure were set. Finding the ship when returning was easy because you could see 30 miles or more if the weather was clear. I guess the radar could reach 5-10 miles, but I never needed to use it. I always ran a plot in my head. The squadron had TBMs which I flew and FMs which are a single seat fighter built by General Motors to a Grumman design. The IBM had two crewmen for me to command. One had a 50 cal. in the turret atop the fuselage; the other had a radio, radar and a 30 cal. gun in the tunnel under the tail. They strafed when possible. The Grumman designed turret on the TBF and the TBM was the first really good turret designed. I drove, navigated, dropped the bombs, and fired the rockets and forward guns. I carried either 10-100 Ib. bombs, 4-500 Ib. bombs or 1-1000 Ib. bomb plus eight 5" rockets and fall loads for 3-50 caliber and 1-30 caliber guns. Most runs were with 100 Ib. bombs. 1000 Ib. were rare. The eight rockets were equal to somewhat more than a broadside delivery by a destroyer. On anti-sub runs I carried depth charges. In all our squadron had about 30 aircraft, there were up to 20 FMs and 12 TBMs. The FM2 fighter had a 38' wing span, 28'-9" length and was driven by a Pratt & Whitney R-1 830-86 engine. It had atop speed of 315 mph and could carry 6-50 caliber wing guns. The TBM was a rather large aircraft with a 54'-2" wingspan, 40' length and 15'-10" height at rest (16'-5 "with the wings folded). To get an ideal of its size, the wing span would equal the width of a square 3000 sq. foot house and the height if parked on the first floor of a house would reach the second floor ceiling. Total weight with the bombs would approach 9 tons. It had a 13'-1" diameter 3 blade propeller. A hydraulic system operated the landing gear, wing flaps, cowl flaps, oil cooler flap, bomb bay doors, wing gun chargers, automatic pilot and wing folding. The turret, tail hook and starter were 12 volt electrical. You had to open the cockpit hatch and rear door by hand. The engine was a radial Wright Cyclone R-2600-20 with air cooled cylinders arranged in two rows. 330 gallons of 100 octane fuel were carried. Additional drop tanks could add 270 gallons, I never carried these. I never ran low on fuel. Cruising at 180 knots on a strike you had about 4 hours of fuel. On a long anti-sub run at 130 knots maximum time would approach seven hours, at 200 knots you would be down to three hours. A three man inflatable rubber raft with all the necessities like food, water and tire patches was provided for any enforced boating. Each member of the crew also had one man yacht equipped with interesting supplies. Properly deployed you could present an impressive flotilla.

Francis Bentinck Heffer
Lt (A) D.S.C. R.N.Z.N.V.R.

Francis Bentinck Heffer who served and flew in an Air squadron with the British Pacific fleet left his fathers farm in Waikanae New Zealand in 1942 to join the British Royal Navy's AIR ARM. Francis, who was called Ben, A short name taken from his middle name was 22 years old. He and others from New Zealand who had joined, was first sent to England. Here they were trained to be Sailors. They were taught navigation, signaling and things that a sailor should know while living aboard a ship. After completing this training it was time to start a new training class in learning the techniques of flying an airplane. Ben and the other men in his training class were split up and sent to different flight training schools. These schools were located in England and in the USA. Ben was in the group sent to the USA. He crossed the Atlantic Ocean aboard the QUEEN MARY ocean liner that had been made into a troop ship at this time. At his new training school near Detroit Michigan, at a small training field, Ben was introduced to the N2S Open Cockpit Stearman bi-plane trainer. After completing his check out in this trainer he was sent to an advanced training base at Pensacola Florida. Here In Florida he trained on the SNJ the Navy's version of the North American Army's AT6 Advanced trainer. After successively completing this course he received his wings. Next stop for Ben was Miami Florida where he learned air gunnery and dogfighting, and air to ground bombing etc. After this he was off to Lewiston Maine. Here he was introduced to the F4 Grumman Wildcat fighter. The British called this fighter the Martlet. He used this plane to practice carrier landings, However, the carrier deck was that of a marked off spot on a landing field They even furnished a signal man at the runway entrance to give the students some corrections for landings or to wave them off if it appeared they were not aligned properly to the runway for landing. This man was often called the batman when aboard ship. Later Ben was moved to Brunswick, Where he and others would be placed into a Squadron and here he learned that the fighter plane that he would be assigned for his Squadron would be the Mkl Corsair, a British version of the American Chance Vought F4U. Ben ended up in 1838 Squadron. He did his carrier landing trials in Norfolk Virginia and upon completing this, He with his plane was loaded onto the escort carrier HMS Begum along with others who had completed their training and they sailed to Britain. Ben and his Corsair, JT331 with his assigned Squadron 1833, was assigned to the British carrier HMS ILLUSTRIOUS with Capt. Sir Charles Lamb in charge of the carrier. After flying combat operations at Sumatra and at the Japanese Oil Refineries at Palemburg, Sumatra, Ben and the ILLUSTRIOUS made their way to Ulithi, in the Caroline Islands in 1945. There with the other ships that made up The British Pacific fleet and Task Force 57, they set sail for Sakishima Gunto in the Rykuyu Islands for there next combat operations. After the war, Ben wrote a book about his memories of his war experiences and named it "FROM COW BELLS TO BELL BOTTOMS".

Lt. (jg) Spencer F. Hatch

Lieutenant (jg) Spencer F. Hatch joined the US Navy Air Corp on July 10, 1942. He became a fighter pilot flying the FM2 Wildcat in combat. He served for seven months in Air composite squadron VC-92 onboard the Escort Carrier Tulagi CVE- 72. He saw combat in the Philippine Island, Iwo Jima, Okinawa and Sakishima Islands of Miyako and Ishigaki Jima.

400 PLANE KAMIKAZE ATTACK
By Spencer F. Hatch

On Sunday, April 8, 1945 the enemy sent about 400 suicide planes from South Japan to hit our ships in the Okinawa area in a desperate effort to turn the tide of the battle. Our ship, the USS Tulagi, was at anchor, along side an ammunition ship near Kerama Retto Island a few miles west of southern Okinawa, taking on supplies. We were the biggest ship in the area and suicide planes were trying to dive into us. I was below deck with other pilots in the ready room. We could hear our 5 inch guns open fire as planes got within range, then soon the 40 millimeter guns would open fire, to be followed by the 20 millimeter guns. Any second we expected a suicide plane to blast through our flight deck into the Pilot's Ready Room. This series continued. I could take it no longer. I wanted to be able to see the action and be in a position to take what ever evasive action might seem prudent. I went up on deck. Enemy planes were coming from different directions. They all seemed intent on getting us. But fire power from other ships would intensify and the suicide pilot would pick out another target or he would get shot down. I crossed back and forth across the flight deck---depending on which direction the nearest plane was coming from.

Then came time when no enemy planes showed on the radar screens. Our ship's Captain radioed to all ships in the area to hold their fire; we were launching planes. Stewart Chapin's division was first in line. Mine was to follow. Stewart was fired off the catapult followed by his wingman. At this point Stewart had circled for a normal rendezvous. At first one ship on the other the other side of the small island opened fire on him, then others. Soon every ship in the area was shooting at him. His plane caught fire. He bailed out. One gunner continued shooting at him in his parachute. What a horrible, helpless feeling. Stewart landed in the water uninjured and was soon rescued by a small ship. We launched no more planes. We pulled anchor and got out to open sea. But while at anchor I saw planes and ships hit all over the area. That day the list of the "trying times" my patriarchal blessing mentions.

On April 13th my close friend, Jack Link, got shot down in flames while making a low run strafing attack on an airfield on Miyako Island. I took the news with a heavy heart until reading Alma 60:13 a few days later. On the 14th my four plane division was assigned to meet a PBY (Seaplane) about 15 miles east of Miyako to fly fighter cover for it and to search for possible American survivors around the island of Miyako. Jack Link was not the only pilot shot down. We met the Seaplane and proceeded to Miyako. I instructed Frank Soars, second section leader, to take his wingman and fly cover for the Seaplane. Tommy Thompson and I went searching for American survivors. We circled the island a couple times looking for anyone in a life raft. We found none. Then we strafed a few enemy ships. Tommy spotted a Zero take off from the airfield. We both took after it in hot pursuit. As we closed on it at great speed the enemy pilot pushed the stick forward and dived his plane into the ocean. As we passed over the spot we could see what appeared to be a partially opened parachute beneath the water surface. I radioed to our carrier, "Splash one, Zero." We continued to search for survivors until our fuel got low. We then returned to our carrier. We had lunch and took off again on another mission. Our assignment was to neutralize the airfield on Ishigaki Island. Miyako and Ishigaki Islands are located about half way between Okinawa and Formosa (now Taiwan). The enemy was flying suicide planes from Formosa to these islands and from them they were taking off early in the morning to hit our ships in the Okinawa area. Our Squadron Commander led the bombers and he had me lead the fighters. As I recall we had 12 bombers and 8 fighters.

On April the 14, 1945 about 20 planes were sent from our carrier to neutralize the airfield on Ishigaki Island. Our Skipper, Lt. Comdr. Wallace led the bombers. I led the fighters. We approached the airfield from the north. The fighter planes went in first, in a moderate steep dive, with me in the lead plane out in front. As a result I drew the heavy fire from the island. Tracers were shooting under me, over me and on both sides. Like a garden sprinkler aimed into the air with sun glistening on the many water droplets. And I knew for every tracer I could see there were 4 or 5 bullets (not tracers) that I could not see. My aim and purpose was to get the ground gunners before they got me. We strafed as many of the ground guns as we could get in our sights and silenced many of them. The bombers came in behind us. It was this type of action that cost my friend, Jack Link, his life the day before over the airfield at Miyako Island. The bombers dropped part of their load and recovered. We were all accounted for. On the next run we came in from the south. Again,

I was the lead fighter plane in the attack. We strafed and fired our rockets at gun installations. The bombers followed and bombed the airfield with the rest of their bombs. Lt.(jg) Victor T. Buettner's bomber (TBM) lost a wing on the second run. He had time to bail out. His two crewmen went in with the plane; they did not have a chance. Buettner's chute opened and he landed near the north end of the runway. I made a quick strafing over the area to keep ground forces down and then rallied the fighters and we made repeated strafing runs on every gun we could see---especially in the area where Buettner landed. We made passes from west to east indicating the direction Buettner should travel to get off the island for a rescue pick up at sea. We strafed until we ran out of ammunition. I went down one last time for a close look at the parachute to be certain he got free from the harness. He did. No one was near the chute.

Recovering from this last run at low altitude but at high speed my plane was hit twice. One large shell grazed the main spar of the plane and exploded blowing a large hole in the left side of the fuselage behind the armor plating protecting the pilot. The explosion knocked out my radio but did not damage the flight controls. The second shell passed through my right wing missing the wing tank less than half an inch. I took strong evasive action, regained altitude, rendezvoused the fighters and passed the lead (visually) over to Frank Soars. We returned to the carrier. My four plane division spent 10 hours in the air that day with most of it under combat conditions. For this action, together with action on March 28th when I escorted the Skipper on the leaflet drop over Okinawa, our Squadron Commander recommender me for the Silver Star. In its place I was awarded the Distinguished Flying Cross. I believe if the citation had been accurately written, they would have awarded the Silver Star. Buettner did bail out and he survived the crash. But he was not able to make it to the water even though he tried. Part way to the water as he paused to catch his breath, he was surrounded and taken captive. He was released after the war.

The second part of my citation reads: "On April 14, when a bomber of his squadron was shot down during an attack on an enemy airfield, he launched a low- level, solo strafing attack in face of intense hostile antiaircraft fire to check enemy ground forces and allow possible survivors of the crash escape. Later, rallying his division, he led them in repeated strafing runs over the area until a close search revealed no survivors. His leadership and fighting spirit under enemy fire were keeping with the highest traditions of the United States Naval Service".

The part about a close search revealing no survivors was not true and it was not what I reported. Little wonder the Silver Star was not awarded. The citation reads like we risked our lives in an effort to assist no one. I was also awarded 3 Air Medals for combat.

MEMORIES
By Alvin Kernan

Take off in the dark from the USS Suwanee climbing into the rising sun never failed to lift spirits, and on a beautiful clear day when you could almost see the islands, Ishigaki and Miyako, they were going to bomb, Catbird Flight, 5 dark blue Hellcats and 5 Avengers, climbed to 20 thousand feet a proceeded south by west to Ishigaki. By their appointed time they were above the dirt strip. A few planes were parked in the revetments and the fighters went in on a steep dive to strafe and rocket them before they could take off. The Japanese were prepared, the guns had been manned and flak filled the air ahead of windshields with a laced tracery of red and white fire. One plane took some hits in its starboard wing, but the plane never faltered, and it poured its fire home, lifting its nose slightly to sweep a succession of revetments and planes. A few planes were burning as the fighters roared out over the leechy marsh and began the climb to altitude for their dive bombing runs. As they went up and up the Avengers were coming down, bomb bays open, each to drop a load of 12 small 100 pound bombs the length of the field and make it unusable by planes. By the time the Avengers were through with their work, the fighters were dropping their single 500 pounders on the facilities and the field, and when they pulled out and went out to sea and began straggling back to the ship. Everyone was exultant how easy it had been and how effective. "No planes will stage from Ishigaki for a long time" was the general sentiment, but within a few hours the holes in the field made by the bombs were filled up for the next flight coming in at noon. So it went day after day and week after week. Neither side yielding an inch.

Alvin Kernan was a Turret gunner on a US Navy TBM Avenger that flew from the USS Suwanee CVE-27 in 1945. His Air Group 40 was assigned bombing missions against the Japanese Sakishima Gunto Airfields. Alvin is the author of a WW-II book titled: "Crossing the Line".

Quentin Schenk
US Navy TBM Avenger Pilot
Squadron VC-93

Navy Pilot Quentin Schenk flew strikes against Okinawa and against Sakishima Gunto. During this time his squadron was stationed on escort carriers; Petrof Bay CVE-80 and Steamer Bay CVE-87.

"Strafing these islands was miserable duty. Small arms fire was dangerous. We would bomb the runways and that night the coolies would fill in the holes, so shortly we would have to bomb again. Our task was to keep the kamikazes from using the facilities."

"We had to clean up what the Essex carriers neglected to do. They shot most of the airplanes out of the sky, and sank most of the shipping. Then we came in and gave protection to the fleet and kept the kamikazes down on those nasty little islands and did tedious seven hour patrols looking for submarines and warships. Our time over the Sakishimas was the costliest and most frightening of the entire combat period of the squadron, for we had to fly low and slow to try and locate the kamikaze planes on the islands, thus making us vulnerable to intense small arms fire directed against us."

"We experienced very little anti-aircraft fire which made it that much more difficult. If we had encountered AA fire we could have identified the source and taken it out. It was terrifying to fly through that rain of small arms fire day after day, not knowing if you would be next shot down. With small arms fire it didn't destroy the plane, but hit an oil line or some other part of the plane that would disable it and force the pilot to go down."

"We never landed on the island if we possibly could help it, but headed for the ocean which was our friend. If possible we would be picked up by a submarine or a seaplane. We were warned to stay away from Formosa which we were told that was occupied by headhunters and if we had to ditch on one of the islands we would be tortured and then executed. I have felt fear over Okinawa, but nothing compared to the fear experienced over the kamikaze islands."

George P. Adams
"PRESS"
TURRET GUNNER
VMTB-143

George "Press" Adams joined the Marines in 1942 at the age of 18 and became a "Turret Gunner" aboard the Grumman TBF Avenger and was assigned to VMTB232. He was stationed at land bases at Guadalcanal, Munda and Bougainville from August 1943 thru April 1944. In 1945, Press was assigned to VMTB-143, and stationed aboard the USS Gilbert Islands Escort Carrier CVE-I07. This Escort Carrier with Marine squadron VMTB-143 participated in the battle of Okinawa. Here Press flew as the turret gunner on the newer, TBM Avenger. His plane flew against targets at Okinawa and in June of 1945 the Gilbert Islands Escort Carrier moved to the Sakishima Gunto area, where Avengers made bombing runs against Nobara, Hirara and Sukuma airfields on the island of Miyako Jima and Ishigaki and Miyara airfields on the island of Ishigaki Jima "Our airplanes were in the air almost every day. If we were not on a bombing run to one of the islands then we were on Anti-submarine patrol." According to Press, he lost four of his good friends when two Avengers were shot down at Sakishima Gunto.

Appendix A

U.S. Pilots and crewmen Killed, Captured or missing at Sakishima Gunto between 1 April and 23 June 1945

NR- Not recovered (Remains not known to have been recovered)

MIA- Missing in action   KIA- Killed in action

Name	Service No	Squadron A/p	Ship	Date lost	Location	Status

Lt. Cdr. John Ostrum USN 82602 AG-24 F6F Santee 10 April 45 Ishigaki Jima

Ensign Joseph F. Florence USNR 382837 AG-24 TBM Santee 23 April 45 Miyako Jima KIA (note 1)

Amm3c Richard J. Murphy USN 2586091 AG-24 TBM Santee 23 April 45 Miyako Jima KIA NR

ARM3c Charles E. Boley USNR 7558593 AG-24 TBM Santee 23 April 45 Miyako Jima KIA NR

LT. Glenn W. Freeman USNR 299072 AG-24 F6F Santee 25 April 45 Ishigaki KIA NR

Lt. John Gray USNR 124139 AG-24 F6F Santee 29 May 45 Ishigaki KIA NR

Lt.(jg) Walter H. Baskett USNR 320806 VF-33 F6F Sangamon 30 April 45 Ishigaki Jima MIA NR

Lt.(jg) Jack H. Bateman USNR 325878 VF-33 F6F Sangamon 18 April 45 Ishigaki Jima KIA NR

Lt. (jg) Richard F. Eckstein USNR 326189 VF-33 Sangamon 22 April 45 Ishigaki Jima KIA NR

Lt. Frank Collura USNR 124403 AG-40 TBM Suwannee 25 April 45 Miyako Jima KIA NR

AOM1c Cletus H. Powell USN 3601993 AG-40 TBM Suwannee 25 April 45 Miyako Jima KIA NR

ARM3c Clifford A. Steward USNR 8087391 AG-40 TBM Suwannee 25 April 45 Miyako Jima KIA NR

Lt. Carroll R. Campbell USN 146666 AG-40 TBM Suwannee 27 April 45 Ishigaki Jima KIA NR

AMM1c James R. Loughridge USNR 4027716 AG-40 TBM Suwannee 27 April 45 Ishigaki Jima KIA NR

ARM2c Edward A. Zahn USNR 7066284 AG-40 TBM Suwannee 27 April 45 Ishigaki Jima KIA NR

Lt. (jg) M. F. Denman USNR 337547 AG-40 F6F Suwannee 28 May 45 Miyako Jima POW (note 2)

AMM3c James D. Christmas Jr. USNR 8459780 AG-40 TBM Suwannee 31 May 45 Miyako Jima MIA NR

ARM#c R.S. Baird USNR 8426601 AG-40 TBM Suwannee 31 May 45 Miyako Jima MIA NR

2nd LT. Douglas H. Merrin USMCR 035081 VMTB-233 TBM Block Island 10 May 45

Sgt. Joseph L. Butehorn USMCR 473293 VMTB-233 TBM Block Island 10 May 45 Miyako Jima MIA

S/Sgt Edward T. Gunning USMCR 395254 VMTB-233 TBM Block island 10 May 45 Miyako Jima MIA

2nd Lt. Jack Marconi USMCR 032266 VMTB-233 TBM Block Island 29 May 45 Ishigaki Jima KIA

S/Sgt Joe F. Surovy USMC 333397 VMTB-233 TBM Block Island 29 May 45 Ishigaki Jima KIA

S/Sgt Ben D. Cannan USMC 402718 VMBT-233 TBM Block Island 29 May 45 Ishgaki Jima KIA

Lt. Cdr. Richard W. Robertson USN 823408 AG-25 F6F Chenango 8 April 45 Ishigaki Jima KIA (note 3)

Major Robert C. Maze USMCR 06770 VMF-511 FG1D Block Island 27 May 45 Ishigaki Jima KIA NR

1st LT. Robert A. Goldberg USMCR 030855 VMF 511 F4U-1D Block Island 27 May 45 Ishigaki Jima MIA NR

Lt. Vernon L. Tebo USNR 121397 VC-97 TBM Makassar Strait 15 April 45 Ishigaki KIA (note 4) NR

ARM1c Warren H. Loyd USNR 3422351 VC-97 TBM Makassar Strait 15 April 45 Ishigaki Jima KIA (note 4) NR

AOM1c Robert Tuggle Jr. USN 6174722 VC-97 TBM Makassar Strait 15 April 45 Ishigaki Jima KIA (note 4) NR

Lt. (jg) Donald E. Glasgow USNR 305801 VC-84 TBM Makin Island 28 April 45 Miyako Jima KIA NR

ARM2c Glenn F. Cota USNR 8606888 VC-84 TBM Makin Island 28 April 45 Miyako Jima KIA NR

continued

AMM2c George Douvos USNR 5641043 VC-84 TBM Makin Island 28 April 45 Miyako Jima KIA NR

PHOM1c Harry M. Hansen USNR 7000408   VC- 84 TBM Makin Island 28 April 45 Miyako Jima KIA NR

Ensign George J. Vigent Jr. USNR 363776 VC-93   FM-2 Steamer Bay 15 June 45 Miyako Jima KIA NR

Lt. R.E. Weeks   VC-96 TBM Shamrock Bay 22 June 45 Miyako Jima MIA

ARM3c Gene G. Kaylor USNR 8572582 VC-96 TBM Shamrock Bay 22 June 45 Miyako Jima MIA NR

AOM2c Herbert J. Gericke USNR 7106902 VC-96 TBM Shamrock Bay 22 June 45 Miyako Jima
MIA

Lt. (jg) William F. Waters   VC-97 FM-2 Shipely Bay 15 June 45 Ishigaki Jima MIA

Lt. (jg) Norbert J. Link USNR 306371 VC-92 FM-2 Tulagi 13 April 45 Miyako Jima KIA NR

Crewman Harold A. Morrissey VC-92 TBM Tulagi   14 April 45 Ishigaki Jima KIA

Crewman Darrell L. Booth   VC-92 TBM Tulagi   14 April 45 Ishigaki Jima KIA

Sgt William Boyd Jr.   VMTB 143 TBM Gilbert Islands 3 June 45 Ishigaki KIA

2nd LT. Logan M.White Jr.   USMCR 031359 VMF 512 FG-1D Gilbert Islands 8 June 45 KIA

1st. Lt. Kelvern O. Misamore USMCR 021300 VMF 512 TBM Gilbert Islands 12 June 45 KIA

Sgt. Otto R. Schaefer USMCR 496852 VMF 512 TBM Gilbert Islands 12 June 45 KIA

Sgt. Chancel A. Hall USMCR 819907 VMF 512 TBM Gilbert Islands 12 June 45 KIA

ARM2c Euclide A. Desjarlais USNR 2046205 AG40 TBM Suwannee 29 April 45 KIA NR

Notes

1. Ensign Joseph F. Florence was captured after he bailed out of his plane. He was forced to work disarming bombs. He was shot and killed for no apparent reason by the IJA on 11 July 1945. At this time his body was buried near Nobarudake at Miyako Jima. After the war some remains were returned to the US.

2. Lt. (jg) M.F. "Max" Denman was captured after he bailed out of his plane. He was sent to the prison camp OFUNA near Tokyo VIA Taiwan. He was released after the war.

3. Lt. Cdr. Richard Robertson survived after bailing out of his plane. It was determined that he drowned while waiting to be rescued.

4. Lt. Tebo, crewmen Loyd and Tuggle were captured by the Japanese Navy and met a violent death at the hands of their captures at Ishigaki Jima. It is not known if they bailed out or went in with their crippled plane. A memorial has been placed on the island for these three Navy men.

Disclaimer

Any information missing from the list of names above was either unknown or unavailable at the time of this writing. The above information was compiled from research information available to the Author of this book. There may be other names that are not listed above.

Appendix B
Japanese Airplanes

Betty   Mitsubishi G4M, two engines, seven seat medium naval attack bomber.

Dinah   Mitsubishi Ki-46, two engines, two seat Army night fighter and Reconnaissance.

Frances   Yokosuka P1Y1 *Ginga*, meaning Milky Way. Two engines, three seat Naval fighter bomber.

Jill   Nakajima B6N *Tenzan*, meaning Heavenly Mountain. Single engine, three seat Naval torpedo bomber.

Kate   Nakajima B5N, single engine, three seat Naval bomber and torpedo bomber.

Myrt   Nakajima C6N *Saiun*, meaning Painted Cloud. Single engine naval fighter and reconnaissance with pilot and three crew members.

Nick   Kawasaki Ki-45 *Toryu*, two engines, two seat Army night fighter.

Oscar   Nakajima Ki-43 *Hayabusa*, meaning Peregrine Falcon. Single engine, single seat Army fighter.

Spruce   Tachikawa 95-1, Army intermediate trainer.

Tony   Kawasaki Ki-61 *Hien*, meaning Flying Swallow. Single engine, single seat Army Fighter.

Topsy   Mitsubishi Ki-57. Transport.

Val   Aichi D3A, single engine, two seat carrier and land based naval dive bomber.

Zeke   Mitsubishi A6M *Reisen*, meaning Zero- Sen. Single engine, one seat naval fighter.

Bibliography

Jablonski Edward, **Air War**, Vol-1, Garden City, NY, Doubleday & Co.,1979.

Polk David, **Escort Carriers of the U.S. Navy**, Paducah, KY, Turner Publishing Co., 1993.

Heffer Francis, **From Cow Bells To Bell Bottoms**, Tauranga, New Zealand, Canrig Publishing, 1998.

Morison Samuel Eliot, **Victory in the Pacific**, 1945, Vol-14, Champaign, IL, University of Illinois Press, 2002.

Hargis Robert, **US Naval Aviator 1941-45**, Elms Court, Chapel Way, Botley, Oxford OX2 9LP, United Kingdom., Osprey Publishing 2002.

Y'Blood William T., **The Little Giants,** Annapolis, Maryland, Naval Institute Press, 1999.

Kernan Alvin, **Crossing the Line,** Annapolis, Maryland, Naval Institute Press, 1997.

Fisch Arnold G. Jr., **Military Government in the Ryukyu Islands 1945-50,** Washington D.C., U.S. Government Printing Office, 1988.

Polmar Norman, **Aircraft Carriers, Vol-1**, Washington D.C., Potomac Books Inc., 2006.

Dresser James, **Escort Carriers and their Air Unit markings during WWII in the Pacific**, Ames Iowa. Compiled by James Dresser 1980.

Hata Ikuhiko, Yasuho Izawa, Shores Christopher, **Japanese Army Air Force Fighter units and their Aces**, London, Grub Street 2002.

Appleman Roy E, Burns James M., Gugeler Russell A., Stevens John, **The war in the Pacific, Okinawa the last stand,** Historical Division United States Army 1948, Washington D.C., US Government printing office 1977.

Nichols, Major Chas. S. Jr. USMC, Shaw Henry I. Jr., **Okinawa: Victory in the Pacific**, Historical Branch, G-3 Division H.Q. U.S. Marine Corps, Washington D.C., Government Printing office 1955.

Eadon Stuart, **Kamikaze**, Bristol, Crecy Books Limited 1995.

Inoguchi Captain Rikihei, Nakajima Commander Tadahi, Pineau Roger, **The Divine Wind**, Annapolis, Maryland, Naval Institute Press 1994.

Senha Sakae, **Sakishima Gunto Sakusen (Chapter of Miyako)**. Kiru Printing Co. and Okinawa History Publisher Association, Okinawa Japan, 900-0021, Izumizaki 2-10-8, Naha 1975.

US Government literature quoted is from
Military naval air and ship action reports and diaries.
Obtained from the National Archives at College park MD.

INDEX